APPROACHING HOOFBEATS

The Four Horsemen
of the
Apocalypse

Also by Billy Graham

Angels: God's Secret Agents
Till Armageddon

APPROACHING HOOFBEATS

The Four Horsemen
of the
Apocalypse

Billy Graham

HODDER & STOUGHTON
LONDON SYDNEY AUCKLAND TORONTO

Unless otherwise indicated, scripture quotations are from the New International Version of the Bible (NIV), published by Hodder & Stoughton, copyright © 1978 by the New York International Bible Society. Used by permission. Quotations from the Revised Standard Version of the Bible (RSV), copyrighted 1946, 1952, © 1971, 1973 by the Division of Christian Education of the National Council of the Churches of Christ in the U.S.A., are used by permission. Quotations from the *New Testament in Modern English* (Phillips) by J. B. Phillips, published by the Macmillan Company, are © 1958, 1960, 1972 by J. B. Phillips. Quotations from the *New English Bible*, © The Delegates of the Oxford University Press and The Syndics of the Cambridge University Press, 1961, 1970, are used by permission. Quotations from The Amplified Bible (Amplified) are copyright © 1965 by Zondervan Publishing House. Quotation from *The Holy Bible*, translated by Ronald Knox, is copyright 1944, 1948, 1950 by Sheed & Ward, Inc. Quotations marked KJV are from the Authorized or King James Version of the Bible.

British Library Cataloguing in Publication Data

Graham, Billy
   Approaching Hoofbeats
   1. Eschatology
   I. Title
   236   BT821.2

ISBN 0-340-35759-2

Contents

1	*The Thunder of Distant Hoofbeats*	17
2	*Is There Any Hope?*	29
3	*A Call to the Churches*	41
4	*The Throng Around the Throne*	63
5	*The White Horse and Its Rider, Part I*	73
6	*The White Horse and Its Rider, Part II*	83
7	*The White Horse and Its Rider, Part III*	103
8	*The Red Horse and Its Rider*	121
9	*The Black Horse and Its Rider*	149
10	*The Pale Horse and Its Rider*	179
11	*Hope in the Holocaust*	207
12	*The Grand Finale*	221
	Bibliography	237

Introduction

Horses have always fascinated me. They are among the most beautiful and intelligent animals of God's creation.

In the Bible horses are often associated with biblical prophecy. In this book we are going to be exploring the implications of what have become known as the "four horsemen of the Apocalypse." These four animals and their riders are anything but beautiful. They are terrible and terrifying. The scenes in which they are described are among the most dreadful in the Bible. Many great painters of history have tried to depict this aspect on canvas—but no artist can fully portray the wonder and horror of these events.

Some theologians and Bible scholars have thought these scenes as described by the apostle John to be a description of past events. However, most evangelical scholars interpret them as having to do with the future—as do I. In my view, the shadows of all four horsemen can already be seen galloping throughout the world at this moment; therefore, I not only want to apply these four *symbols* of events yet to come, but also to put our ears to the ground and hear their hoofbeats growing louder by the day.

I have asked people from various parts of the world what they thought about the future. Most of them hold a pessimistic view. Editorials in the world press are much more gloomy than the American press. Constantly the words *armageddon* and *apocalypse* are being used to describe the events of the future. Orwell's *1984* is referred to time after time.

The four horses are described in Revelation 6. They are almost an exact repeat of the first four signs of the end of the age that Jesus gave in Matthew 24. The *first horse* has to do with counterfeit religion. The *second* deals with war and peace. The *third* has to do with famine and pestilence. And the *fourth* represents the trauma of death and the sufferings of Hades.

Horses and horsemen are mentioned some three hundred times in the Bible. But the most famous are the four horses—white, red, black, and "pale"—ridden by the "four horsemen of the Apocalypse" and described by the apostle John in Revelation 6. Imagine them as war-horses with heaving flanks and flared nostrils, rearing and pawing the air with their terrible hooves. This kind of horse stands out in both the biblical and historical narratives. It strikes fear in the heart of the onlooker. The increasing sound of their powerful hooves reverberates across our world today. I ask you to join me as we explore what the "four horsemen" are telling us—and God's answer to the world's dilemma.

The Book of Revelation has always interested me, with its clanging symbolism, roaring thunder and flashing lightning. It is also the only book in the Bible for which we are promised a blessing if we read it.

I cannot pretend that I understand it all. In *Approaching Hoofbeats* I only cover the first six chapters. You will find very little, for example, about important events concerning the second coming of Christ—events such as the Rapture, Tribulation, Millennium, and so on. As I have already said, this book is concerned primarily with the four horsemen of the Apocalypse and their symbolic warnings to us today, and with how the hoofbeats can be heard growing louder with each passing day. My major emphasis was not necessarily to interpret these passages as much as to make them relevant to the great problems we face as individuals and as a world.

This has been a rather difficult book for me to write. In writing it I have become more deeply aware of the enormous problems that face our world today, and the dangerous trends which seem to be leading our world to the brink of Armageddon. I also have become more deeply convicted about the responsibility those of us who are Christians have to declare and live the gospel and to fight against both individual and corporate evil.

In this book I have tried to share my concern, and indicate some of the ways Christians should act in Christ's name to improve our world and prepare people for the future world that the Scriptures promise.

At the same time, I want to make it clear that while I am very concerned about these social ills and want to do everything I can to combat them, I have not changed my priorities. My priority is the same as it has always been: to proclaim the saving gospel of Jesus Christ so that people may respond in faith to Christ and become children of God throughout all eternity.

While this book deals with most of the social issues of our day, it is primarily a call to repentance. I certainly am not suggesting that the church should abandon its primary mission of preaching the gospel and devote itself instead to social concerns. God's primary calling to His people is to proclaim—by word and deed—the matchless gospel of Christ. In the midst of a world torn by chaos and suffering, may we be faithful in doing all that God has called us to do.

Without the help of a few of my associates and friends I could not have written this book. We should say it is "our" book. Especially do I want to thank Al Bryant of Word for carefully going over the manuscript several times. Thanks to my new friend, Mel White, author, film producer, and seminary professor, for his willingness to take my original manuscript, then interview me for hours on a tape recorder over several days and make the manuscript more readable; to my associate, Dr. John Wesley White, for his help especially on the last chapter; to Dr. John Akers, my able assistant in much of my ministry; to Dr. Art Johnson, President of Tyndale Theological Seminary in Holland; to my wife, Ruth, who made many helpful suggestions; to Millie Dienert, for reading the manuscript and checking out Scripture verses to see that they were accurately quoted; to T. W. Wilson for his helpful suggestions; to Stephanie Wills, who not only helped with the research, but typed the manuscript many times, and also to our faithful staff in Montreat for the many hours they spent checking the manuscript; to the Meads of Dallas, Texas, for their hospitality; to our friends at Trans World Radio for their friendship and support.

It is my prayer that this book will be used as a warning of things to come. It is also my prayer that it will give hope and comfort to those who put their trust in God through Jesus Christ.

I can hear the hoofbeats of these horses much louder than when I first began writing this book. . . .

A Parable

Mt. Saint Helens belched gray steam plumes hundreds of feet into the blue Oregon sky. Geologists watched their seismographs in growing wonder as the earth danced beneath their feet. Rangers and state police, sirens blaring, herded tourists and residents from an ever-widening zone of danger. Every piece of scientific evidence being collected in the laboratories and on the field predicted the volcano would soon explode with a fury that would leave the forests flattened.

"Warning!" blared loudspeakers on patrol cars and helicopters hovering overhead. "Warning!" blinked battery-powered signs at every major crossroad. "Warning!" pleaded radio and television announcers, shortwave and citizens-band operators. "Warning!" echoed up and down the mountain; and lakeside villages, tourist camps and hiking trails emptied as people heard the warnings and fled for their lives.

But Harry Truman refused to budge. Harry was the caretaker of a recreation lodge on Spirit Lake, five miles north of Mt. Saint Helens's smoke-enshrouded peak. The rangers warned Harry of the coming blast. Neighbors begged him to join them in their exodus. Even Harry's sister called to talk sense into the old man's head. But Harry ignored the warnings. From the picture-postcard beauty of his lakeside home reflecting the snow-capped peak overhead, Harry grinned on national television and said, "Nobody knows more about this mountain than Harry and it don't dare blow up on him. . . ."

On 18 May 1980, as the boiling gases beneath the mountain's surface bulged and buckled the landscape to its final limits, Harry Truman cooked his eggs and bacon, fed his sixteen cats the scraps, and began to plant petunias around the border of his freshly mowed lawn. At 8:31 A.M. the mountain exploded.

Did Harry regret his decision in that millisecond he had before the concussive waves, traveling faster than the speed of sound, flattened him and everything else for 150 square miles? Did he have time to mourn his stubbornness as millions of tons of rock disintegrated and disappeared into a cloud reaching ten miles into the sky? Did he struggle against the wall of mud and ash fifty feet high that buried his cabin, his cats and his freshly mowed lawn—or had he been vaporized (like 100,000 people at Hiroshima) when the mountain erupted with a force 500 times greater than the nuclear bomb which leveled that Japanese city?

Now, Harry is a legend in the corner of Oregon where he refused to listen. He smiles down on us from posters and T-shirts and beer mugs. Balladeers sing a song about old Harry, the stubborn man who put his ear to the mountain but would not heed the warnings.

Note: Full information on all sources cited in the text is given in the bibliography at the end of the volume.

APPROACHING HOOFBEATS

The Four Horsemen
of the
Apocalypse

1

The Thunder of Distant Hoofbeats

On a barren, rock-strewn island in the Aegean Sea almost 2,000 years ago, another old man put his ear to the ground and heard the earth rumble ominously. Unlike Harry Truman at Spirit Lake near Mt. Saint Helens, John the apostle on the Isle of Patmos heard the thunder of distant hoofbeats and sounded the alarm. And that alarm, John's words of warning, are as clear and as urgent today as they were twenty centuries past.

Picture it. Tradition tells us that John's face is wrinkled, burned almost black by the sun. His arms are gnarled, his knees knobby. His feet and hands are rough and callused. He is a political prisoner of Rome in exile off the coast of Asia Minor (modern Turkey). John carries granite chipped from cliffs above the sea to a dock beneath the Roman citadel. It guards the narrow isthmus between the Bay of Scala and the Bay of Merika. The gravel will be used to build foundations for the temples and palaces of the Emperor Domitian or to pave his roads across the empire.

We can imagine that John, stumbling under the loaded straw basket strapped to his forehead, uses both hands to grasp his staff and pick his way painfully down the treacherous trail. Even the Roman guards must wonder at the determination of this gray-bearded Jewish Christian who works alongside the other prisoners by day, then spends his evenings writing stories they cannot understand.

"On the Lord's Day I was in the Spirit," John wrote, "and I heard behind me a loud voice like a trumpet, which said: 'Write on a scroll what you see and send it to the seven churches: to Ephesus, Smyrna, Pergamum, Thyatira, Sardis, Philadelphia and Laodicea'" (Revelation 1:10, 11).

And so, in his cavelike prison cell, John, the seer, spent every free moment recording the seismographic warnings of a world bulging and buckling just beneath the surface. His ancient world was not unlike our own.

The Vision

These stories of urgency and warning, written over the next eighteen months of John's island exile, were copied and sent as instructed to the seven churches in Asia. Eventually, this Apocalypse of St. John was titled by its opening line, "The Revelation of Jesus Christ" or simply "Revelation" and became the last and perhaps most controversial New Testament book.

Often in the history of the church the Book of Revelation has been neglected, misunderstood, or misinterpreted by far too many Christians. William Barclay wrote, "The Revelation is notoriously the most difficult and bewildering book in the New Testament; but doubtless, too, we shall find it infinitely worthwhile to wrestle with it until it gives us its blessing and opens its riches to us" (*The Revelation of John*, Vol. 1, p. ix).

Because of the vast technological advances of the past few years, the Book of Revelation is more easily understood. Many of the things that I used to think were symbolic are now realities in our world. For some strange reason, the Book is not being taught and preached on as much as it was in the earlier part of this century. And yet, at the beginning of the Book of Revelation (1:3), the Scripture says, "Blessed is the one who reads the words of this prophecy, and blessed are those who hear it and take to heart what is written in it, because the time is near."

The morning I wrote these words I had read in the paper a quote by one of the great literary and political leaders of our time. He used the very same expression, "The time is near. But I probably will not live to see the end."

That is the irony. The book of Revelation may be difficult and demanding to read, yet it is the only biblical book whose author promises a blessing to those who read it.

I am an evangelist, not a scholar. But I have spent a lifetime variously intrigued, inspired and informed by the warnings of this dramatic book written under inspiration by John on the Island of Patmos. In my study at home, I have read thousands of commentary pages, articles and word studies on Revelation. In my devotions I have let John's words flow over me, listening to God's voice speak through John's island voices. Until now I have resisted adding my feeble efforts to the great minds of the centuries who have grappled with the meaning of John's visions. But I can resist no longer.

Perhaps it is because I, too, like John, am growing older. There is something ominous in the air and my bones, like John's, vibrate with the horror and hope of it. Of course, he wrote 2,000 years ago. I know that his culture and mine are light years apart. He was a real man who wrote in a real moment of time to real people living in cities where now only ruins stand. And his message to them was clear. They understood it because he spoke in their language referring to people and events in their time.

But John wrote to me and to my time as well. His series of visions, dreams and nightmares are not meant to confuse or confound me. After all, *apocalypse* is a Greek word combining *calypto* (to veil, to cover, to conceal) with *apo* (from). Thus, *apocalypse* means "to remove the veil," "to uncover," "to reveal," "to make clear." His warnings were clear to people then. How we need that clarity now!

Once in the Louvre Museum in Paris I stood inches away from a large impressionistic painting by Renoir. Globs of paint seemed splattered incoherently across the canvas. "What in the world is that?" I wondered aloud. And my wife answered, "Stand back, Bill, and you will see it." I had stepped too close to the masterpiece and each individual detail, each oil splotch, each brush mark kept me from seeing the whole. I was bogged down by details. But when I stood back, the mysterious puzzle disappeared and the beautiful vision of the artist formed in my brain.

For too long, too many of us have stood too close to the Apocalypse of John. We have turned that great masterpiece into a series of blotches and brush marks. We have tried to outguess each other at the modern meaning of every star, every dragon, and every number—and we have lost the grand design of the prophet's vision and have missed the urgency of his warning.

Lately, there has been something magnetic to me about the writings of the apostle John; they keep drawing me back, haunting me, hounding me. Again, perhaps it is because I, like John, am growing older. But it is more and more obvious that the world I see around me is no longer so real or important as the world I cannot see—but it is real all the same.

I have not been banished to the isolation of a rocky island ten miles long and six miles wide. I have been banished to an endless itinerary of jet planes, hotels, coliseums, boardrooms and television studios. I am not surrounded by criminals and political prisoners. I am surrounded by ordinary people—businessmen, housewives, teachers, students, laborers, public servants, soldiers. I am not as often alone with the sounds of screeching sea gulls, or crashing waves, as I would like to be. Very often I am inundated with the sounds of the city and of men and women in the city drowning themselves in activity and noise. I can stand on a corner in New York or Paris or London or Tokyo and I can see hopelessness, fear and boredom on the faces of hundreds. It would seem, on the surface, that John and I have almost nothing in common. Yet I can almost hear the voices he heard. I hear the approaching hoofbeats of the distant horsemen. I hear their warnings and, like John, I have no choice but to deliver them.

The Man of Vision

Who was this wizened old man—poet, prophet and pastor? What drove him to write a letter that 2,000 years later still boggles the minds of believers and unbelievers alike? The argument about the

20

identity of the author of Revelation has raged over the centuries. But earliest Christian tradition, preserved by Justin Martyr, Clement, Origen, Irenaeus, Eusebius, Jerome and others, has it that the author was John the apostle. Modern scholars from John Walvoord to Bishop Robinson agree. And so do I.

Most of that little band who had lived with and learned from Jesus for three years were now dead. Each one had been martyred for his faith in the risen Christ. But, Amy Carmichael writes, to John the beloved disciple "was entrusted the long martyrdom of life."

Let us try to imagine what it might have been like. That wrinkled old man whose hand trembles as he scratches out Greek letters onto scraps of parchment in his prison cave was once the teenage Galilean fisherman who dropped his nets and, filled with hope, followed after Jesus to become a fisher of men. That exiled ancient squinting by candlelight at his growing manuscript once stood beside Jesus on the Mount of Transfiguration and later, flushed with power, argued to be secretary of state when Jesus set up His kingdom in Jerusalem. That tired visionary who sprawled exhausted on the rough-hewn table in his cell once stared at a wooden cross upon which the corpse of his Master hung. Numb with hopelessness and powerlessness, John felt his dreams die there. His aching body, roused by his guards to begin another day in the quarries, once stood in the empty tomb of Jesus and knew hope born in him again!

Now John is roughly herded from the prison cave. After breakfasting on a bowl of gruel, he is chained together with his fellow exiles and marched by Roman guards up the steep winding trail to the quarries. Now the cave is empty, but his pile of rough parchment pages are stacked neatly in a secret hollow or beneath a straw sleeping mat. One day those pages will be smuggled off the island. One day Christian volunteers will copy down what John wrote and deliver the Revelation of Jesus Christ to the churches of Asia. And from those churches the Apocalypse of John will spread round the world to you and to me.

Controversy will grow! Great church gatherings will be held to test Revelation's place in the growing corpus of sacred Christian writings. Is this vision inspired? Is it authoritative? Is it trustworthy? How is it to be interpreted? Some will rise to condemn John's vision to the fire. Others will rise to speak on its behalf. But when the dust settles, the words written by John in his damp island home of Patmos will be given equal place in the canon or approved works of Scripture. And, in the act, they will be placed forever as a word not limited in time and space, not limited by language or culture, but a word "God-breathed . . . useful for teaching, rebuking, correcting and training in righteousness, so that the man [or woman] of God may be thoroughly equipped for every good work" (2 Timothy 3:16, 17).

It is ironic how the debate has raged. It is even more ironic how the angelic voices anticipated the controversy when speaking to John on Patmos. Twice at the end of Revelation John records the voice as saying, "Write this down, for these words are trustworthy and true" (Revelation 21:5), and again, "The angel said to me, 'These words are trustworthy and true. The Lord, the God of the spirits of the prophets, sent his angel to show his servants the things that must soon take place'" (Revelation 22:6).

It is one thing to believe that John's words are "trustworthy and true," but it is another thing to understand their full meaning. There are word pictures in Revelation which leave me breathless with their beauty—and totally confused as to their exact meaning! I have heard at least a hundred different explanations for just one particularly difficult symbol in John's language—none of which seemed adequate, I might add. But that should not make us neglect the Book of Revelation or give up trying to understand it. We may not understand *everything*—but that does not mean we can't understand something.

To understand John and the Book of Revelation we need to remember several important things about this remarkable man.

First, John was an apocalyptist. That is, he wrote Revelation in a certain type of poetic language known as apocalyptic language. An apocalyptic writer—such as John—was one who used vivid imagery and symbolism to speak about God's judgment and the end of the world. Among the Jewish people in biblical times writers often used an apocalyptic style. Some parts of the Old Testament (such as portions of Daniel and Ezekiel) make use of apocalyptic language.

The difficulty, of course, is that this style of writing, using vivid word pictures and symbols, is quite foreign to us today. Undoubtedly most of John's first readers had little difficulty understanding what his symbols stood for—and whether or not some of them were symbols at all but were to be taken literally. It takes careful study for us today to understand some of the more obscure parts of his message (much of it quoted from the Old Testament)—and some of them we may never understand fully.

But again, this does not mean John's message is lost to us today—quite the opposite! When we take the trouble to dig into the treasures of Revelation we will be richly rewarded. Don't think of John's vivid language as a barrier to understanding—see it instead as the way he used to paint the picture of God's plan for the future in incredibly vivid colors.

As an apocalyptist John concentrated on one overpowering theme: the end of human history as we know it and the dawn of the glorious messianic age. As such, his message is always one of both warning and hope—warning of the coming judgment, and hope of Christ's inevitable triumph over evil and the establishment of His eternal kingdom.

We need that message today—that sin does not go unpunished, that God will judge. We need to know there is hope for the future when we are in Christ. In a bloody battle scene in Francis Ford Coppola's film *Apocalypse Now*, a messenger wanders into the front lines, looks at the chaos, and asks, "Who's in charge here?" No one answers his question. Many people today, looking at the chaos and evil of our world, wonder vaguely if anyone is in charge of this universe. John's message in Revelation answers clearly: Yes—God is! There is no reason to despair, because God is faithful to His promises of salvation and new life through Christ. My prayer as we look together at God's message through Revelation is that God will convict you of the reality of His judgment to come and give you new hope in your heart through Christ.

Second, John was also a prophet. The apocalyptists despaired of the present and looked only to the future. The prophets, on the other hand, often held out hope for the present—hope that God's judgment could be delayed if people would but repent and turn to God in faith and obedience. That does not mean the prophets offered an easy way out of all difficulties, as if somehow all problems would vanish if people would just profess their faith in God. Instead, like Winston Churchill standing amidst the bombed ruins of London, the prophets offered "blood, sweat, and tears" for those who would follow God. It would not be easy to serve God and fight against the evil of this present dark and sinful world, and yet the prophets knew that God would be victorious in the end and His people would share in that victory.

And so John was a prophet, calling his generation—and ours—to repentance and faith and action. He knew that men will never build the kingdom of God on earth, no matter how hard they might try. Only God can do that—and some day He will, when Christ comes again. But John also knew that God's judgment on this world could be delayed if we would repent and turn to Christ.

That sinewy old man on Patmos, chosen by God to receive and declare His special message, was therefore both apocalyptist and prophet. Why shouldn't he be both? After all, as a young Jew he had heard from the Old Testament of God's eventual judgment on the earth and the coming reign of the Messiah. He also had listened to the call of the prophets—Amos, Isaiah, Jeremiah and the others—who urged men with all their strength to turn back to God. Then one fateful day John had heard the call of Jesus Christ and responded by following Him. In Jesus, he discovered that the message of the apocalyptist and the prophet were united. In Him the apocalyptist's declaration of coming judgment and ultimate victory joined with the prophet's message of repentance and obedience to God in the face of present evil. "In this world you will have trouble," Jesus told His disciples. "But take heart! I have overcome the world" (John 16:33).

Again, we need to hear John's message as a prophet, declaring a message not only of the future but of the present. We need to hear his call to repentance and his challenge to live for God, taking our stand for purity and justice and righteousness no matter what others may do.

24

Third, John was also an evangelist. John's concern was not with a sterile message with no power to influence lives. John was concerned about people. He was concerned with the problems they were facing every day as they sought to be faithful to God. He was concerned with the pressures and persecution many of them encountered as Christians. He was concerned about people because he knew God loved them and sent His Son to die for them.

He also was an evangelist. The word "evangelist" comes from a Greek word which means "one who announces good news"— in this case, the Good News of the gospel. To some John's message of the future may have sounded gloomy and depressing. John knew, however, that the worst thing he could do would be to assure people everything was all right and that there was no need to be concerned about the evil in the world or God's judgment. But John's message is ultimately a message of good news—the Good News of salvation in Jesus Christ.

Our chaotic, confused world has no greater need than to hear the message of good news—the gospel of Jesus Christ. John's message in Revelation focuses not just on events that will happen in the future, but on what can happen now when Jesus Christ becomes Lord and Savior of our individual lives. John's message focuses supremely on Jesus Christ, the Son of God, who died for our sins and rose again from the dead to give us eternal life. What John declared at the end of his Gospel could also have been applied with equal force to his words in Revelation: "But these are written that you may believe that Jesus is the Christ, the Son of God, and that by believing you may have life in his name" (John 20:31).

John was also a pastor. Revelation was the apostle's last letter to the people he knew and loved best. He began the letter with seven personal notes, one to each of the seven little groups of Christians, scattered across Asia Minor, to whom his letter is addressed. Read the personal notes. See how well John knew his people and how deeply he loved them, but feel his fear for them and for us as well.

It is easy to picture how those first-century Christians began their life in Christ. I have preached in more than sixty nations of the world. I have seen thousands of people listening to the

Good News of Jesus' life, death and resurrection. I have watched many literally run to accept Christ as Savior and Lord of their lives. I have witnessed their enthusiasm and been thrilled by their early and rapid growth. Then, with John, I have watched first love die. I have seen men and women eagerly embrace the faith, then watched them slowly abandon it, giving in again to immorality, idolatry and self-destruction. And I have witnessed others who accepted Christ and remained faithful to the end—but found terrible suffering and sacrifice along the way.

I look back on my many years as an evangelist, and I wonder, have I made the Christian faith look too easy? Even before I heard the expression, I have constantly borne in mind what Bonhoeffer called "cheap grace." Of course it is "by grace you have been saved, through faith . . . not by works, so that no one can boast" (Ephesians 2:8, 9). Of course our salvation was a result of what Christ has done for us in His life and death and resurrection, not what we must do for ourselves. Of course we can trust Him to complete in us what He has begun. But in my eagerness to give away God's great gift, have I been honest about the price He paid in His war with evil? And have I adequately explained the price we must pay in our own war against the evil at work in and around our lives?

John worried about his flock as he wrote his vision of this world (where evil reigns) and of the world to come (where God will restore righteousness and peace again). He wrote of the war between the worlds and of the men and women who fight and die on the battlefield in that war. At the center of his vision, he wrote of Jesus, the Lord of the world to come, who has entered this world to rescue humankind (wherever they find themselves on the battlefield), to guide them through enemy lines and to deliver them safely home again.

Revelation is not an academic paper produced for some scholarly professional meeting. It is not a poem created by a gifted genius to entertain and divert. It is not the diary of a senile old man driven to wild hallucinations by his isolation and loneliness. Revelation is a pastor's letter to his floundering flock, an urgent telegram bearing a brilliant battle plan for a people at war. It reflects all the realistic horror and heartbreak of a bloody battlefield strewn with corpses. It is frank and it is frightening, but it is a plan for victory—if not for every battle, certainly for the war.

That's why I must write this book. With John, I have heard the distant sound of hoofbeats. I have seen the evil riders on the horizons of our lives. I am still an evangelist whose one goal is to proclaim new life in Christ, but there is serious trouble ahead for our world, for all of us who live in it, and in the four horsemen of the Apocalypse there is both a warning and wisdom for those troubled days ahead.

2

Is There
Any
Hope?

Recently my wife and I were in Europe and were reading the British, French and American papers. Within a two-week period we clipped out more than a score of articles that used the word *apocalypse* or *armageddon*. Reporters, commentators, editors—the men and women working in modern media—seem hypnotized by the notion of the end of the world as we know it. A recently widely circulated book on nuclear war strategy is called *The Wizards of Armageddon*. The *London Times* featured one article entitled "The Shadow of Armageddon." The story raised the grim specter of a future race war in Britain. Other columns, editorials, news stories and letters to the editors were permeated by the common fears: nuclear war, economic chaos, the misuse and drying up of the earth's nonrenewable resources, runaway crime, violence in the streets, mysterious new killer viruses, terrorism, radically changing weather patterns, earthquakes, floods, famines, destruction and death. Everywhere I go I find people, both leaders and ordinary individuals, asking one basic question: "Is there any hope?" And the answer comes roaring back from the world's press: "There is no hope for planet earth!"

One morning in the woods near our home I walked with

the morning paper in one hand and the Apocalypse of John, the Book of Revelation, in the other. The saintly seer on Patmos was writing for just such a time as this. His visions ring with hope. Although his letter was addressed to the seven churches in the Roman province of Asia, more accurately to the handful of Christian believers who made up the churches in each town, his letter is written to us as well. And though his news to them and to us for the long haul of history was hopeful good news, his vision for the immediate future was not. He wrote honestly to his Christian friends of the disaster ahead and how they were to face it. We need to take his words to heart.

The News Is Good—and Bad

I have spent my lifetime proclaiming one central truth: there is good news for the people of planet earth. At the heart of that good news is Jesus Christ. He is God in human flesh, and the story of His life, death and resurrection is the only good news there is to proclaim these days. I have spent my life on nearly empty street corners and in packed coliseums across the world telling people that good news. You can be forgiven. You can be at one with your Creator again. Regardless of your past, you can be guaranteed a future through faith in Jesus as Lord and Savior of your life. I like announcing that good news, but if I am to take John's island visions seriously this time I cannot write just the good news! There is also bad news.

John, too, was an evangelist. I am sure he would have been content to finish his days writing of the past. Imagine the untold stories of Jesus that he might have shared with Christians of his day (and with us). After all, John was an old man. The old are supposed to reminisce. He could have added to the books he had already written (the Gospel of John and probably the three letters of John as well), filling his parchment pages with memories of those wonderful days with the Master beside the Sea of Galilee and in the hills around Jerusalem. He was an eyewitness on the scene when God walked the earth in human flesh healing the sick, casting out evil spirits and raising the dead. What a wonderful, hope-filled book he might have written. But it was not to be. This time Jesus interrupted John on Patmos and told him to share the bad news along with the good.

A Pilgrimage to Patmos

To understand the visions of John, to get hold of both the good news and the bad news at their core, to understand the warning, the hope and the direction in those visions, we must return to Patmos on a personal pilgrimage. We must walk the beaches with the old man and see his visions again, close up and in living color. We must ask what they meant to John and to that handful of Christian believers scattered across the empire. Then, we must ask what John's visions mean to us.

Imagine it. "On the Lord's Day," he wrote to that handful of believers, "I heard behind me a loud voice like a trumpet" (Revelation 1:10). From the text we learn that this revelation by Jesus to John began on "the Lord's Day." Perhaps, in their "benevolence," John's Roman captors allowed this Jewish seer his ancient Old Testament practice of keeping one day out of seven holy. Perhaps, that day, they had already herded the other grumbling non-Jewish prisoners to their hot quarry labors and left the old man to walk alone along the Aegean Sea. I can imagine him there praying the ancient prayers, singing the ancient psalms, quoting from memory great portions of the ancient words of wisdom and remembering the new life and meaning Jesus had given these ancient practices.

A Pastor's Heart

Suddenly, John stands and walks nervously down the beach. He is worried about the Christian believers on the mainland only miles away. How he longs for this separation from them to end. After all, he had the heart of a pastor. How many men and women, boys and girls sitting in those seven places of worship had probably been led to faith in Christ through John's own preaching?

He felt responsible for them and for their spiritual growth. Others, directly and indirectly, had helped raise up those churches, but the others were dead: Paul, beheaded with a Roman sword; Peter, crucified upside down on a rough wooden cross; John's own brother, James, beheaded by Herod Agrippa; and young Mark, dragged through the streets of Alexandria and burned, his body bruised and still bleeding. Unconfirmed news of the deaths or disappearances of John's close friends and co-workers must have left him lonely and even more fearful for the future of the churches they had planted together.

At first it had been safe and rather simple to be a Christian in a world dominated by the Roman Empire. The Caesars had even granted special privileges to the Jews. Most of the earliest Christian believers were Jews who shared in those privileges. Under the Pax Romana (the peace Rome built across the world with Roman might and Roman law) the church had spread. Roman authorities had even saved Paul's life in Jerusalem when Caesar's soldiers rescued him from a mob infuriated by his preaching (Acts 21:31, 32). Peter had written to the earliest Christians that they were to fear God and "honor the emperor" (1 Peter 2:12–17, RSV)—although the emperor was often evil and persecution was breaking out.

But toward the end of the first century all benevolence had ceased. Rome was losing her grip on the world. The emperors and their courts had grown more and more extravagant. The royal treasuries had been drained. New taxes were levied by the Roman senate to help offset their balance-of-trade deficit. When protest and rebellion followed, Rome answered with the sword.

It was no simple task for Rome to maintain an empire made up of so many differing races, religions and cultures. Nationalist movements, political conspiracies, terrorism and open attack grew until the empire was threatened from within and from without. And out of the emperor's growing paranoia to maintain Rome's power and keep her subjects in check, one simple test of loyalty evolved. On certain feasts and holidays row upon row of subjects lined up to walk past the area's Roman magistrate, toss a pinch of incense into a fire in the golden bowl at his feet and mutter, "Caesar is Lord."

Jesus—or Caesar?

Most citizens of the empire were glad to pay tribute to the emperor and to the empire that had brought them this period of peace. But for the Christian, another loyalty oath was at the center of his or her faith. "Jesus is Lord," not Caesar. In spite of their gratitude to the empire and to the emperor, in spite of the admonitions of Paul and Peter to worship God and honor the emperor, this act of Caesar worship was impossible. And because of their refusal to put Caesar before Christ, Christian believers began to be persecuted.

William Barclay writes, "This worship [of Caesar] was never intended to . . . wipe out other religions. Rome was essentially tolerant. A man might worship Caesar *and* his own god. But more and more Caesar worship became a test of political loyalty; it became . . . the recognition of the dominion of Caesar over a man's life, and . . . soul" (*The Revelation of John*, Vol. 1, pp. 21–22).

Imagine a village in the suburbs of Ephesus or Laodicea. Christian believers are at work tanning leather, dying cloth, harvesting crops, raising families, studying math and history—at worship, at work or at play. Then, suddenly, hoofbeats are heard clattering up the nearby cobbled streets. The horses are reined in by a Roman centurion and his honor guard. A leather camp table is unfolded. An incense burner is placed upon the table. A flame is lit. Heralds sound the trumpets. There is no place to hide, no time to decide. Believers must join their neighbors in that line. Just ahead the village mayor tosses his incense into the flames and exclaims proudly, "Caesar is Lord." Others follow. The line ahead grows shorter. The moment of decision draws near. Will the Christian avoid the conflict and protect his life and security with the simple act of obedience? Will he mutter "Caesar is Lord" and sneak back home to safety? Or will he recognize that act as a symbol of a wider disobedience, refuse the incense, proclaim "Jesus is Lord" and pay the price for his disloyalty to the state?

Did John wander up and down the beach at Patmos that Sabbath remembering the centurion, the incense and the terrible decision of ultimate loyalty each believer had to make? Who knows? Perhaps it was in just such a line, surrounded by his neighbors and friends, that John himself failed the emperor's test and, in punishment, was exiled to the island prison. We don't know the charges leveled against the apostle that led to his exile, but we do know why John said he was there: "I, John, your brother and companion in the suffering and kingdom and patient endurance that are ours in Jesus, was on the island of Patmos because of the word of God and the testimony of Jesus" (Revelation 1:9).

It was not easy to be a Christian then. It is not easy now. Late in the first century, during the time of John's exile, the persecutions of the Christian church by the Roman Empire had begun in earnest. It was difficult to keep the faith then. It is now. There are grand and awful moments before a centurion's blazing fire. And there are little and awful moments almost daily when one longs to give in to the values of this world, to give up the high standards of our Lord, to give way to the various temptations that pressure every man, woman or young person who believes. Even Christians are tempted to surrender to the passions or the pleasures that pursue us all.

A Daily Decision

We think of modern Christians living under atheistic or totalitarian regimes as being the only ones who must daily decide their ultimate loyalties. It is not true. Every Christian in every nation—totalitarian, democratic or somewhere in between—decides daily to be loyal to Christ and the world He is building or to give in to this age and its values.

No wonder John was anxious. The believers then had (and now have) a constant and confounding choice. Those infant Christians in the churches of Asia lived in a world (not unlike our own) where their belief in Christ often left them at odds with the political powers, the economic realities and the social norms. The day-by-day choices were difficult and demanding. Great suffering lay ahead. Would they keep the faith? Would they stand firm or would they give up under the pressure and the pain of following

Jesus? Every day today—as then—the Christian will face many decisions. Will he give in to the materialism, the selfish pleasures, the dishonest practices of this present age? What do you do when you face these decisions? Is your steadfast desire to do God's will, or do you give in to the steady pressures of those around you? The Bible says, "Don't let the world around you squeeze you into its own mold, but let God remold your minds from within, so that you may prove in practice that the plan of God for you is good, meets all his demands and moves toward the goal of true maturity" (Romans 12:2, Phillips).

Suddenly, John heard the voice "like a trumpet." We are dealing with mystery here. I can't tell you how the visions came or in what real or symbolic form they appeared to the seer. When I read the beginning of John's revelation on Patmos (Revelation 1:12–20) I try to picture it in my mind. We don't know if John, "in the Spirit," simply sat quietly on the Patmos beach and saw the visions in his mind's eye. There is a tradition that the Spirit of God came to John in a dark cave and lifted him up from that cave to four different locations just as Jesus was led by Satan to the mountaintop in His desert temptations. It is even possible that the visions all took real form and substance to John—more real than the holograms in Disneyland's Haunted House where specters dance through walls and young and old watch open-mouthed at the lifelike apparitions before them.

A Picture on Patmos

I do believe, however, that John saw vividly what he describes, that everything he saw was from God and that each vision is as important and as full of meaning and application today, to you and to me, as it was to those seven churches in Asia. Come with me to Patmos. Picture John praying desperately for the churches in his care. Suddenly he hears a voice, trumpet clear, speaking to him. The biblical account ignores the first words of the speaker. Perhaps it was a simple greeting, not unlike the angel greeting Mary before giving her good news. Perhaps it was the glory of the Lord shining round about or a host of angels from heaven, not unlike those that caused the shepherds to shake with fear before their good news. We don't know what the figure said, but we do know the first response of John to his "good news." He was terrified.

As he whirled to "see the voice" his eyes were blinded by light from seven great lamps. Standing in the light was a man, his eyes blazing, his head and hair "white like wool." The figure's feet were "like bronze glowing in a furnace, and his voice was like the sound of rushing waters." The figure held seven stars in his right hand. Out of his mouth came a sharp double-edged sword and his face was "like the sun shining in all its brilliance" (Revelation 1:12–16).

John fell before the figure "as though dead," stunned and awed by what he saw. That man (standing in the light with a robe "reaching down to his feet" and "with a golden sash around his chest") was Jesus. Yet John did not recognize his Master. It was the very same Jesus who had first appeared to John by the Sea of Galilee. Three years they had been together; still John did not recognize the Savior. This was the very same Jesus who had appeared to John and the others in a locked upper room, His resurrected body changed yet still bearing open wounds on hands, feet and side from the nails of the cross and a cruelly thrust Roman spear. This was the very same Jesus who had taken on the powerlessness of a human being to share humanity's suffering, to feel humanity's weaknesses and temptation, and to deliver humankind from evil. Yet John, long-time disciple, close personal friend and intimate associate, had no idea that this giant, glowing figure was his risen Lord.

Then, gently, as a mother wakens a child from night terrors, the figure leaned over the panic-stricken John, touched his shoulder and said, "Do not be afraid. I am the First and the Last. I am the Living One; I was dead, and behold I am alive for ever and ever! And I hold the keys of death and Hades" (Revelation 1:17, 18).

What is going on here? Well, imagine what was going on in John. Had he, only moments before this mysterious encounter, been fearing for the future of the church? Then suddenly the risen

Christ Himself appears to deliver the word that is needed as desperately now as it was almost twenty centuries past. Had the seer been wondering if in fact there was sufficient power available to him and to his flock to withstand in that evil day, when suddenly the Creator and Sustainer of the universe reveals Himself as the One who holds the key, the One who holds the power over the very worst fears that plague humankind—death and eternal lostness?

"Write, John!" commanded the Lord of Power. Then, He clearly specified to whom the letter should be sent: to the leaders of the churches ("the angels of the seven churches"—which literally means "pastors") and to the members of the churches from which this light would shine to brighten the entire world ("the seven lamp-stands"). "Write . . . what you have seen," commanded the figure bright as the sun. "Write what is now and what will take place later" (Revelation 1:19).

God Is Still in Control

This is the *good news.* Imagine how you would feel if you were John. At one moment, John is worrying about his Christian friends struggling to survive in those awful times of hard choices and bloody persecutions. The very next moment, he is standing before the Lord of History who assures him by His very presence that He is still in control of this world. He still has plans for His people, and He is about to tell us what we can do to participate in His plan for the redemption and the renewal of planet earth. Perhaps right now you are facing some particular problem, and you even are at the point of despair. But Christ comes to you and says, "I am Lord! There is no circumstance beyond My power, and you can trust Me."

Then almost immediately, there is bad news with the good. The irony of what follows, the words John was instructed to write, reminds me of my last visit to California. The state had suffered through the worst winter in memory. Winds had howled, felling power lines and plunging cities into darkness. Seas had bashed and buffeted beachside communities, swallowing houses and piers, parks and highways in a powerful, murky tide. Rain had fallen, causing rivers to drown people and animals, whole towns and croplands. It was a terrible time and the media were filled with stories on how to cope with the present storm.

Yet the front-page news in the *Los Angeles Times* warned worse times were coming. Scientists at the California Institute of Technology warned people across the entire state to prepare for an earthquake of major proportions. The instructions were clear. Lists of emergency supplies were recommended. How they should be stored for easy retrieval was described. How people should respond when the earth began to shake was outlined clearly. "Get away from buildings with glass windows. Stand in a strong archway or rush into an open space. Don't exit your houses without guarding against heavy tiles and pieces of plaster falling from above. Turn to the emergency radio station. Gather your medical supplies and help your neighbor—for the roads will be closed and emergency vehicles will be stranded. You may have to wait for help for several days."

Picture the poor Californian, wading through the flooded ruins of his beachfront home, being warned that soon an earthquake will tumble what remains into the sea. That is the double-edged predicament which faced the Christian believers in the seven churches of Asia. This is the bad news with the good. They are already facing terrible trouble. That reality is acknowledged and warning given in the seven individual letters to the churches (Revelation 2, 3). But worse trouble is coming. That second warning echoes from the hoofbeats of the horsemen of the Apocalypse as the seals are opened and the future revealed.

It is good news to know that God has a plan for the redemption of the world. But first, the prophet warns his people to set their lives in order. That's his immediate, short-term advice, complete with specific directions as to how it might be accomplished. John catalogs their sins and warns them of the consequences. He exhorts them to overcome. (In the next chapter we will look at these seven letters of advice to the first-century Christians and see how relevant they are to you and me.)

Second, warns the prophet, there are even worse times ahead. We are to prepare to meet them. That's the long-range warning of the four horsemen of death and destruction already riding in their direction and in ours. (The rest of this book will be focused on those horsemen, their significance to the first-century church and their significance to us.) There's good news in knowing we can overcome the present sin, weakness and suffering in our lives and in so doing grow tough enough to overcome the sin, weakness and suffering that lies ahead.

My wife was born and raised as the daughter of missionary parents in China. She witnessed firsthand how God prepared His church there during times of trouble to withstand the even greater troubled times ahead. And the Christians in China not only survived the years of crises and conflict; they have multiplied and grown stronger under the difficult times of restrictive laws and suffering. So, in the good news and in the bad, there is great hope for the future. Through John's visions on the island of Patmos we are given signposts that will lead us all along our way.

3

A Call
to the
Churches

Imagine it! On Patmos, the apostle John lies prostrate where he had fallen before the mighty presence of the risen Lord. With one hand John might have shielded his eyes against the blazing light. The great figure whose eyes shone like fire, the seven great lamps blazing around Him, and the sun reflecting off the sea blurred all the images together into one blinding light. John must have wiped his eyes in wonder as he tried to focus on the scene, to take it in, to grasp its meaning.

We don't know what happened next. Perhaps Jesus moved out of the light, reached down for John's gnarled hand and gently lifted the old man to his feet. Perhaps their eyes met for a moment as they had met half a century earlier. And in that flash of recognition John may have seen past the blinding splendor and recognized the risen Lord—the same Jesus who had walked beside him, arm in arm, on a Galilean beach and in the streets of Jerusalem. Possibly John felt the same compelling love of Jesus he had known as they walked the trails and byways of Galilee and Judea. Perhaps he felt Jesus' arm on his shoulder as the Lord led him up the shoreline and past the grove of palm trees to his prison cave. Maybe John stumbled about in the darkness of his exile home searching for the oil lamp and lighting it, flattening out a new piece of parchment and inking the end of a freshly shaved quill. Possibly he sat for a moment before the driftwood slab that served him as desk and altar, waiting for the Lord to begin His message.

You may imagine the details of John's dream in another way. The details aren't important. But it helps me to picture John there with the risen Lord, for whatever form the vision took—whether a very private, personal revelation by our Lord in John's mind's eye or this very literal experience on a Patmos beach—to get a feeling for this moment, to see what actually happened on Patmos that day, is to realize the wonder and hope from Christ's revelation, both the good news and the bad.

We have been talking about John's vision of Jesus. But are we necessarily to expect God to give us a vision like that? No. God has given us His Word, the Bible. Do you want to know God more deeply and intimately? Do you want to discover His will for your life? Then read and study the Scriptures daily.

We don't know the details. But this one thing we know. The risen Lord spoke that moment to John and told him to write. "Write," He said. "Write. . . . the mystery of the seven stars that you saw in my right hand and of the seven golden lampstands. . . . The seven stars are the angels [leaders or pastors] of the seven churches, and the seven lampstands are the seven churches" (Revelation 1:19, 20). Then He begins the series of short letters to the seven churches in the Roman Province of Asia (now modern Turkey) that you have read about in the second and third chapters of the book of Revelation. "To the angel of the church in Ephesus," commands the risen Lord, "write" (Revelation 2:1)!

The preceding details are unimportant. The important part is what Jesus told John to write. What was happening on Patmos that day elevates the words of those seven short letters into God's eternal Word, as trustworthy and as authoritative to our times as they were to John's. And what we learn from these words goes beyond the words themselves to lessons about God that stir at the very heart of Revelation.

First, He sees and cares about us as individuals. Imagine it! He knows those people by name. Our risen Lord cares about each believer intimately. Look at the details in each letter. He named names. He described events. He commended the churches for their successes. He scolded them for their failures. He gave them warm, loving, confronting counsel. What hope that gives to me, to each of us. He knows us as a mother knows her child. The risen Lord did not withdraw far off somewhere in the universe. He is present in His Spirit in every believer. He knows each believer by name, and when we search His Word, when we stop to hear His voice, He will be specific to us now as He was specific to them then.

Second, He sees us as sharing our lives with other believers in the church. He was concerned about each of those individual churches in the cities and towns of Asia. He didn't dictate those letters to key leaders across the world or to official gatherings of bishops or clergy. He wrote to individual churches, small clusters of believers, leaders and followers together. At the heart of these letters is God's assumption that we belong together at work and at worship in a local church. I am convinced that the cluster of believers of which you are a part, those brothers and sisters in Christ with whom you join to pray and study, give and witness, is the basic unit through which God is working to redeem the world. He cared about each of their individual churches then. He cares about each of our individual churches now. He cares deeply about how we relate to Him, to each other, to our communities and to our world. That He cares about each of our churches (as He cared about those seven churches then) should give us great hope!

Third, the issues to which the risen Lord spoke then are the very same issues about which He would speak to us now. Our problems are not unique. Our sins, our temptations, our weaknesses, our needs are no different from theirs. That, too, gives me hope; for in His revelation through John to the churches of Asia, Jesus was anticipating the struggles we would face and speaking to us as well. The call and the warning He gave them is the call and the warning we must hear today.

Fourth, although the form of each letter is practically the same—

the greeting, the title of the risen Christ, a word of praise (except to Laodicea), a word of criticism (except to Smyrna and Philadelphia), the warning, and the promise—*the content of each letter is different.* He knew that every church was facing its own unique struggle to be His body in the world and so He addressed each church uniquely. He didn't mass-produce advice. We can gain hope from this. His words to them are His words to us, but we too face our own unique struggle; therefore, we must search the letters to find exactly the right word at the right time that applies to us and to our struggle, remembering that some of the advice may not apply to us at all, at least not yet, not now.

By now, you must be wondering, when will we ever get to the four horsemen of the Apocalypse? When will we hear the hoofbeats? Why all this talk about Patmos, the "good news with the bad," and the seven churches of Asia? I'll tell you why. Those distant hoofbeats, growing louder by the day, are the riders who would destroy the earth and all of us who live upon her. To face these riders, to make war upon death and bring new life—life in Christ— to the people of the earth, will require certain preliminary steps.

That's why Christ began His vision with these seven short letters to the Christians in Asia. He knew what their future held. He knew the price they would have to pay in their war against evil. And He knew those churches were not prepared to pay that price. They were not yet strong enough to face the horsemen. He knew that unless they spent time and energy getting prepared, they would not survive those riders of death and destruction. He knew that unless they learned better how to overcome, they might themselves be overcome by the riders. So, in the letters are the clues that they and we must follow as we face the riders galloping down upon us. In the letters are His words of power that will help us overcome the destruction they would bring upon the earth.

To simplify, I've combined the letters into three groups. When you've finished this chapter, go back and search the letters for those words that speak to your situation. Turn now to Revelation 2:1–7 and Revelation 3:14–22. Read the letters John received from Christ for the church in Ephesus and the church in Laodicea.

The Call to Holy Passion—Ephesus and Laodicea

Ephesus was a large seaport city on the Aegean Sea. The apostle Paul himself helped found the church in this great commercial and religious center. At the heart of the city was the temple to Artemis (Diana), one of the seven wonders of the ancient world, a temple four times the size of the Parthenon in Athens. Paul almost lost his life in his courageous stand against the idolatrous worship of Artemis (Acts 19). He invested two years of his life in the people of Ephesus and the growing young church there, and the investment paid in rich dividends for the kingdom of God. Ephesus became the center from which the Good News of Christ spread throughout Asia. The church at Ephesus was known throughout the empire for her fervor and for her faith (perhaps 50,000 members).

Do you remember that wonderful moment in Acts when the elders from the church in Ephesus met Paul in Miletus to say their last good-byes to him? He was on his final journey to Jerusalem, and from there to Rome where he would meet his death. The elders held onto the apostle and wept as he shared his final thoughts with them. At the heart of his advice that last day were these words: "After I leave," he warned them, "savage wolves will come in among you and will not spare the flock. . . . So be on your guard" (Acts 20:29–31).

Apparently, they had taken Paul's words to heart. More than half a century later, Christ's letter to them in the Revelation indicated He was pleased that they had "tested those who claim to be apostles but are not, and . . . found them false" (Revelation 2:2). Too, at Miletus he had instructed them "to help the weak" and in Revelation Christ commended them for "your deeds, your hard work and your perseverance" (Revelation 2:2). Still, in spite of their obedience and their endurance, something had gone wrong. "You have forsaken your first love," He warned them. "Remember the height from which you have fallen! Repent and do the things you did at first" (Revelation 2:4, 5). Remember—repent—or be removed.

Laodicea

If you had followed the Maeander River due east from its headwaters near Ephesus and taken the first major tributary to the right about four miles, you would have found the city of Laodicea. This, too, was a prosperous town in the times of John's exile. On the road between Rome and its southern provinces, Laodicea became a center of banking and exchange. A prestigious medical center known around the world for its healing eye salve was another Laodicean claim to fame. And in the hills around the city grazed sheep of such pure black wool that the most expensive and stylish clothing of the empire was made from the rich, black fabrics woven there. How ironic (and how perfect an example of our risen Lord's attention to detail) that He would say to the church in Laodicea, "you are . . . poor, blind and naked" (Revelation 3:17).

We don't have the early history of the young Christian church in Laodicea. But we know how highly Christ must have valued their potential in kingdom building, for this church felt His wrath in the visions to John with a white-hot intensity. "You are lukewarm—neither hot nor cold—I am about to spit you out of my mouth," Christ warned them (Revelation 3:16). Then, in an almost immediate counterpoint, Christ continues with one of the best-known and most poignant invitations in biblical literature: "Those whom I love I rebuke and discipline. So be earnest, and repent. Here I am! I stand at the door and knock. If anyone hears my voice and opens the door, I will go in and eat with him, and he with me" (Revelation 3:19, 20).

Both the Ephesian and the Laodicean Christians had lost their holy passion. The same thing had happened to Jerusalem in Jeremiah's day when he wrote, "The word of the Lord came to me . . . 'I remember the devotion of your youth, how as a bride you loved me and followed me through the desert, through a land not sown' " (Jeremiah 2:1, 2). In other words, the people of that day had also lost their first love, and God had rebuked them.

The "first love" of the Ephesians had settled into a kind of faithfulness to doctrinal purity. They could probably spot a heresy or a heretic a mile upriver. They probably knew the creeds by heart and passed them on faithfully from generation to generation. But Christ's letter says, "Repent!" Repent of the coldness of your hearts and your lack of zeal. Repent of your lovelessness and your lack of concern for others.

Apparently the first passionate prayers of the Laodiceans had settled into comfortable prayers of gratitude. Christ mocked their prayers with "You say, 'I am rich; I have acquired wealth and do not need a thing.' But you do not realize," He warned, "that you are wretched, pitiful, poor, blind and naked" (Revelation 3:17).

One vacation, Ruth and I had been invited to the home of some wealthy socialites. They had gathered together a large group of their neighboring vacationers for a party, and asked me if I would say a few words. I explained the gospel simply and briefly, reminding them that pleasure and possessions are not lasting— that only the person who knows Jesus Christ as Savior can know true happiness. As I concluded, one attractive woman known for her casual morals and high life style, young and smartly dressed, laughed gaily. "But, Billy," she protested, "what about those of us who are perfectly happy?"

From God's point of view, that woman was spiritually wretched, pitiful, poor, blind and naked, as the years ahead were soon to prove. Christ says to people like her as well, "Repent!"

For the churches in Ephesus and Laodicea, the problem was *the problem of spiritual passion.* "You have forsaken your first love," John writes the Ephesians. "You are neither cold nor hot," he writes the Laodiceans. What began as a wholehearted commitment to Christ and His work gradually cooled. We don't have any of the details, only these fragments of history from Revelation, but we can picture it from our own experience.

I remember the first time I saw Ruth. With me, it was love at first sight. I can still remember the excitement I felt. I remember the first time I held her hand. I remember the thrill of the first kiss, our eyes shining with love for each other. I remember my stomach churning, heart pumping, blood boiling during our honeymoon and for years afterward. First love is wonderful. But the first flames of physical passion inevitably change.

Our love has been one of commitment. The word *love* is an

active, not passive, verb. It should not be confined to the physical. It is a lifetime of commitment. Ruth and I can sit on our front porch on a summer's evening and hardly say a word, but we are communing with each other, and communicating. The passion is even deeper. But we have known so many who did not have that spiritual commitment to each other. Their love was only physical. The first flames of the honeymoon inevitably went cool, then the day-to-day routine settled in. The passion of first love died, and with the passion died the practices associated with it.

Remember that moment you first heard of Christ and believed in Him as Lord and Savior of your life? Remember kneeling at a parent's bedside, at a local church altar or in the quiet of a redwood retreat, or coming forward in an evangelistic crusade? Remember joining the church and feeling the loving arms of a Christian community reach out to receive you? Remember your baptism and the joy you felt in this act of faith?

Remember sharing your testimony for the first time? Remember leading someone you loved into the faith? Remember studying the Word with relish and pouring out your heart in prayer? (When I accepted Christ someone handed me a little booklet entitled *Biblical Treasures.* It had Scripture memory verses and even hymns. I remember milking the cows on my father's dairy farm, singing those hymns and memorizing those Scriptures.) Remember making your first generous pledge to the church, or joining hands and hearts with a small group of your brothers and sisters in Christ to sing "Amazing Grace" or to work for the poor and oppressed in your neighborhood? Remember your "first love" and all those acts of worship, witness, work or fellowship that flowed spontaneously from the time of your "first love"?

Christ was calling the Ephesians and the Laodiceans away from respectable, comfortable, passionless, lukewarm religion. He wanted them totally committed to Him, wholeheartedly available. He called them back to the holy passion and the joy of the first love. They had settled instead for mere theological respectability and material comfort. He wanted them alive, depending, risking, passionate again. For it is in that "first love" commitment that they would find the strength to face the horsemen.

Of course, John was addressing the believers in Ephesus and Laodicea who had lost their "first love." Let me here interrupt to ask an even more basic question. Perhaps you have never known Christ personally as your Savior and Lord, never loved Him that way. Perhaps you have never known the wonder of seeking Christ's forgiveness for your sins or the joy of being forgiven. Before you go any further in reading this book, you could know all of this right now.

You may ask, "What do I have to do?" First: Admit your need ("I am a sinner"). Second: Be willing to turn from your sins (repent). Third: Believe that Jesus Christ died for you on the cross and rose from the grave. Fourth: Through prayer, invite Jesus Christ to come in and control your life (receive Him as Savior and Lord).

You see, it's that simple! God loves you. Christ died for you. You repent of your sin. You receive forgiveness. And you discover the joy of that "first love."

Recently I met a well-known lawyer on an airplane. He was drinking everything the stewardess served to drown his pain. It wasn't working. He told me that he was a church member in good standing, but, he said, "I need to clean up my act. I really would like to serve God." I immediately recognized that he did not even know the Lord. Sitting across the aisle was my associate T. W. Wilson. Since I was studying and preparing for an important engagement at the end of the flight, I turned the man over to T. W. who explained to him the way to salvation.

The man went back to his home church and asked if he could say a few words on a Sunday evening. He admitted to the whole church what a hypocrite he had been. Then he looked out over the congregation and said, "A lot of you are the same kind of hypocrite I've been." He said, "I've cleaned up my act. I've made my peace with God." Recently I heard he had given his testimony in another church. He had found for the first time, even though he had been a longtime church member, his "first love."

For the rest of us for whom that "first love" stage is long past, John has very specific advice. John writes in the Spirit to the Ephesians, "Remember therefore from whence thou art fallen, and repent, and do the first works" (Revelation 2:5, KJV). We don't know from the record what those first works were. But we can guess from our own experiences with "first love" in courtship or marriage. Remember your desire to be at your best, to please, to be in the company of the other always? Remember the growing sense of awe and wonder and surprise? Remember all the actions, large and small, that went with that love?

"You don't send me flowers anymore," says one lover to another whose love has grown cold and whose forgetfulness gives his secret away. "How did we get here from there?" asks one despairing spouse of another when their anniversary is forgotten, when the warm feelings have died, the marriage is on the rocks, and "first love" days are only memories. Christ sees Himself and His church as lovers. The Old Testament is full of ardent expressions describing God's relationship with His people. The church is the bride of Christ in New Testament terms.

In this Revelation warning, Christ is a jealous lover calling out to the Ephesians and the Laodiceans to return and renew their "first love." He doesn't ask that they return to the *feelings* of those first days. You can't rejuvenate those same physical feelings of first love twenty or thirty years after the honeymoon is over— but you can do the *acts* of "first love." Love is more than feeling. Love is a commitment. Love is doing. "For God so loved the world he gave," John had written earlier. "My little children, love not in word only, but in deed." You can do the works of first love again, and in the process rekindle the intensity of that love.

Think back. What specific works were a part of your "first love"? I think, for example, of being with the one you love. Talking with the one you love. Listening to the one you love. I remember the times that I have gone off to a quiet place to talk with God alone, to actually walk with Him. Many times before some of the crusades I have held, I have wandered into the woods or the mountains to pray and to talk and to think.

I remember that before the London Crusade in 1954 I spent a great deal of time on the front porch of what we at Montreat call "Chapman Home." It was the old home of one of the great evangelists of another generation, J. Wilbur Chapman, and the place where the famous hymn, "Ivory Palaces," was written. I used to sit on that front porch and pour out my heart to the Lord—and I would hear Him speak and give me assurance that He was going to be with us in that crusade. We were still young and inexperienced, and yet we were trying to reach one of the great cities of the world for Christ. It was supposed to be a month-long crusade. We stayed three months and, by the end, tens of thousands had found Christ. The crusade made news all over the world and encouraged Christians everywhere.

I remember the New York Crusade where we stayed sixteen weeks at Madison Square Garden. How many problems we faced! How many crises came even before the crusade began! How I used to walk the trails around my home and pour out my heart to the Lord. In some of the darkest hours I could feel the touch of His hand on mine as I reached up through the darkness.

This was a return to "first love."

When was the last time you set an afternoon aside simply to be alone with the Lord, to walk and talk with Him as you might your very best friend? From my earliest days of faith, I loved to read, study and memorize the Word. I was eager to learn what He wanted of me, and quick to obey. When was the last time you turned off the noises that can drown out His still, small voice and took time to read and memorize the biblical passages which bring new life?

I remember how I loved to be with the members of my church for worship and fellowship. It's so easy to drop out of regular worship, to move from your hometown and your home church and never find a new community of believers to replace it. How quickly, alone and cut off from worship, our interest dries up and "first love" cools. Perhaps you remember the joy of sharing your faith in those early days, or working in the streets to help the poor, or teaching, or giving—how easy it is to stop those works that spring spontaneously out of "first love." How easy it is for "first love" to die!

"Remember the height from which you have fallen!" John writes in the Spirit. "Repent and do the things you did at first" (Revelation 2:5). You may not feel like working at first love. It may seem like drudgery to read and memorize the Word. It may be inconvenient to take time out regularly to be alone and pray. It may feel awkward to find and join a church in your neighborhood. You may resist getting involved again. It's easier to hide out and not be asked to give or teach or work or lead. But beware; you have been warned. Unless you get about that business again of returning to your "first love" or doing those "first love" works, you are in danger of "being removed" and being threatened by the horsemen even now thundering in our direction.

The Call to Righteousness—Pergamum, Thyatira, Sardis

North of Ephesus, clustered about the Hermus River Valley, lie the three cities in this next group of letters from Revelation. Pergamum, a coastal city, was the capital of the Roman province of Asia. It was a city crowded with heathen temples and the home of the first temple of the imperial cult of Rome, the place where Caesar was worshiped as a god. Thyatira was inland on the Lycus River, a commercial center on an important trade route. Many trade guilds had their headquarters in Thyatira. Membership in the guilds was necessary to work and the immorality of the guild banquet orgies was widely known and fully accepted. Sardis, a wealthy commercial city, was also known for its loose, luxurious life style. The city had twice been captured by enemies for its slackness in spite of the well-fortified hilltop citadel built to guard the citizens from invasion.

Whereas the Christians at Ephesus and Laodicea were orthodox and comfortable but lacking in spiritual passion, apparently these next three churches were victims of runaway physical passion that led to idolatry and immorality.

But let's not jump to conclusions. In the cave that day, the Lord of Power inspired His servant John to write to the Christians at Pergamum. It is always interesting to me that to most of these churches He commended them before He rebuked them. For example, to those at Thyatira He said, "These are the words of the Son of God, whose eyes are like blazing fire and whose feet are like burnished bronze. I know your deeds, your love and faith, your service and perseverance, and that you are now doing more than you did at first" (Revelation 2:18, 19). To Pergamum, although

He had very little good to say, He did promise, "To him who overcomes, I will give some of the hidden manna. I will also give him a white stone with a new name written on it, known only to him who receives it" (Revelation 2:17). In other words, there was a small minority in Pergamum who held on to their first love. He said the same about Sardis: "You have a few people . . . who have not soiled their clothes" (Revelation 3:4).

Christ found something or someone in all three churches to commend. Sometimes we oversimplify the problem. We think of these three ancient churches as being fallen, sinful, unlike our churches in every way. But it wasn't true. There was much about these churches that was commendable. Still they were in serious trouble (especially in light of the problems ahead) and didn't even know it. The parallels between their churches and our own may be far too close for comfort.

To the Christians in Pergamum, John writes, "I have a few things against you: You have people there who hold to the teaching of Balaam, who taught Balak to entice the Israelites to sin by eating food sacrificed to idols and by committing sexual immorality. Likewise you also have those who hold to the teaching of the Nicolaitans" (Revelation 2:14, 15).

To the people in Thyatira he writes, "I have this against you: You tolerate that woman Jezebel, who calls herself a prophetess. By her teaching she misleads my servants into sexual immorality and the eating of food sacrificed to idols" (Revelation 2:20).

To the Sardis church he writes, "You are dead. Wake up! Strengthen what remains . . . for I have not found your deeds complete in the sight of my God" (Revelation 3:1, 2).

What is going on here? What is so seriously wrong in Pergamum that the risen Lord Himself threatens that unless they "repent" He will fight against them with the sword in His mouth? What is happening in Thyatira that causes our Lord to warn, "I will strike her children [the followers of the false teacher in that church] dead. Then all the churches will know that I am he who searches hearts and minds, and I will repay each of you according to your deeds" (Revelation 2:23)? Or what's happened in Sardis that He says to them, "If you do not wake up, I will come like a thief, and you will not know at what time I will come to you" (Revelation 3:3)?

There are clues in John's short letters that will solve the mystery of Christ's anger at these three churches. Balaam was an Old Testament prophet who led God's people off their trail to the Promised Land and into the towns and practices of God's enemy, the Moabites (see Numbers 22–24, 31). One commentator describes Balaam as an example of compromise with false religion. The Nicolaitans were first-century followers of a similar false prophet who taught the Christians to give in to the practices of tipping their hats to the false gods of the city (and their immoral sexual practices) so that the gospel might be more acceptable to the people.

Jezebel had been a foreigner (a Phoenician princess) who centuries before had married a king of Israel and insisted on practicing her faith in the false god, Baal, alongside the worship of the God of Israel. She had dared to encourage the people of Israel to worship her false god and practice his immoral ways. Now someone in Thyatira whom John nicknamed "Jezebel" was teaching those first century Christians to give in to the worship of the gods of the city and to their immoral sexual practices. The people were standing by, allowing, even obeying, her.

Picture the predicament of those first century believers. They lived in towns where many different gods were worshiped. Their neighbor's home had shrines to various deities; in little nooks and in grand temples stood statues and symbols of family gods, ancestral gods, ancient mythical gods and the modern god of Rome—Caesar himself. A Christian couldn't walk through a neighbor's house without passing a pagan shrine. He could hardly buy meat that hadn't been sacrificed to a pagan god. He couldn't conduct business without walking through the temple of the patron gods of his union or guild. In the market or at business, he couldn't avoid the devout throngs of people before the temples of Diana or Isis. He couldn't cross the city without passing the sentries and the priests who tended the place of worship set aside to worship Caesar.

Why offend neighbors by ignoring—or worse, by condemning—their own personal gods? It would only mean a token offering, an orange placed at a neighbor family's shrine or a pinch of incense at the feet of Caesar's giant marble form. It would only mean standing at the pledge of allegiance or bowing at the prayer or unobtrusively joining in the hymn to the deities of friends, neighbors and co-workers at a social or political or commercial event. Why be rigid? Why not worship the one true God in private while simply nodding good-naturedly in the direction of the false gods on every corner? Was this really idolatry?

And why all the fuss about sexual immorality? Again, picture their predicament. Outside Antioch, that town where the first Gentile church was established, was a beautiful parklike sanctuary called Daphne. Amongst great lawns, flower gardens, fountains and cypress groves stood temples to Diana and Apollo. Leading citizens from the business, professional and political worlds met there to rest, to conduct business and to worship. Temple prostitutes were provided as a courtesy. What John called sexual immorality was to the first century common practice—even part of worship for the unbeliever. Men had wives and concubines. The wives were for raising families. The concubines were for sexual pleasure. Everyone knew her role.

What was the problem? Why was the risen Christ, through John, so angry at their occasional adultery? It kept sexual needs satisfied. It kept Christian tradesmen from looking like fanatics— or worse, like fools—during guild parties and initiations. Why were the sexual standards of Christ's revelation to those early Christians so tough, so rigid and so demanding? And why is idolatry (worshiping the values of this world) so often tied together with immorality (giving in to our sexual passions)?

Review the up-and-down history of the people of Israel. God rescued that motley crowd of Jewish slaves and started them toward the Promised Land. And they, filled with gratitude to God, "believed his promises and sang his praise" (Psalm 106:12). Then almost immediately their gratitude to God faded, and grumbling replaced it.

Grumbling and gratitude are, for the child of God, mutually exclusive. Be grateful and you won't grumble. Grumble and you won't be grateful. The psalmist writes, "They soon forgot what he had done and did not wait for his counsel. In the desert they gave in to their craving; in the wasteland they put God to the test" (Psalm 106:13, 14).

When Israel felt passionately about God and His great mercies to them, when they sought His guidance and obeyed His commands, they were victorious over their enemies. But when their holy passion for God and His will died, they were defeated. When Moses disappeared on the top of Mount Sinai and was gone so long, they immediately reverted to idolatry and had Aaron make a golden calf from the jewels they had taken from Egypt. And when Moses came down from the top of the mountain he found them in an orgy of idolatry and immorality.

Why? There is only one passion that can help us control the many other passions which plague us; that is the passion to know and obey God. When this primary passion grows cold, we give in to the lower passions that would control us. When we get out of close relationship with Christ, we try to fill that aching void and loneliness with other things. We read about it every day in the newspaper and watch it on our television screens.

It is like the prodigal son who tried to fill his stomach with the husks that the pigs were eating. I meet people constantly who are going to one round of parties after another: gambling, drinking, abusing drugs, partaking of a thousand and one things that this world has to offer. But nothing satisfies.

Today there are many people, even in so-called Christian countries, who are turning to Satan worship to try to fill this longing that only God can satisfy. Not even human love can satisfy the longing for God's love that we feel. Instead of turning back to the Father's love, we begin a mad, promiscuous search for the perfect human lover. Idolatry (worshiping anything or anyone besides the true God) is closely connected to and often the cause of immorality (giving in to sexual passions).

On Patmos, the risen Christ sounded His warning to the churches of Asia. He ordered them to stop giving in to the pressures to conform to the values of the people around them. "Repent!" commands John. "Wake up!" he warns them. "Hold on!" he cries. And his cry echoes down through the ages to you and to me.

Look at the condition of marriage within the context of today's

Christian homes and churches. The staggeringly high divorce rate is almost the same among believers as among unbelievers. Every day a new rumor crosses my path of another leader in the church whose marriage is in shambles. All too often, in both the spiritual and in the marital dimensions of life, it is simply a matter of letting "first love" grow cold (the problem of the Ephesians and the Laodiceans) and of giving in to the values of this age and to its immoral practices (the problem of the Christians in Pergamum, Thyatira and Sardis).

It is an interesting, if not frightening, test to compare the current levels of our holy passion to know Christ and His will in our life with our current practices. Inevitably, I find the person who is passionately following the Master will be better able to master his or her passions than the person whose "first love" has died. Invariably, I find the person who is involved in irresponsible, destructive and debasing practices is the person who is falling out of love with Christ and is trying to fill the empty space with other things, even trying to fill the spiritual emptiness with sexual excitement. It will not work! Only God's love can fill our empty space. Human love will always fall short and fail—and sex or materialism alone will not even come close to filling it.

The Scripture makes it clear that our "first love" is always to be our Lord. The true church of Christ is called "the bride of Christ." This analogy is found throughout the Scripture. For example, many people find themselves confused by the passionate poetry of the Song of Solomon. They'll never understand this book until they understand that this is a love story of Christ and His church or, in the Old Testament, God and Israel. Someone has said that if one book of the Old Testament could be called "holier" than the others, it is the Song of Solomon. It is the holy of holies of the Old Testament.

For those who would worship the one true God, the command is clear. "You shall have *no other* gods before me" (Exodus 20:3, italics mine). God's instructions regarding sexual morality are equally clear. Old and New Testament literature cry out for sexual purity. Hebrews 13:4 says, "Marriage should be honored by all, and the marriage bed kept pure, for God will judge the adulterer and all the sexually immoral." In 1 Corinthians 6 Paul writes, "Flee from sexual immorality. . . . he who sins sexually sins against his own body. Do you not know that your body is a temple of the Holy Spirit . . . ? You are not your own; you were bought with a price. Therefore honor God with your body" (vv. 18–20). Adultery (sexual relations with anyone but your own spouse) and fornication (sexual relations apart from a loving, lifelong commitment) are expressly forbidden; for they are inevitably destructive, dehumanizing and demeaning to God's creation. God's Word promises that sexual immorality, though a short-term source of physical pleasure and emotional escape, in the long run will lead to disappointment, heart-break and even death. The Bible is clear: "You shall not commit adultery" (Exodus 20:14).

It seems that almost all entertainment, and even advertisements, give just the opposite message; they tell us to enjoy ourselves now, take care of this life and ignore the next. We've become used to such expressions as "You only live once," or "You only have one time around." Richard Pryor recently was quoted as saying, "Enjoy as much as you can. Even if you live to be ninety that's not as long as you're going to be dead."

In our fallen world, satanic influences are everywhere persuading us toward idolatry (worship of the values of this age, the false gods among us) and sexual immorality. Right moral living (righteous-ness) is not easy. It demands difficult choices. It requires self-forgetfulness. At times it may create tension between what we want to be for God and others and what we crave for ourselves. In that awful struggle to overcome, friends and families may come to our aid. Pastors and counselors and fellow Christians may assist us. Setting goals, practicing disciplines, building new interests and diversions, creating systems of reward to modify our behavior—all may help. But in the struggle for righteousness, there is nothing more helpful than being passionately related to Christ through His Spirit—and being passionately committed to finding and doing His will in our lives.

Those children of Israel who got off the trail, who let their "first love" die, who gave in to the values of this world, never reached the Promised Land. The Bible says "their bodies were scattered over the desert" (1 Corinthians 10:5).

The price we pay in broken lives and shattered dreams when we let that "first love" die goes far beyond what we can imagine when we begin giving in to the worship of pagan values and the practice of pagan sex. But worse, in this condition of spiritual poverty and sexual immorality there is no way we will be able to stand against the approaching riders who threaten not only our well-being and the well-being of our families, but also the future of the world in which we live. However, we have the glorious promise to him that overcometh, "a new name."

But perhaps as you read this you have had to admit to yourself that you have sinned against God and need His forgiveness. Perhaps you have fallen into sexual sin, or you have allowed worldly desires and pleasures to fill your heart and mind. Jesus said, "I tell you that anyone who looks at a woman lustfully has already committed adultery with her in his heart" (Matthew 5:28). Whatever your sin, you need to repent and turn to Jesus Christ in faith for forgiveness and new life.

The Problem of Suffering—Smyrna and Philadelphia

Smyrna, now the city of Izmir, Turkey, was and is one of the great business and trade centers in that area of the world. Almost two centuries before Christ, Smyrna welcomed Rome and served Caesar with unquestioning loyalty. The city was perhaps the most beautiful in the entire region. Many religious cults were headquartered there, including the cult of Caesar worship. Although eleven cities bid for it, the Roman senate built a temple to the Emperor Tiberius in Smyrna. A great and powerful Jewish minority also lived there and joined with Rome in making life difficult for Christians of both Gentile and Jewish background.

Philadelphia, due east from Smyrna, was built on a plateau looking out across the valley of the River Cogamus. This prosperous city was called the "gateway to the East," and through its gates passed caravans to and from Rome, the capital of the empire. To them, John writes, "I have placed before you an open door." (Revelation 3:8). Here, too, the Jewish synagogue was strong and hostile toward the young Christian church. We know almost nothing about either of the Christian churches in Smyrna or Philadelphia except from these two short letters dictated to John by the risen Christ on the island of Patmos.

We do know that both churches were faithful. There is not one word of criticism in the letters to the Christians in either church. John writes to Smyrna, "I know your afflictions and your poverty—yet you are rich!" (Revelation 2:9). And to Philadelphia, he writes, "I know that you have little strength, yet you have kept my word and have not denied my name" (Revelation 3:8). Apparently, both churches were small; both had few economic resources; both faced hostile environments (John—a Jew himself—scathingly refers in both letters to the "synagogue of Satan"). And for both churches more troubled times lay ahead.

The irony of these two letters is immediately apparent. In the difficult times to come—or, as John writes to Philadelphia, in "the hour of trial that is going to come upon the whole world to test those who live on the earth"—one church (Smyrna) will face terrible suffering. The other church (Philadelphia) will escape unscathed. All the assumptions we can make about suffering are tested by these two short letters. Both churches seem equally faithful. Yet one will suffer "even unto death." The other will not suffer at all.

But this seeming inequality has precedent in the Scriptures. In Hebrews 11 we have a long list of people whom God delivered. But in verse 35 the writer says, "Others were tortured and refused to be released." In the book of Acts, for example, James was beheaded, while Peter was delivered.

In these passages and others we are reminded that suffering has a mysterious, unknown component. John, too, assumes that suffering is a natural part of Christian faith. He doesn't question why one church will suffer and another church won't. He doesn't even expect God to rescue Smyrna from suffering, yet he credits God with protecting Philadelphia from the suffering that lies ahead.

John simply delivers the bad news to Smyrna—"the devil will put some of you in prison to test you and you will suffer persecution for ten days. Be faithful, even to the point of death"—and the good news to Philadelphia—"I will also keep you from the hour of trial" (Revelation 2:10, 3:10). Suffering is simply a fact. And to both churches Christ's advice is simple. To Smyrna John writes, "Be faithful, even to the point of death, and I will give you the crown of life" (Revelation 2:10). And to Philadelphia he writes, "Hold on to what you have, so that no one will take your crown." (Revelation 3:11).

There are several assumptions here that we must not forget in our own days of trouble that lie ahead. First, expect suffering. Don't feel surprised or put upon or proud or afraid. Suffering is part and parcel of the Christian life. Second, don't look at anyone else and what he or she does or doesn't have to bear; comparisons are demoralizing either way. Third, recognize that it doesn't take great wealth or social influence to be faithful (note how few resources these two churches had), but it does take patience and endurance. Remember: one of the fruits of the Spirit is patience (Galatians 5:22). Fourth, remember that one day all earthly suffering will end and that second death, the eternal death of the spirit, will not touch us. Fifth, keep in mind that, when one bears suffering faithfully, God is glorified and honored. The suffering servants of Christ will be honored in a special way and given a new name which "no man knows except he that receives it." Christ said to the church at Philadelphia, "Him who overcomes I will make a pillar in the temple of my God. Never again will he leave it. I will write on him the name of my God" (Revelation 3:12).

Some years ago the great Canadian photographer, Yousuf Karsh, sent me a book of his photographs. On the wrapping paper the customs official had stamped the words, "Value of Contents." Under that had been written, "Autographed by the author." Inside, it was autographed to me.

Our value is the fact that we are going to be autographed by the Author.

I don't understand the reasons for suffering and persecution. I don't know why the churches in one part of the world bear terrible pain and deprivation while other churches are fat and rich and almost pain free. I don't know why some of the young evangelists who gathered in Amsterdam in 1983 carry scars from where they have been beaten and burned for Christ's sake while my life has been free from physical persecution. I don't know why Corrie ten Boom watched her sister die in prison or Joni Eareckson Tada is paralyzed from the neck down—while I have never known a night in jail and I can run the beaches or walk the mountain trails freely.

Perhaps you have faced pain or suffering you did not understand. You may even have become angry at God for allowing it to happen when others seem to have escaped such problems. But don't let the acids of bitterness eat away and destroy you. Instead, learn the secret of trusting Christ in *every* circumstance. Learn to say with Paul: "I have learned to be content whatever the circumstances. I know what it is to be in need, and I know what it is to have plenty. I have learned the secret of being content in any and every situation, whether well fed or hungry, whether living in plenty or in want. I can do everything through him who gives me strength" (Philippians 4:11–13).

I was traveling in an Eastern European country recently. The Orthodox priest who accompanied me while there said, "Every believer has a cross. I know what ours is. But I wondered what yours was." And looking out over the crowd of reporters he said simply, "Now I know!"

All I know from the short letters in Revelation is this: Christ commands us to "Overcome!" in the strength He alone can supply as we turn to Him in faith, trusting His promises.

"Overcome!" cries the risen Savior from the island of Patmos— and in the distance I can hear the hoofbeats of the four horsemen riding rapidly in our direction bringing destruction and death. "Overcome!" writes John at the end of each letter to the seven churches and to us who, like them, will be asked (and soon) to suffer outrageously for Christ and His kingdom's sake. "Overcome!" read leaders from each of the seven churches to their flocks, who then went on to join the saints and martyrs known and unknown through the ages. These have heard the call to suffering and have taken it seriously. "Overcome!" echoes the Word directly to us to join with those who have been laughed at or ignored, humiliated, stripped, tried unfairly, imprisoned, beaten, tortured and killed.

4

The
Throng
Around
the Throne

One of the most moving moments in my life as an evangelist is that moment when I stand before thousands of people and invite them to come forward to receive Christ as Savior and Lord. I can see the struggle on their faces as the Spirit of God touches their hearts one by one and moves them down the aisle to the place of public commitment. I can often see the tears of repentance on their faces as they stand with a counselor beside them in front of the platform. Sometimes I see their joy as they stand forgiven by their loving Savior, reborn and redirected. And I can see the relief on most of their faces. On some occasions they even embrace their counselor and waiting friends and walk from the auditorium or stadium as infant members of Christ's body, the church. On the other hand, I see some faces which indicate that they are confused and doubting and even wondering why they came forward. Many of these people actually find Christ in the extensive follow-up system we have.

On Patmos that day, I believe our Lord was thinking of those new believers, then and now. Christ knew the horror and the heartbreak that lay ahead for the faithful in those seven churches of Asia and in every church across the earth that would be raised up in the centuries ahead. Christ knew the price they would pay to "overcome." He knew they would need His power in the present struggle and His promise for that day ahead when He would wipe away their tears and they would live with Him forever. So, as He ends those seven letters, He gives an invitation not to unbelievers, as I do, but to the Christian. This invitation from Revelation is, I think, the most beautiful and powerful invitation in the entire biblical account.

Picture it. John had just written those strong, difficult words from his Lord to the churches. He knew what each member of those same churches had suffered in his or her own personal struggle to be faithful. Perhaps he was wondering if the risen Christ wasn't coming down too hard on them. Try to imagine that moment. Did our Lord see the look of concern on the old man's face? Did He lean down over the place where John was writing and whisper, "Those whom I love I rebuke and discipline. So be earnest, and repent" (Revelation 3:19)? Did John look up from that last invitation to repent and wonder how those simple believers in Asia would ever be able to live up to these marching orders from this risen Lord? What will give them the power to overcome? Did Christ see the question in the old man's face, hold out His arms in a gesture of invitation and say those next wonderful words, "Here I am! I stand at the door and knock. If anyone hears my voice and opens the door, I will go in and eat with him, and he with me" (Revelation 3:20)?

The Promise of His Presence

This promise of His presence in those future times of trouble is a promise Christ gave to the churches. Too often we use these words in invitation to the unbeliever, but here they are spoken to *believers* in those struggling churches of Asia. In those troubled days ahead, for them and for us, Christ Himself is standing just outside the door waiting to be invited in. He is waiting to enjoy a meal with us, waiting to share our sorrows, to renew our courage, to come in and talk with us. We are not alone. We never shall be. He has promised them, and us, to be there just outside the door, always knocking. All we need do is open the door to Him. What is your need today? Do you need forgiveness for your sins? Do you need the salvation Christ offers you freely as a gift through faith in Him? Do you need to make a new and deeper commitment to God and His will for your life? Whatever your spiritual need, right now Christ is knocking at the door of your heart. He is Lord of the universe—and He wants to be Lord of your life as well. When Jesus was on trial Pontius Pilate, the Roman governor, turned to the crowd and asked, "What shall I do, then, with Jesus who is called Christ?" (Matthew 27:22). That is the question you must answer also. No one else can make that decision for you. Turn to Christ, and by faith invite Him into your life right now as your personal Savior and Lord.

John stared tear-blinded at those words of promise he had just written. But the Lord was not finished. Perhaps He leaned down before John and fixed His gaze on those tired eyes, the eyes that had seen so much suffering and so much death, the eyes of the old disciple in exile from family and friends, the eyes of a pastor worried about his flock and their future.

At that moment, did the Lord smile down at His old friend with the shaky hand writing there before him? "To him who overcomes," said the Lord, "I will give the right to sit with me on my throne" (Revelation 3:21).

Did John's mind flash back to those many years ago when he and his brother James, young and full of hope, had begged the Master for the honor of sitting on His right and left when He came into power? Did He remember Jesus' answer then? "Can you drink the cup I am going to drink?" "We can," they had blurted out naively, never dreaming the suffering that lay ahead. "You will indeed drink from my cup," the Lord replied then, "but to sit at my right or left is not for me to grant. These places belong to those for whom they have been prepared by my Father" (Matthew 20:22, 23).

The Price That Was Paid

Now John has learned the price. John has truly drunk the cup.

He has spent his lifetime in suffering with the Savior. Did the risen Lord reach out and put His hand on the trembling hand of John and repeat the promise to him and through him to us all: "To him who overcomes, I will give the right to sit with me on my throne, just as I overcame and sat down with my Father on his throne" (Revelation 3:21)?

Smiling now, heart pounding with hope, John writes the last words of that final letter. "He who has an ear, let him hear what the Spirit says to the churches" (Revelation 3:22).

What happened next boggles the mind and staggers the imagination. John has just finished writing the seven short letters when the risen Lord disappears. Perhaps John searched quickly around his cave, then hobbled out into the sunshine. "After this I looked," John writes, "and there before me was a door standing open in heaven. And the voice I had first heard speaking to me like a trumpet said, 'Come up here, and I will show you what must take place after this'" (Revelation 4:1).

The words that follow have baffled Bible scholars for centuries. "At once," writes John, "I was in the Spirit" (Revelation 4:2). Again, we don't know what "in the Spirit" means to John. But never mind. What he saw is clear. How or where he saw it must remain a mystery. Our task is to prayerfully consider the meaning of his vision—to John, to the believers then and to all of us who follow Christ now.

A Vision of the Future

Nestled into the two chapters, between the practical orders to the churches and the terrible warning of the four horsemen of the Apocalypse, is this next vision that lies at the center of the Christian believer's hope and at the heart of the entire Revelation. If John was worried about the world and its condition, if John was concerned about the future and how his flock could overcome it, if John was perplexed about the power of evil and the apparent weakness of good on this planet, the next vision made all the difference. And if you are worried about the world and its condition, if you are concerned about the future and how you will overcome it, if you are perplexed about the power of evil (in the world and in your life) and the apparent weakness of good, then this next vision could make all the difference for you as well.

"There before me was a throne in heaven with someone sitting on it," wrote John. He was hard pressed to describe the person he saw sitting on the throne. He described something about jasper, a transparent crystal-like stone, and carnelian, a fiery red stone. Apparently, John was nearly blinded by the glory on and surrounding the throne. An emerald rainbow encircled it. From the throne came "flashes of lightning, rumblings and peals of thunder" and before the throne, reflecting back the entire incredible scene, was a sea of glass as clear as crystal (Revelation 4:2–6).

Surrounding the throne were twenty-four other thrones. Seated on them were twenty-four elders dressed in white and wearing crowns of gold. Around the throne were four living creatures. The first was like a lion, the second like an ox, the third had a face like a man. The fourth was like a flying eagle (Revelation 4:7). Each of the four living creatures had six wings and was covered with eyes all around. The visual impact of that moment must have been overwhelming. For nineteen centuries Bible commentators have analyzed that scene, describing in detail the names of the elders (usually assumed to be the twelve Old Testament patriarchs and the twelve New Testament apostles) and the living creatures (usually seen as seraphim and cherubim, angelic beings created to carry out God's commands).

John didn't bother to analyze what he saw. But what he heard he reported in detail. Those strong, angelic creatures never stopped chanting these words:

> Holy, holy, holy
> is the Lord God Almighty,
> who was, and is, and is to come (Revelation 4:8).

Whenever the living creatures gave "glory, honor and thanks to him who [sat] on the throne and who lives for ever and ever," the twenty-four elders fell down before Him and worshiped Him and lay their crowns before Him, saying,

You are worthy, our Lord and God,
   to receive glory and honor and power,
for you created all things,
   and by your will they were created
   and have their being (Revelation 4:11).

The Mystery and the Majesty

For this one moment in time, the old apostle was ushered into the presence of the Mystery behind the universe. There is no way to describe God. John could only describe the response to God by both the angelic and the human beings before him. Yes, there was description of color and beauty, of majesty and power. But even as he stood before Him, God remained a mystery to John and to us—the Mystery who was and is and will always be, the Mystery behind our creation and our preservation, the Mystery worthy of our glory and honor and power.

The risen Christ had called John into the presence of God so that the old man could know, and through him we could know, this fact: Behind the universe there is a Power worthy of our praise and of our trust. In spite of rumors to the contrary, we are not creatures abandoned on a planet spinning madly through the universe, lost in galaxies upon galaxies of gaseous flaming suns or burnt-out cinder moons. We are the children of a great and wonderful God who even now sits in power accomplishing His purposes in His creation.

Hope at the Center

At the heart of this mystery is great hope. The national powers that we see hellbent for destruction—amassing weapons, killing and being killed—are not the ultimate power. Nor are the individual figures who rule in our lives the ultimate powers; mothers, fathers, teachers, pastors, counselors, politicians, diplomats, bankers, police officers, social workers, wardens and jailors, probation officers, tax collectors, dictators and their soldiers, kings and presidents will all one day stand powerless before this God of John's vision.

The Revelation is carefully calculated to restore and renew hope in John and in each of us. I'm not sure how John beheld that vision, but I am certain of the truth it represents. There is a God behind creation, and though in many ways He remains a mystery, I am confident that He has created the planet on which we live, that He has created me and that what He has created He loves and has a plan to save. If He didn't, He wouldn't be worthy of our praise. As George Ladd wrote about this scene: "However fearful or uncontrolled the forces of evil on earth may seem to be, they cannot annul or eclipse the greater fact that behind the scenes God is on his throne governing the universe" (*A Commentary on the Revelation of John*, p. 70). God is in control! That awesome truth penetrates every chapter John writes—and it can make the difference for you if it penetrates every area of your life. You can trust your life and your future to God, because He alone knows the future. You can trust Him, because He loves you and because He is ultimately in control of this universe. How do I know He loves you and me? I know it because He sent His only Son to die on the cross for our sins. "For God so loved the world that he gave his one and only Son, that whoever believes in him shall not perish but have eternal life" (John 3:16). And how do I know He is in control of the universe? I know it because Jesus Christ broke the power of evil and sin through His resurrection from the dead. Christ is alive!

John stood staring in awe and wonder as suddenly God held out a scroll "with writing on both sides and sealed with seven seals." A mighty angelic voice trumpeted out the question, "Who is worthy to break the seals and open the scroll?" Apparently what followed in the silence of that awful moment left John weeping, for there was "no one . . . worthy to open the scroll or look inside" (Revelation 5:1–4).

Why the tears? Imagine it. Picture yourself standing before this God of power and mystery who created the universe, who created you. Remember the old camp song, "We'll talk it over in the by and by. We'll talk it over, my God and I"? It is the dream of man from the most primitive days of faith to communicate directly with his Creator. It is everyone's dream to speak with God. "I'll ask the questions," continues that old song, "He'll tell me why. When we talk it over, my God and I."

Mute before the Mystery

But at that very moment when God Himself was holding out a communique, a letter, a news flash, a story, a list, no one was worthy to open it. So John wept. Is there no one who can tell us what is written on the scroll? Is there no one worthy to bear God's message to us?

Suddenly, one of the twenty-four elders approached the weeping John and said, "Do not weep! See, the Lion of the tribe of Judah, the Root of David, has triumphed. He is able to open the scroll and its seven seals" (Revelation 5:5). Immediately, John turned in the direction the elder was pointing. What did he expect to see? A lion, of course—the traditional Jewish symbol of the conquering Messiah who would come to deliver his people from evil. Instead, John writes, "I saw a Lamb, looking as if it had been slain, standing in the center of the throne" (Revelation 5:6). Again, John beheld a mystery. Who was the Lamb standing on the throne? Years before, John himself had written of Jesus, "Look, the Lamb of God, who takes away the sin of the world" (John 1:29). That Lamb was Jesus. The Messiah, God's anointed One, His only begotten Son, had two roles to play in the redemption of this earth. First, He came in the humble form of a man. In that form He suffered and died. And somehow through His perfect sacrifice the penalty for mankind's sinfulness was satisfied. Second, He would reign as Lord, the promised Messiah, the Lion of David in splendor and in power.

A Vision and a Dream

Now, John was watching a vision of that perfect sacrifice, the Lamb of God "in the center of the throne." Suddenly John saw as in the strange but perfect logic of a dream, the Lamb reach out and take from the hand of God the scroll no one dared to open. Suddenly, the elders and the angelic forms all fell down before the Lamb in a chorus of praise. The universe echoed in "a new song":

> You are worthy to take the scroll
>   and to open its seals,
> because you were slain,
>   and with your blood you purchased
>   men for God
>   from every tribe and language and
>   people and nation.
> You have made them to be a kingdom
>   and priests to serve our God,
>   and they will reign on the earth (Revelation 5:9, 10).

Then, joining in that song, John heard "ten thousand times ten thousand angels" all encircling the throne and joining in that song of praise to the Lamb who was bridging the gap of silence between God and His creation:

> Worthy is the Lamb, who was slain,
> to receive power and wealth and
>   wisdom and strength
> and honor and glory and praise! (Revelation 5:12).

The vision widened. The song swelled. John says in wonder,

> I heard every creature in heaven and on earth, and under the earth and on the sea, and all that is in them, singing:
>> To him who sits on the throne and
>>   to the Lamb
>> be praise and honor and glory and
>>   power,
>>   for ever and ever! (Revelation 5:13).

And again, the elders all fell down before the throne and worshiped and the four angelic creatures lifted their voices in a solemn "Amen!"

This vision of Revelation 4 and 5 between the letters to the churches and the reading of God's mysterious scroll has two great spiritual truths we must not forget. The first I've already mentioned.

There is a powerful God at the center of creation who is worthy of our trust and worthy of our praise in the troubled days ahead. Now, second: at the heart of understanding this God is Jesus, our Savior and Lord. The presence of God blinds us in His glorious splendor. We can't break through the world and fully grasp who He is. But in Jesus, the Lamb, we see all of God we need to see. From Jesus we learn all of God we need to know.

This two-sided vision is an all-important source of hope we can cling to in the awful days ahead. It would be a mistake only to see God isolated, high and lifted up on a throne surrounded by lightning and thunder. What hope have we in that kind of powerful but distant, impersonal God? That generator at the center of the universe would be about as loving as the boiler in a high-rise or as comforting as the turbines in a giant hydroelectric dam. It would be a mistake of equal danger to see Jesus only as a wonderful man who suffered and died, who gave us the perfect example of what humankind should be—a good man assassinated by villains as Lincoln or Gandhi were slain. For Jesus was not simply a good man. He is that same powerful God revealing Himself in weakness and in love. The two are one on that throne: power and love. In John's vision we see the Father made known through the life, death and resurrection of Jesus, the Son. Who can explain this mystery? No one. Scholars through the centuries have tried. Great church councils have been convened to discuss and debate it. A forest of trees has been cut down to print the millions of pages written to get underneath the mystery of this moment. It remains a mystery still, but a mystery full of hope!

John isn't asking us to put our brains aside. But for this one shining moment he would simply have us join that great throng around the throne. He would have us bend our knees in praise. He would have us lift our voices in song. For what we see, in the shape of a Lamb sharing God's throne ablaze with lightning and echoing with thunder, is a colorful picture of a truth almost beyond expressing: Jesus, the slain Lamb of God, is the only one worthy to open God's scroll, to speak God's Word to us. And Jesus, the risen Lord, is the only one powerful enough to see us through the future that this scroll reveals.

5

The
White Horse
and Its Rider—

Part I

The Rider Who Deceives

Picture John somewhere above Patmos caught up in his vision to the very throne of God. The Lamb is about to open God's book. The four creatures bow in silence. The twenty-four elders tremble in anticipation. The choir of ten thousand times ten thousand angels stops its singing and stands on tiptoe waiting to see what happens next. Then, as John, an eyewitness on the scene, reports in Revelation, "the Lamb opened the first of the seven seals" (Revelation 6:1).

What should happen then is obvious. A page of writing should appear peeled back from the leather scroll and John and the creatures and the elders should all crowd around to read that page. But this is no ordinary book! This is an illustrated, God-inspired volume whose pictures leap full-blown from the pages and thunder across their vision. Apparently, there is a brief moment between that time when the Lamb breaks open the seal and the time when the four horsemen of the Apocalypse can ride. In that instant they await God's command like racehorses poised in the gate. The four horsemen cannot ride at their own command because of God's sovereign control; they pause for God's order to begin their journey.

In that pause, as the riders await God's command to ride, we learn several great lessons about these judgments.

First, we learn that the judgment of the four horsemen is in part conditional. As I have written this book I have pondered repeatedly a very basic question about these judgments. It is this: Are these judgments which John foresees inevitable? Will they definitely happen? Or can these judgments somehow be delayed or even completely averted? In other words, are they *unconditional*—definitely going to take place no matter what happens? Or are they *conditional*—able to be diverted if certain conditions are met, such as our repentance and faith?

This is not an easy question to answer, and I am aware sincere students of the Bible may not all agree. However, after careful study I have come to the conclusion that the answer is—*both!* At some time in the future—a time unknown to us—the terrible hooves of the four horsemen will finally trample across the stage of human history with an unprecedented intensity, bringing in their wake deception, war, hunger and death on a scale which staggers the imagination. God will use those four horsemen in an awesome act of judgment on the earth, and like a tremendous tidal wave smashing on the shore, nothing will be able to prevent it. Some day, the Bible says, judgment is certainly coming. "For he has set a day when he will judge the world with justice by the man he has appointed" (Acts 17:31).

Until this time that God has appointed, however, there are many occasions when God seemingly delays or averts His hand of judgment for a period of time because men have repented and turned to Him in faith and obedience. Throughout the centuries the hoofbeats of the four horsemen have echoed and re-echoed across the pages of history: deception, war, hunger and death have haunted the human race to one degree or another since the day Adam and Eve chose to rebel against God. At times those hoofbeats have hammered loudly, bringing suffering and death on a massive scale. At times they have become much fainter. Why? I believe it is because there are times when God delays His judgments, possibly even for several generations, because many have listened to

74

His message of warning and turned to Him in repentance and faith.

A good example of this is seen in God's dealings with the people of the ancient Assyrian capital of Nineveh. They were an evil, pagan people who worshiped idols and often fought against God's people. God sent the prophet Jonah to Nineveh to proclaim His coming judgment to them: "Go to the great city of Nineveh and proclaim to it the message I give you. . . . Forty more days and Nineveh will be destroyed" (Jonah 3:2, 4). But when the king of Nineveh heard Jonah's message he repented and ordered the whole people to repent as well. As a result God's judgment was averted. Only later, when evil increased in the generations after Jonah and the people failed to repent, did God's judgment finally fall on Nineveh. God's judgment is often this way. Some day it will come in all its fullness and finality—but in the meantime it may be that God's hand of judgment will pause when we repent, just as this first horse pauses before being let loose on the world in full measure.

Therefore as we approach our study of the four horsemen and their judgments, we must not feel that we are to sit back and do nothing to fight evil just because some day they will come with full and final force upon the earth. Yes, God's final judgment is inevitable—but He alone knows when it is, and until that time we are to learn the lessons of the four horsemen and act in such a way that God may be pleased to delay His judgment and allow our world more time to hear His Word and turn to Him.

Perhaps an illustration will help (although it is not perfect). We know that death is inevitable for each of us. But when we get sick we don't say, "Oh, well, I'm going to die eventually anyway so I might as well do nothing about my illness." No! We seek the best medical help we can obtain, because we hope we will get over our illness and live for many more years. In the same manner, God's ultimate judgment on this world is inevitable. But at the same time when we hear the hoofbeats of the four horsemen approaching, God would have us listen to their warning and repent before it is too late. In His grace He may be pleased to turn aside His judgment for a time, just as He has done in the past.

How near are the horsemen right now? I do not know! All I can say with certainty is that every sign points to one fact: the hoofbeats of the four horsemen are approaching, sounding louder and louder every day. That is why I have titled this book *Approaching Hoofbeats*, because the indications of God's judgment are growing stronger and stronger with each passing hour. May God open our ears to hear and our eyes to see their warning before it is too late!

Second, we learn that the judgment of the four horsemen is corrective. God's judgment in some ways is similar to pain in our physical bodies. Some of you reading this have had the experience of realizing one day that you had a vague pain some place in your body. Perhaps you ignored it at first, but as time went by it became more and more intense until at last you could dismiss its insistent voice no longer. You realized that the only intelligent thing to do was to go to a doctor and find out the reason for your pain. For some of you the doctor's examination revealed a potentially deadly cancer eating away at your body. Only surgery could remove it—but once it was removed your health returned and you were well again. The pain had been like an alarm clanging in the night, warning of impending disaster. The purpose of that pain was *corrective*—to let you know something was wrong so you would take action to correct the underlying problem.

In the same way, God's judgments are meant to be *corrective*. They are meant to remind us forcefully of our need of God and the demand to follow His principles for living. God can use trials and difficulties (even if they sometimes are not His direct judgments on us) to teach us and make us into better persons for His glory. "My son, do not make light of the Lord's discipline, and do not lose heart when he rebukes you, because the Lord disciplines those he loves. . . . No discipline seems pleasant at the time, but painful. Later on, however, it produces a harvest of righteousness and peace for those who have been trained by it" (Hebrews 12:5, 6, 11).

The four horsemen of the Apocalypse point inevitably to deeper moral and spiritual problems which affect our lives. May God use their warning to make us face these problems and turn to God, who alone can bring us forgiveness and the strength of the Holy Spirit to live a new life.

There are four horsemen. Each is unique. Each carries his own agenda.

In these next chapters we will look closely at the horsemen to ask ourselves what God is saying through each of them to each of us. In every age we have seen precursors of the horsemen riding over the earth. They had a very specific agenda for those first-century churches in Asia. They have a very precise program for us today as well.

They point the way for us. We must dare to look in the direction they are pointing, for they ride as messengers from God for these last two decades of the twentieth century to lead us to the real issues at hand. We must have the courage to face those issues. We can no longer evade them. The final judgment cannot be that far away!

Somewhere above Patmos, the seal was broken. The four horsemen were ready to mount their steeds. Then John heard one of the four creatures, created to serve God at His seat of power, cry impatiently, "Come!" Did John gasp and stagger backward as into his presence strode a giant white horse? Did the rider rein in that beast? Did it stand for a fleeting moment, chomping at the bit, hooves pounding in place impatiently, thundering against the pavement? Did John gaze with wonder at the large bow in the rider's hand? And in that instant did one of God's creature-servants place the crown of victory on the rider's head? The text reports that "he [the rider] was given a crown" (Revelation 6:2). Then, as suddenly as he had appeared, the rider kicked the great heaving flanks of the pure white stallion and raced toward the earth "as a conqueror bent on conquest."

For John, the image must have been unmistakably clear. He had perhaps watched the invading armies of Rome enter Jerusalem with the conquering centurion riding a prancing white steed and carrying in his hand the bow, a sign of victory and of power. Perhaps this is even a subtle historic flashback to an event that happened in the Roman Empire just before John's exile on Patmos. The Romans feared their Parthian neighbors, who threatened the far eastern borders of the empire. The Parthians rode swift white horses and were deadly accurate with their bows and arrows. In A.D. 62 a large Roman army had been overrun by the Parthians and forced to surrender to the Parthian king, Vologases. Apparently the Parthians were such skilled bowmen that even from a galloping horse, bow held waist high, an archer could pierce an enemy on another moving horse across a battlefield. William Barclay says that there is still an old English expression, a "Parthian shot," which means "a final, devastating blow to which there is no possible answer."

Who is this rider on the white horse? Is this rider on the white horse Christ, as some have suggested? For centuries biblical scholars and commentators have argued about the identity of this rider. You will note that he is wearing a crown of victory and carrying a bow of great destruction in his hand. In Revelation 19 Christ is pictured on a white horse wearing many crowns, and this has led some to believe that the rider on the white horse here in Revelation 6 is also Christ.

However, after careful study I do not believe this to be the case. In the Greek language the crown worn by the rider of Revelation 6 is called *stephanos*, which was the crown of victory worn by a conqueror. The crowns Christ wears in Revelation 19, on the other hand, are *diadema*, or the crowns of royalty. Furthermore, although the rider on the white horse bears a resemblance to Christ, the appearance is actually deceptive because a deeper look reveals his true nature. He is "a conqueror bent on conquest," greedily riding roughshod over all who stand in his way in his lust for power.

Who, therefore, is the rider on the white horse? He is not Christ, but a deceiver who seeks to capture the hearts and souls of men and women. He is one who seeks to have people acknowledge him as Lord instead of the true Christ.

We should always remember that one of the Bible's strongest indictments of Satan is that he is a deceiver, implacably opposed to the truth of God. Jesus said concerning Satan, "He was a murderer from the beginning, not holding to the truth, for there is no truth in him. When he lies, he speaks his native language, for he is a liar and the father of lies" (John 8:44). In Revelation 20 John speaks of God's final judgment on "the devil, who deceived."

The rider who deceives has been at work in the world since the dawn of human history. He was at work in the Garden of Eden when Satan accosted Adam and Eve and by his diabolical power of deception convinced them to turn their backs on God and disobey His clear command. As a result of that action the human race fell from its sinless glory, bringing death and despair in its wake.

Adam and Eve, the first human beings, were created by their loving Father free to obey or defy their Creator. In obedience they would have found life everlasting. In defiance they found destruction and death. Early in his time on earth, man discovered that the world is a torrid war zone. A worldwide battle rages between forces of God and Satan, between light and darkness, between good and evil. Every man, woman, boy or girl who lived, who lives, or who will live is caught in the crossfire. Evil stalks the earth seeking to dominate and to destroy God's creation. At the same time our Creator, in His love and mercy, works to save that which He has created. The Garden of Eden was "round one" of that battle. It has since escalated into what Dr. Arno C. Gaebelein referred to as "the conflict of the ages." Some day Satan and his works will be completely destroyed and Christ will be victorious—but until that time the battle still rages.

Immediately following Adam and Eve's disobedience God was on the scene to condemn the evil act and to promise redemption to His children from its consequences.

Picture it as Moses gave us the record in Genesis 3:9–21. Adam and Eve had disobeyed God. They would pay the price of their disobedience. But even as God in judgment banished them from the garden, His love had already planned a way back—at a staggering cost to Himself. It was the death of His Son on the cross.

It is a fact of sin that it always affects someone else. The tragic consequences of Adam and Eve's disobedience, which had begun in the Garden of Eden, pursued them relentlessly. In Genesis 4 we have the account of Cain, in a jealous rage, murdering his brother, Abel.

Cain, envious of Abel, heard God's voice: "Why are you angry? . . . If you do what is right, will you not be accepted? But if you do not do what is right, sin is crouching at your door; it desires to have you, but you must master it" (Genesis 4:6, 7). At that precise moment, did Abel hear approaching hoofbeats? All we know is that evil won the battle. And while the blood of Abel still stained the hands of Cain, God said, "What have you done? Listen! Your brother's blood cries out to me from the ground" (Genesis 4:10). Again God condemned the heinous act! Again God intervened in mercy to rescue the evildoer. Again the deceiver fled in transitory triumph, although scarred by his sin for the rest of his life.

Or again the one who deceives was at work among the Israelites as they fled from their slavery in Egypt, persuading them that a golden calf could save them or that they should return to the fleshpots of Egypt. The deceiver roamed the Sinai wilderness, spreading his lies among the children of Israel to make them doubt God's promises and deflect them from entering the Promised Land, throwing them instead into the clutches of God's enemies. Yes, and he lingered long enough to leer as the bones of those who had defied God's commands grew white in the hot desert sun. Then he moved aside again, for the will of God cannot always be frustrated by evil. Again in cloud and fire God called the faithful back to the trail and onward to that land of promise.

Back and forth the battle has raged: God urging man to follow Him to safety and to peace; evil darting in and out of the ranks on his white horse, waylaying the careless, luring away, lying, deceiving and bringing death to those who follow him. The horseman who deceives rode up to Samson, the herculean Hebrew judge, and seduced him subtly through the arms of Delilah. The horseman who deceives rode up to David, the king of all Israel, and promised him undisturbed pleasure through the murder of Bathsheba's husband. Then David's royal scepter was plagued by a sword that wouldn't go away. The horseman who deceives rode up to Judas and promised him power through the betrayal of God's only Son, but Judas soon discovered that he was putting the hangman's rope around his own neck. It would drop him into hell! The horseman who deceives rides into our lives today as he has ridden throughout history. *The hoofbeats of the white horse are at this moment being heard louder and louder up and down the streets of our troubled world.* He promises us whatever we want if we will but disobey God and follow him in the tragic train of captives plodding unceasingly to their doom. *And we must do all we can, with God's strength, to resist his alluring deceptions.* Peter warned, "Be self-controlled and alert. Your enemy the devil prowls around like a roaring lion looking for someone to devour. Resist him, standing firm in the faith" (1 Peter 5:8, 9).

6

The White Horse and Its Rider—

Part II

The Rider Who Deceives from Outside the Church—
False Religion

Jesus Christ Himself once said to His disciples, "Watch out that no one deceives you. For many will come in my name, claiming, 'I am the Christ,' and will deceive many" (Matthew 24:4, 5). One of the ways this first rider deceives is through counterfeit or false religion.

One afternoon in Paris, Ruth answered a knock on our hotel room door. Two men stood there. One explained in broken English that the other was "the messiah" who had come to see me on a "divine errand." After that pathetic encounter with another of the deranged people who have come my way, claiming to be "the messiah," Ruth remarked, "He claimed to be the Christ, but he couldn't even speak to us in our own language." There is a vast menagerie of masquerading messiahs in the world today—both men and women claiming to be *the Christ*. Some of them are mental or emotional cripples. Others scheme and dream with ever more menacing sophistication and power. But all are counterfeit.

The Bible promises that this line of false christs will grow longer until the final embodiment of Antichrist appears at the head of the procession. He will be Satan's man. Imitating Christ, he offers peace—but he is as false as the peace he offers. His golden age will be short-lived. The Scripture teaches that Satan is an imitator.

This rider's method is that of deception. He promises peace to the world, but it is a false peace. He will be a superman imposing a supersystem with an iron fist. Jesus said, "I have come in my Father's name, and you do not accept me; but if someone else comes in his own name, you will accept him" (John 5:43).

The world that has rejected God's Christ is ready to receive the Devil's christ.

The Bible teaches that some time in the future there will be a great superman called the Antichrist. As we read in 1 John (2:18) "the antichrist is coming." On the other hand, previous to the actual Antichrist's coming, John prophesied there will be "the spirit of the antichrist" (1 John 4:3), and there will be "many antichrists" (1 John 2:18).

Obvious Deception: Satanism

Some of the deceivers around us are more obviously in league with Satan and the satanic than others. Some even make no overt attempts to deceive. They speak directly of the tempting powers of evil and call men and women to worship at the feet of Satan himself. Overt worship of Satan is perhaps the most easy deception to see through. In his book, *Those Curious New Cults*, William J. Petersen, former editor of *Eternity* magazine, discusses Satanism. "The most infamous blasphemy of Satanist ritual is the Black Mass" (p. 80). Petersen describes how, in the Black Mass, the participants try to reverse everything they know about Christianity. The crucifix is hung upside down. The altar is covered in black instead of white. Hymns are sung backwards. The rite is performed by a defrocked priest and, whenever the Lord or Christ is mentioned, he spits upon the altar, or worse. To make the blasphemy even more despicable, sexual rites are added. Sometimes a child is even slain. During the ceremony, the worshipers renounce their faith, acknowledge

Satan as Lord and, when the ritual concludes, the high priest closes with a curse rather than with a blessing.

Regardless of how obviously evil or how repulsive all this may seem to you, remember there are multiplied thousands of Satanists in the world today. In my travels throughout the world I have seen innumerable varieties of Satan worship. For example, one night in Nuremberg, West Germany, we were holding a crusade in the same stadium in which Hitler used to stage his infamous war rallies. It was difficult indeed to sit in that place and hear in the echoes of memory the masses shouting, "Sieg, Heil!" We realized that from this place the Third Reich had marched out to exterminate millions of Jews and other prisoners held for political, religious and psychological reasons. But we were having 60,000 people a night in that open arena. They were singing Christ's praises and we were preaching the Word of God. Thousands were committing themselves to Jesus Christ as Savior and Lord. The presence of God's people there seemed to exorcise the old demons that had stalked those aisles thirty years before.

Then one night, as I sat on the platform, Satan worshipers dressed in black assembled just outside the stadium doors. Using ancient, evil rites, they tried to put a hex on the meeting. The rumor of their presence spread. Christians prayed. And in answer to those prayers, nothing came of the incident.

Another night in Chicago 300 Satan worshipers approached McCormick Place with the specific intent of taking over the platform and stopping the crusade service which was in progress. They announced their plan in advance, but I didn't dream they would actually try to storm the platform. We had just sung the second hymn of the evening. George Beverly Shea had sung a gospel song and Cliff Barrows was about to lead a massed choir in a great anthem of praise. At that moment a policeman rushed to the stage and whispered something in the ear of the mayor of Chicago, who was present that night to welcome us.

At the same moment, the Satan worshipers forced their way past the ushers at the rear of that spacious auditorium and were proceeding down the back aisles toward the platform. There were more than 30,000 young people in that Youth Night service. Only those seated near the back saw the Satan worshipers enter. The mayor of Chicago turned to me and said, "Dr. Graham, we'll let the police handle these intruders."

We never call in the police for crusade duty if we can help it. "Let me try it another way, Mr. Mayor," I suggested. I then interrupted the choir's song and addressed the 30,000 young people there in McCormick Place. I explained, "There are about 300 Satan worshipers now entering the auditorium. They say they're going to take over the platform. You can hear them coming now."

The crowd could hear the rising chant of the Satan worshipers. Everyone turned to see them moving with determination down the aisles, past the ushers who were working to restrain them. They were causing a considerable disturbance by then. I continued addressing the crowd. "I'm going to ask you Christian young people to surround these Satan worshipers," I exhorted. "Love them. Pray for them. Sing to them. And gradually ease them back toward the entrances through which they have come."

I will never forget that moment! Hundreds of young Christians stood to their feet and did exactly as I had asked. Some grabbed hands and began to sing. Others put their arms around the Satan worshipers and began to pray for them. Others calmly shared their faith with them. Everyone else in McCormick Place sat praying as God's Spirit moved through His people to confound the work of Satan in our midst. I stood watching in silence. I waited and prayed until peace was restored and the service could resume.

It happened again in Oakland, California, in the football stadium. Hundreds of Satan worshipers again invaded the meeting to distract and disturb thousands who had come to hear of Christ and His plan of salvation. We did the same thing we had done in Chicago. Again, hundreds of Christians stood and gently led the worshipers of Satan from the stadium. I asked the young people to surround them and to love them. They did! Later that week I received a letter from one of the leaders of the Satanist group thanking me for what I had done. He wrote, "I think you saved our lives." The power of those Christian young people came not in the impact of evil and violent force, but in their quiet, loving, prayerful resolution.

Christianity and the Cults

In recent years we have seen some encouraging things within the churches. Many are growing dramatically. Evangelical seminaries are bulging at the seams. Countless thousands of small group Bible studies have sprung up all over the nation. At the same time, in recent years there has been a growing dissatisfaction on the part of some people—especially young people—with the typical Christian church. They have grown up in an age of discontent and distrust. There's been the Vietnam War, the Bay of Pigs, and the apparent corruption of much of the general political process. There's been Jim Jones and the People's Temple. There's been scandal within the church, including the misuse of money or funds. The list of reasons for discontent goes on and on. Disillusionment follows. And with disillusionment rides deception. The first horseman offers two primary alternatives to true faith in God.

The first alternative is *to ignore religion altogether.* When we feel alienated, isolated, unloved, lonely and adrift in a cold dark universe, we don't seek God through Christ. We simply work to escape. That's why drugs are misused, why promiscuous sex runs rampant, why alcoholic overdose is commonplace. Without faith in God, a person is alone. He or she may do everything possible to fill the loneliness, but nothing works. As St. Augustine put it, "Thou madest us for Thyself, and our heart is restless, until it repose in Thee" (*The Confessions of Saint Augustine*, Book 1, p. 1).

The second alternative is *to plunge into a synthetic, false religion,* a counterfeit offered by the first horseman of the Apocalypse. Look at the phenomenal growth of the Eastern religions in North America. Filmmaker Ralph Thomas, director of the cult exposé film, "Ticket to Heaven," researched heavily into the "2,200 cults in North America." He believes that "millions of young people are involved and even more millions of friends and parents out there have someone involved. It's almost impossible to turn around," he writes, "without encountering someone who has a niece, a nephew, a friend, or a child in the cults." A Korean cult leader, for example, has demonstrated that false messiah movements are escalating rather than passing. The *Wall Street Journal* (3 February 1982) insists that this cult, which originated in Korea, is no laughing matter! Indeed the cult is veritably "a present-day curiosity of the business world . . . a spreading network of companies with interests in publishing, entertainment, fishing, food retailing and banking." His churches are spreading rapidly in many countries, drawing impressionable young recruits. Today the cult has thousands of members in the United States, and it realizes an income of millions of dollars annually.

Director Thomas's film tells the story of a devoted follower and demonstrates how devotees are recruited through typical standard brainwashing techniques. Included among them are "therapy, food deprivation, sleep deprivation, isolation, touching, holding, feeling, chants and games that involve hyperventilation and spacing out, and digging into a person's personal life. This leads to a nervous breakdown after two or three days, the first sign of successful brainwashing."

This second false option to Christian faith—the rise of the cults, especially cults of Eastern origin—is on the increase. There is an endless and growing list of false options to the true faith. What are we to do? We Christians cannot simply turn our backs or fold our arms in judgment or derision. Many of us have been part and parcel of the growing disillusionment that young people have with traditional Christian faith.

Discerning the Deception of False Religions

Suppose a neighbor of yours or a member of your family has become involved in a religious group and is urging you to look at it seriously and become a member. Or suppose someone knocks on your door and with a warm smile asks to share a few ideas about their religious group with you or give you some religious literature. What should you do to avoid being deceived and led astray from the truth of Christ? Let me suggest three questions you should ask.

First, is Christ worshiped as Lord and Savior? The central question today is still the same as that Jesus asked almost two thousand years ago: "What do you think about the Christ? Whose son is he?" (Matthew 22:42). Some cults dismiss Christ completely or suggest He was only a great teacher. Some claim salvation is not to be found in Christ, but only in their leader or founder, or in their teachings. Many cults claim to have a high view of Christ, but deny that He rose again from the dead, or that He was the unique and divine Son of God, or that we are saved only through His atoning death on the cross.

But Jesus declared, "I am the way and the truth and the life. No one comes to the Father except through me" (John 14:6). The apostle Peter summarized the consistent message of the New Testament from beginning to end: "Salvation is found in no one else, for there is no other name under heaven given to men by which we must be saved" (Acts 4:12). Don't be deceived! No human leader, no group, no set of religious teachings or philosophical ideas can save you from your sins and reconcile you to God. Only Christ can do that—and He will, for all who turn in simple faith and trust to Him as Lord and Savior.

Second, is the Bible central as the one true guide to faith and practice? Cults and false religions often ignore or even deny the full inspiration and authority of the Bible as the Word of God. They often substitute instead another book or a set of teachings that are not based on the Bible. Some cults pay lip service to the Bible as the Word of God, but then add a second book to "interpret" the Bible "correctly" according to their own man-made teachings. One prominent cult in America claims it bases its teachings on the Word of God—but has made its own "translation" of the Bible which twists the meaning of the Bible's clear teaching.

The Bible is God's Word, and as such it is our authoritative source of truth about God. It is not the product of men's imaginations—although God used men to write it—but comes from the Spirit of God Himself. "Above all, you must understand that no prophecy of Scripture came about by the prophet's own interpretation. For prophecy never had its origin in the will of man, but men spoke from God as they were carried along by the Holy Spirit" (2 Peter 1:20, 21).

Third, is participation in a local Christian fellowship encouraged and practiced? One common characteristic of many cults is that they claim that they, and they alone, have the whole truth. They therefore strongly discourage their members from participating in the worship and instruction of a Christian church—and may even take violent measures to prevent it.

The church is not perfect. Some within the churches—as we shall see below—have even departed from the basic truths of the Christian faith. But God has His people and the church is essential to His plan. We need other believers—and other believers need us. The Bible says, "Let us not give up meeting together, as some are in the habit of doing, but let us encourage one another" (Hebrews 10:25). Beware of any group which speaks against other Christians and churches and insists it alone has the truth.

Ways Deception Takes Hold

As we have considered these deceptions you may have asked yourself, "Why does there seem to be so much of this today? Why are so many people willing to be swept away by teaching which is false and thereby are turning their backs on God's truth?"

There are, no doubt, many reasons for this. But I am afraid we Christians must confess that at times we have been part of the problem because we are not examples of Christ's love and purity as we should be. Many people—especially young people—have become disillusioned with the Christian faith and the church, and have therefore been open to the rider who deceives.

Throughout history there are examples of Christian believers becoming unwitting allies of the horseman who deceives. Rather than standing against the symbol of the white horse whose hoofbeats we can hear, unknowingly we can assist him. Sometimes it is in word and action. For example, part of the state church in Nazi Germany gave their official blessing to Hitler's Third Reich as it wreaked havoc on Europe. Sometimes our sin is in our silence and inaction. Jim Jones was an ordained clergyman. Surely some ecclesiastical court should have challenged his credentials before those 913 lost their lives so tragically in Guyana. Instead, Jones was left unhindered, a representative of the rider who deceives.

Today, too, Christian believers are in danger of *helping* the rider on the white horse to deceive. In his fine book, *Unholy Devotion: Why Cults Lure Christians*, Harold Busséll says: "In our fervor to point out (the cult's) errors of doctrine, we have virtually ignored our own shortcomings and vulnerabilities." I will briefly illustrate some of the ways too many people assist in the deception of others through: 1) half-truths, easy answers and lies, 2) maintaining double standards (saying one thing but doing another), 3) discriminating against certain sins while approving or ignoring other sins, 4) inadequate practical teaching on "the inward journey," 5) inadequate practical teaching about the "outward journey."

The Problem of Half-Truths, Easy Answers and Lies

One of the primary reasons young people reject Christ and follow after the rider who deceives and his cultic allies are the half-truths, easy answers and lies we Christians have sometimes told in our attempts to "sell the faith." I have listened to too many sermons, read too many Christian books and seen too many Christian films with happy-ever-after endings. Some even declare that if you become a Christian you will get rich or always be successful. In our attempts to share the faith we have given the impression that, once you have accepted Christ as Savior and Lord, your problems are over. That is not true. Becoming "new" in Christ is a wonderful beginning—but it isn't the end of pain or problems in our lives. It is the beginning of our facing up to them. Being a Christian involves a lifetime of hard work, dedicated study and difficult decisions.

After the apostle Paul's wonderful conversion on the road to Damascus, I doubt if he ever dreamed what hardship and suffering lay ahead. Even though God had told Ananias (who was to disciple Paul), "I will show him how much he must suffer for my name" (Acts 9:16), he could not have known what lay ahead in not only living the Christian life, but serving Christ. In 2 Corinthians, the sixth chapter, he recounts some of his sufferings—not in discouragement and complaining, but in joy and victory: "In great endurance; in troubles, hardships and distresses; in beatings, imprisonments and riots; in hard work, sleepless nights and hunger; . . . through glory and dishonor, bad report and good report; genuine, yet regarded as impostors; known, yet regarded as unknown; dying, and yet we live on; beaten, and yet not killed; sorrowful, yet always rejoicing; poor, yet making many rich; having nothing, and yet possessing everything" (vv. 4, 5, 8–10).

He gives even more detail in 2 Corinthians 11: "Three times I was beaten with rods, once I was stoned, three times I was shipwrecked, I spent a night and a day in the open sea, I have been constantly on the move. I have been in danger from rivers, in danger from bandits, in danger from my own countrymen, in danger from Gentiles; in danger in the city, in danger in the country, in danger at sea; and in danger from false brothers. I have labored and toiled and have often gone without sleep; I have known hunger and thirst and have often gone without food; I have been cold and naked. Besides everything else, I face daily the pressure of my concern for all the churches. Who is weak, and I do not feel weak? Who is led into sin, and I do not inwardly burn? If I must boast, I will boast of the things that show my weakness" (vv. 25–30).

For Paul the Christian life was one of suffering. The same could be said of a multitude of Christ's followers, many of whom were killed for their faith. So when Christ said time after time that one must "deny himself and take up his cross and follow me" He was indicating that it is not easy to be His true follower. The apostle Paul warned, "Everyone who wants to live a godly life in Christ Jesus will be persecuted" (2 Timothy 3:12). He offers no cheap grace, no easy life. As someone has said, "Salvation is *free* but not cheap."

Charles T. Studd was a famous sportsman in England, captain of the Cambridge XI cricket team. A century ago he gave away his vast wealth to needy causes and led the "Cambridge Seven" to China. His slogan was, "If Jesus Christ be God and died for me, then no sacrifice can be too great for me to make for Him."

During the first decade of this century, Charles Borden left one of America's greatest family fortunes to be a missionary in China. He only got as far as Egypt where, still in his twenties, he died of typhoid fever. Before his death he said, "No reserves, no retreats, no regrets!"

A generation ago, Jim Elliot went from Wheaton College to become a missionary to the Aucas in Ecuador. Before he was killed, he wrote, "He is no fool who gives up what he cannot keep to gain what he cannot lose."

The Christian faith brings its own "blood, sweat and tears" to those who would follow Jesus Christ. Christ calls us to discipleship. When we come to Him, He takes away one set of burdens—the burden of sin, the burden of guilt, the burden of separation from God, the burden of hopelessness. But He also calls upon us to "Take my yoke upon you and learn from me" (Matthew 11:29). It is not a yoke that is too heavy for us to bear, for Christ bears it with us: "For my yoke is easy and my burden is light" (Matthew 11:30). Nevertheless, Christ calls us to follow Him, regardless of the cost, and He has never promised that our path will always be smooth. There is no life that is without its own set of burdens. I have chosen Christ not because He takes away my pain but because He gives me strength to cope with that pain and in the long range to realize victory over it. Corrie ten Boom said, "The worst can happen but the *best* remains." When we oversell the material and spiritual benefits of the Christian faith, we ally ourselves with the horseman who deceives.

I remember a wonderful young man who came to one of our crusades in a wheelchair. He was suffering from the last cruel stages of terminal cancer, and he was angry and bitter. He had read too many Christian books promising health to the believer. Too many well-meaning Christians had promised him a full healing from his disease. His loving parents had carried him from Christian leader to Christian leader who would pray dramatically for his immediate healing, but to no avail. The boy had prayed and fasted and believed—and still no miracle cure had taken place. Now he was dying. Hundreds had been mobilized to pray. Our crusade would be the last Christian meeting that young man would attend.

Our Youth Night special guest was Joni Eareckson Tada. She, too, had been crippled—in her case, by a tragic accident. She, too, had prayed for healing. And she too, remained confined to a wheelchair—a quadriplegic. When she wheeled herself to the microphone that night she did not oversell the Good News in Christ. She confessed her own early anger at remaining crippled after praying and believing for a miracle. Then she told how God had met her in her pain and given her life a new direction in spite of her disappointment and despair.

Joni dared to tell it like it is. Her honesty set that dying young man free. Letting go of his bitterness and his anger, he stopped seeing himself as a failure, as one who did not have enough faith. He saw Christ in and through his pain. Soon after that meeting he died, and his parents rejoiced that he had not died angry. He simply gave his life back to his loving Father, by giving himself to Jesus Christ, and went to be with the risen Lord, where he has freedom forever from suffering and pain.

That does not mean that God never heals in miraculous ways—for there are certainly times that He does. But there are also many times when He does not. We cannot understand why some people appear to glide effortlessly through life while others seem constantly to be in the throes of pain and sorrow. We cannot explain why some withered bodies are healed while others suffer and die. We cannot know why some prayers seem so wonderfully answered and others seemingly go unheard. We cannot pretend that life in Christ always means victory, miracle and success in this life. When we tell only the stories of victory, we tell only a part of the truth. When we recount only the answered prayers, we oversimplify. When we imply the Christian faith involves no yoke, we lie. And half-truths, easy answers and lies are the weapons of the horseman who deceives.

But in the midst of the suffering, trials and temptations, He will provide His peace, joy and fellowship. We are not all called to suffer for Christ in the same way. In some parts of the world it is very hard to be a Christian—although in our own nation it may be just as difficult to stand against the materialism and self-centeredness of our age. But whatever comes your way, know that Christ is with you. He knows what it is to suffer, for He—the sinless Son of God—suffered the pangs of death and hell for you. He knows what it is to be tempted, and "Because he himself suffered when he was tempted, he is able to help those who are being tempted" (Hebrews 2:18). In the midst of every situation of life He can give an inner calm and strength that you could never imagine apart from Him. "Peace I leave with you; my peace I give you. I do not give to you as the world gives. Do not let your hearts be troubled and do not be afraid" (John 14:27).

The Problem of Double Standards: the Difference between What We Say and What We Do

Another reason the rider who deceives is having a field day is the double standard practiced within the Christian church. I commend that bumper sticker that reads, "Christians are not perfect, just forgiven." We have pointed fingers of accusation at cults and at cult leaders for deceiving their members. "They say one thing and practice another," we complain. Yet look at our own history as Christian believers. Who of us cannot agree with the apostle Paul who said, "I do not understand what I do. For what I want to do I do not do, but what I hate I do" (Romans 7:15)?

Often the outsider can see through our facades. He has heard the stories of Christian churches that have been divided by anger and hatred. He knows about the Christian deacon who left his wife to run away with the church organist. He knows how some of the Sunday morning faithful spend Saturday night. He knows that Christian believers, too, are human. Yet how we work to keep that secret hidden!

We write books about celebrities who are supposedly converted to the faith. All too often, after the book is released, our celebrity Christian is caught in a front-page scandal. We produce films about the wonderful change Christ makes in a couple facing tragedy. Then, as has happened on occasion, just as the film is released that same couple announces their divorce. Ministers, deacons, Christian leaders and celebrities are vulnerable to sin. Why can't we simply admit it? None of us is perfect. None of us lives without occasional sin and failure, and it is hypocritical to say otherwise. At the same time, of course, we must never grow complacent about sin or simply say, "Oh well, everyone else is doing it too." The

Bible commands, "But just as he who called you is holy, so be holy in all you do" (1 Peter 1:15). It also tells us there is forgiveness and new life when we repent and confess our sins to Christ.

My wife just reminded me that the early mountain people in the area where we live used a wooden cradle with slatted sides to put their laundry in. It was set crossways in a rushing creek, the water flowed through the slats and the laundry had continuous cleansing. (As she remarked, this was probably the first automatic washing machine!) A North Carolina bootlegger was converted. When he was taken down to the stream to be baptized he asked if he could please be put crossways to the current so that he would "get washed the cleaner!"

When the sin and failure comes, as it most certainly will, then we have the wonderful promise that "the blood of Jesus, his Son, purifies us from every sin" (1 John 1:7). That promise was written to *believers*. And the word used here, *purifies* (or, in the King James Version *cleanseth*), means "*continuous* cleansing."

The greatest thing you can do when you have sinned is to go immediately to the Scriptures and claim the many promises of God. Memorize some of them.

Another thing I have found helpful is to confide in a very close Christian friend who can share your burden, problem or failure *in confidence*. (However, a word of caution here. Although there are some believers in whom you confide who cannot wait to tell someone else, don't let that be an excuse for hiding your secrets from everyone. Just be sure you can trust the one to whom you talk.) Then, let that person read the Scripture and pray with you.

Why must we pretend with each other? Why must we wear assumed smiles of victory in our public gatherings and weep tears of loneliness and anger when we are alone? If your business fails and bankruptcy threatens, let your brother and sister in Christ be aware of your struggle. If your marriage is tearing apart at the seams, find at least one or two trustworthy believers to share your pain and help you deal in practical ways with the problems you face. The Bible says, "Carry each other's burdens, and in this way you will fulfill the law of Christ" (Galatians 6:2).

It only takes one act of repentance to receive Christ as Lord and Savior. But repentance is not a one-time act. All Christians are guilty of individual and corporate sin. Corporate sin is participating in a group's sin, whether it's a family that ignores a neighbor in need, a church that ignores the needs of its neighborhood, or a nation that ignores the needs of other nations in the world.

Once we confess the fact that we Christians, too, still sin, we see unbelievers in a new light—and they will see us in a new light. We do not look down on their sinfulness from any position of arrogance. We simply reach out in understanding and in love, offering to our fellow sinners the forgiveness and new life that we were freely given in Christ. When we admit that we, too, are not perfect, just forgiven, and share appropriate Scripture, we drive away the rider who deceives, as Jesus did in the wilderness. But as long as we pretend to be perfect and live behind the double standard, we give him room to ride.

The Problem of Discriminating against Some Sins While Ignoring Others

Another way we help the rider who deceives by bringing disillusionment to some who observe us is by condemning some sins but tolerating others. Some of us grew up in churches that had a rigid code of "do's" and "don'ts." These sometimes blinded us to other sins which made our lives inconsistent with our profession of Christ.

But sin is sin in God's eyes, and we must pray that He will open our eyes to see it in our lives and root it out. How, for example, do we treat people who may be struggling against deviant sexuality? The Bible teaches these practices are wrong—but no more so than adultery. Many Christians have had far too little compassion for those who are having a hard-fought struggle against deviant sex. Or again, how do we treat people whose lives have been bruised by divorce—even when they may have been an innocent partner?

Jeannie Mills was a leader in Jim Jones's People's Temple cult. Before joining Jones she had been an active teacher and Sunday school superintendent in her church for over nine years. She had held down two jobs to put her husband through school but when he finally graduated he divorced her and remarried. The church elders called Jeannie to appear before an official meeting where she was told that she could no longer serve in that church because of her divorce—although she was not at fault. Heartbroken, feeling "discarded as an old dish rag" she wandered into the People's Temple and gave her talents to a group that "loved me, and accepted me and used me."

In his prizewinning documentary on the Jones cult Mel White recounts how Jeannie Mills eventually left the cult and established the Human Freedom Center in Berkeley, a rallying point for victims of Jones and other cult victims. But all her suffering went back to the moment when, as an innocent victim of another's sinfulness, she was condemned by her church and thrown by churchmen into the path of the rider who deceives.

But there are other kinds of sins we are prone to excuse. Are we complacent about the way people of another race are treated in our community? Are we indifferent to those who are victims of injustice or grinding poverty in our world? Do we impatiently get up from our overburdened dinner plates and switch off the television news when it pictures the victims of famine in a far-off country? Let us pray that God will make us sensitive to sin wherever it is found. We must reach out in Christian love to those whose lives are battered and bruised by sin, point them to the only One who can bring healing and new life, and welcome them into our fellowship. "For it is God's will that by doing good you should silence the ignorant talk of foolish men. Live as free men, but do not use your freedom as a cover-up for evil; live as servants of God" (1 Peter 2:15, 16).

The Problem of Inadequate Practical Teaching about the "Inward Journey"

The inward journey is that lifelong pilgrimage of spiritual growth and maturity. Too often we see conversion as the end rather than the beginning of life's struggle to know God and to do His will. For example, going forward in a crusade or church to receive Jesus

Christ as Lord and Savior is the first step of the long inward journey. The study of God's Word, the practice of prayer, wide reading of Christian books and articles, memorization of Scripture, poetry, and hymns, gathering together in Christian community, participation in small nurture groups, building intimate and honest Christian friendships—all of these activities are necessary to grow in Christian faith. Yet too often we just assume that people understand and practice these disciplines on their own.

I'll never forget a pastor telling me the story of one of his most faithful members who did not know how to pray. She had been a hardworking, committed member of his church since her conversion in a crusade. She had taught Sunday school and pledged her financial support. She had even brought neighbors and friends to church. One Wednesday evening the pastor asked that woman to lead in closing prayer. After a long, embarrassing silence she ran from the room in tears. For a while the woman disappeared. She wouldn't answer her phone. She didn't return to church. Finally, she called the pastor and made an appointment to see him. In his study, the woman confessed that she had never been taught to pray. She didn't know what to say or how to say it. Everyone had just assumed that she could pray, but she honestly didn't know how. The pastor told me that teaching this person from a totally secular background how to pray was one of the most difficult yet rewarding tasks of his ministry. It gave new meaning to the disciples' question directed to Jesus, "Lord, teach us to pray, just as John taught his disciples" (Luke 11:1).

Each evening in a crusade, I give an invitation for people to commit themselves to Christ. Afterward I talk to them about four important things that must be part of their lives if they are to develop and mature. One of those is prayer. I tell them that they may not be able to pray like a clergyman in the beginning, but that they can start with just a simple sentence. "Lord, I love you"—that's a prayer. Or, "God, help me"—that's a prayer. Since the disciples had to be taught to pray, we, too, ought to study the Scriptures and learn to pray.

All too often cult leaders sweep down into the lives of these babes in Christ and offer them rigorous spiritual discipline. While we are taking for granted that all is well with new converts, cults assume that their new members know nothing. They start from scratch and build into the newcomer all the skills he or she needs to feel a part of that particular cultic system.

By assuming too much, we leave our new believers open and vulnerable to cults with their skillful systems and pat answers. It is important for local church leaders to keep in touch with the spiritual state of their membership, to see the level of biblical knowledge or to determine how well and how often people pray.

A recent survey showed that in 85 percent of the seminaries of this country there were no classes on prayer. How many local churches offer classes on developing the skill and practice of prayer? One church had a "week of waiting"—an *entire week for prayer!* The rider who deceives gloats when we assume our people are alive and growing. He is all too free to ride into our ranks and to make victims of us all if and when our inward journey, our spiritual growth and maturity, are not a primary concern to us all.

The Problem of Inadequate Practical Teaching about the "Outward Journey"

The outward journey is an expression that I think originated with Elizabeth O'Connor, the historian of the Church of the Savior in Washington. To grow on an inward journey, the journey to know God, is not enough. We are also called to follow Christ onto our streets and into our neighborhoods. We are called to serve Christ in bringing His message of redemption to the world. The outward journey, that journey which takes us beyond our own small world to the world in need, is the inevitable outworking of a genuine inward journey. The cross points in two directions—toward God and toward my neighbors.

The Church of the Savior requires that each member be actively working in an outreach project—whether evangelism through a coffeehouse, a retreat ministry, rebuilding houses or feeding the poor, caring for orphans, widows and transients, being involved in the primary concerns of education, public housing or environment. Sometimes we act as though attending church on Sunday morning and putting an offering in the basket are all that God requires of us. We make the faith seem undemanding. And we forget Jesus standing before the rich young man saying, "sell everything you have and give to the poor. . . . Then come, follow me" (Mark 10:21).

The rider who deceives revels when we make the faith too easy. Faith involves trust and commitment. The crowd at the fringe of the cross is easily led away. But those who mix their blood and sweat with the blood and sweat of the martyrs are those who are not easily deceived. The more involved a believer is in a daily devotional life and in the lives and needs of others, the more he or she will grow in faith and in practice. The less involved, the more likely he or she is to be deceived.

Many sincere people leave the church and join the cults because the cults make demands. People want a challenge. They respond to a call to hardship. The cults offer practical ways that the followers can serve others—we talk a lot about "cross-bearing" but seldom give our members practical, difficult tasks of Christian service. It may seem ironic, but if we don't make demands, the rider who deceives will rein in and provide practical programs of caring as the first step of deception.

7

The
White Horse
and Its Rider—

Part III

Those Who Deceive from Within the Church

We have looked at the rider who deceives *outside the church* and how we inside the church can often unwittingly assist him. Now it is time to discuss a more difficult dimension of this rider on the white horse, the rider who deceives from *within* the church. Believe me, deception is on the rise within the Christian church and we ignore it to our peril.

Sometimes it is difficult—even for a Christian—to recognize the deceivers. Jesus spoke of false prophets who "perform great signs and miracles to deceive even the elect—if that were possible" (Matthew 24:24). Paul tells of the coming Antichrist, whose activity in the last days will be marked by "all kinds of counterfeit miracles, signs and wonders" (2 Thessalonians 2:9).

Satan's greatest disguise has always been to appear before men as "an angel of light" (2 Corinthians 11:14). The underlying principle of all his tactics is deception. He is exceedingly crafty and clever in the art of camouflage. For Satan's deceptions to be successful, they must be so cunningly devised that his real purpose is concealed. Therefore, he works subtly.

As I said before, his deception began in the Garden of Eden. The woman said, "The serpent deceived me, and I ate" (Genesis 3:13) From that time to this, Satan has been seducing and beguiling.

Paul warned Timothy, "Evil men and impostors will go from bad to worse, deceiving and being deceived" (2 Timothy 3:13). He also cautioned the church at Ephesus, "Let no one deceive you with empty words, for because of such things God's wrath comes on those who are disobedient" (Ephesians 5:6). And he exhorted them to be "no longer . . . infants, tossed back and forth by the waves, and blown here and there by every wind of teaching and by the cunning and craftiness of men in their deceitful scheming" (Ephesians 4:14).

The Bible teaches that there will be more and more false teachers, prophets and even false religious conferences in the church as the age draws toward its end. As the apostle Peter said, "There will be false teachers among you. They will secretly introduce destructive heresies, even denying the sovereign Lord who bought them—bringing swift destruction on themselves. Many will follow their shameful ways and will bring the way of truth into disrepute. In their greed these teachers will exploit you with stories they have made up. Their condemnation has long been hanging over them, and their destruction has not been sleeping" (2 Peter 2:1–3).

Satan does not want to build a church and call it "The First Church of Satan." He is far too clever for that. He invades the Sunday school, the youth department, the Christian education program, the pulpit and the seminary classroom.

The apostle Paul warned that many will follow false teachers, not knowing that in feeding upon what these people say they are taking the devil's poison into their own lives. Thousands of uninstructed Christians are being deceived today. False teachers use high-sounding words that seem like the height of logic, scholarship and culture. They are intellectually clever and crafty in their sophistry. They are adept at beguiling thoughtless, untaught men and women.

These false teachers have departed from the faith of God revealed in the Scripture The Bible states plainly that the reason for their turning away is that they gave heed to Satan's lies and deliberately chose to accept the doctrine of the devil rather than the truth of God. So they themselves became the mouthpieces of Satan, speaking lies.

Writing to Timothy, the apostle Paul warned, "The Spirit clearly says that in later times some will abandon the faith and follow deceiving spirits and things taught by demons. Such teachings come through hypocritical liars, whose consciences have been seared as with a hot iron" (1 Timothy 4:1, 2).

Paul also wrote again in Timothy (2 Timothy 4:3, 4), "For the time will come when men will not put up with sound doctrine. Instead, to suit their own desires, they will gather around them a great number of teachers to say what their itching ears want to hear. They will turn their ears away from the truth and turn aside to myths."

Satan is a liar and a deceiver. He is a great imitator. As we have seen as far back as the Garden of Eden, Satan's purpose was not to make Eve as ungodly as possible, but to make her as godlike as possible without God. Satan's plan has always been to imitate God. The Scripture says, "Satan himself masquerades as an angel of light. It is not surprising, then, if his servants masquerade as servants of righteousness. Their end will be what their actions deserve" (2 Corinthians 11:14, 15).

The Bible teaches that God is clothed in a blazing light. When the disciples saw Christ on the Mount of Transfiguration, it says, "They saw his glory" (Luke 9:32). God came to Adam and Eve clothed in light. Satan imitated God by transforming himself into an angel of light. Adam and Eve were fooled and deceived.

Satan is still transforming himself into a false angel of light and Satan's representatives are also being transformed as ministers of righteousness. While propagating that which brings death and darkness to the mind and heart of the sinner, they profess to be representatives of the God who is light. They claim to be propagating doctrines that come from the God of light, the living God. This is a part of satanic deception—the satanic system that imitates the program of God.

In his newly published *The Life and Times of Grigorii Rasputin*,

Oxford scholar Alex De Jonge characterizes the prerevolution Russia of seventy years ago. He says, "The whole country seemed possessed by demons and redeemers, and who could tell the difference?" That is the way it will be, we are taught in Scripture, before the appearance of the actual Antichrist who will precipitate Armageddon. There will be many who pretend to be christs. These we cannot mistake recognizing because they will themselves claim to be messiahs. But every one of these antichrists will harden hearts to Jesus Christ and soften up the way for the revelation of the true Antichrist.

It is difficult for us to accept the fact that Satan can use a preacher or a clergyman as one of his tools, proclaiming another gospel than the gospel of Jesus Christ. Yet that can be the case. That does not mean we should be strongly critical of every church or every pastor, constantly suspicious and looking for heresy in a proud, judgmental way. We should thank God for the thousands and thousands of pastors who faithfully proclaim the Word of God in churches of many different denominations. At the same time, we must not be naive about Satan's ability to deceive. That is why the apostle John warned, "Do not believe every spirit [or teacher], but test the spirits to see whether they are from God, because many false prophets have gone out into the world" (1 John 4:1). We "test the spirits" as we compare their teaching with the truth of God's Word, the Bible.

The Deceiver and Modern Materialism

Millions of people today have been deceived by false religions and counterfeit cults. But is false religion the only way the rider on the white horse deceives today? Not at all! For many people today the problem is not false religion, but a total lack of any religious views at all. They may say, "Yes, I believe in God," when a Gallup poll is taken—but He has no influence on their lives. They are what someone has termed "practical atheists" living life just as if God did not exist.

And yet in another sense they are very "religious" because they constantly worship the idols of modern civilization We usually think of an idol as a religious figure carved out of wood or stone, perhaps in some primitive tribe far removed from civilization. But we have our "idols" today, because an idol is anything that you worship in place of the living God. Some people worship the idol of beauty or sexual pleasure. Some people worship the idol of money and security—although I have observed that the more money some people have the more insecure they become. Some people worship at the shrine of power, constantly scheming for ways they can dominate others.

There are literally thousands of ways Satan deceives people today. Some are very obvious because they cause a person to get involved in practices which are clearly wrong in God's eyes, and which are clearly seen as wrong by others as well. Others, however, are very subtle and clever, and we may even be unaware of them—or at least think we have concealed them from others. When Satan came to Adam and Eve in the disguise of a serpent, the Bible says, "Now the serpent was more crafty than any of the wild animals the Lord God had made" (Genesis 3:1). But whatever guise Satan's temptations and deceptions take, they still are wrong and will ultimately lead a person to destruction.

Often Satan's biggest deception is convincing people that they can sin and get by with it. Millions today believe that they can turn their backs on God and never pay any price for their foolishness. The Bible warns, "Do not be deceived: God cannot be mocked. A man reaps what he sows. The one who sows to please his sinful nature, from that nature will reap destruction" (Galatians 6:7, 8). The Bible also commands us to avoid anything which is associated with the evil in the present world system which is controlled by Satan and his powers. "Do not love the world [*cosmos*] or anything in the world. If anyone loves the world, the love of the Father is not in him. For everything in the world—the cravings of sinful man, the lust of his eyes and the boasting of what he has and does—comes not from the Father but from the world [*cosmos*]. The world and its desires pass away, but the man who does the will of God lives forever" (1 John 2:15–17).

What is your idol? What really, honestly, dominates your life? What are your priorities, and what are the real (although perhaps hidden) motives in your everyday living? Is Christ on the throne of your life, or is self? You don't have to practice voodoo or be a follower of a strange cult to have been deceived by the rider on the white horse. Jesus warned us to beware of "the deceitfulness of wealth" (Mark 4:19). Anything that entices you away from a wholehearted commitment to Christ is being used of Satan to deceive you.

When you ignore Christ's invitation to confess your sins, to be forgiven and to receive Him as Lord and Savior of your life, you are in danger of being in league with Satan—just as if you wore a black robe and joined in worship with America's self-appointed chief Satanist. Whether you refuse or just neglect to study and obey the words of Scripture, you are as open to deception as if you memorized and practiced the teaching in the *Satanic Bible*. And when you refuse to worship in a Christian church or avoid participation in any local body of the Christian community, you are as open to deception as if you were a card-carrying member of one of the Satanist centers around the country.

I would not be any help to you at all if I minced my words at this point. Lost is lost! And without Christ as your Lord and Savior *you are lost!* You are on the wrong path following in the hoofprints of the horseman who deceives. The white horseman symbolically rides to warn us all of the coming judgment. It will be too late then to retrace your footsteps. The Bible is quite clear. There is one last reality after death. Read it. Hebrews 9:27 warns, "Man is destined to die once, and after that to face judgment." Seek Christ as Savior. Confess your sins right now where you are. Don't wait another second. Invite Christ to enter your life as Lord. Get a Bible and read as though your life depended on it. It does— your eternal life.

Facing Our Vulnerability

Perhaps you have read the words I have written in this chapter about Satan's way of deceiving, such as through false teachings or through his appeal to our lusts and our pride. Possibly, however, you have said to yourself, "This is all very interesting, but Satan could never deceive me. I'm not a member of some false religion. I'm not involved in any sinful life style." The Bible warns us, however, "So, if you think you are standing firm, be careful that you don't fall!" (1 Corinthians 10:12). Satan never gives up in his efforts to deceive.

First, we must admit to ourselves that *Christians, too, are vulnerable to deception.* The Scriptures are filled with wonderful promises: "Do not be afraid, little flock. . . . my grace is sufficient. . . . you have overcome the evil one" (Luke 12:32; 2 Corinthians 12:9; 1 John 2:13). We must remember these promises and believe them. But we must also remember God's warnings. Jesus Himself said that in the last days "false Christs and false prophets will appear and perform signs and miracles to deceive the elect—if that were possible" (Mark 13:22). Paul wrote, "See to it that no one takes you captive through hollow and deceptive philosophy" (Colossians 2:8). Jesus warned us, "Watch out that you are not deceived" (Luke 21:8). God will complete in us what He has begun, and yet we must be on our guard against deception.

Second, we are vulnerable at the point of authority figures. We Christians sit in pews facing the front of the church. We listen— and then we get up and leave. How often do we pause to think about what was said? Do we ask questions of those who address us? Most of the authority figures in our lives can be trusted. And that means that there is all the more reason for us to ask questions. A trustworthy authority figure welcomes our honest questions and will answer them frankly. A cult figure is not interested in questions; he wants loyalty. A cult figure doesn't want to give us options; he wants power over our lives.

Of course, the basic test of the Spirit in an authority figure is clearly stated in the Scriptures: "This is how you can recognize the Spirit of God: Every spirit that acknowledges that Jesus Christ has come in the flesh is from God, but every spirit that does not acknowledge Jesus is not from God" (1 John 4:2, 3). Unfortunately, however, this test alone may not prove adequate, for many—in fact most—cult leaders would acknowledge Jesus in just such a way before going on to replace His authority over us with their own authority.

Victims are often from religious homes and churches in which people are not instructed to question authority figures nor taught to make decisions on their own. When the rider who deceives rides into town, we need to ask him who he really is and what he really wants from us. In all likelihood we will quickly detect why he must not be trusted—why he is a false messiah who would lead us to our deaths.

Third, we are vulnerable at the point of money. It is common for false religious leaders to be very secretive about the finances of their organization. Unfortunately, when legitimate Christian organizations and churches refuse to be completely open about finances they are conditioning people to accept unquestioningly the contention of the cult leader that he is not accountable to anyone for his financial dealings. What is the least attended meeting of the church year? The annual business meeting, of course. Too often even those who attend rush superficially through the budget with little understanding of what it says or means. Yet the annual budget is one document that enumerates our priorities. Without understanding the budget, we don't understand who we are or what we are doing. Worse, by not understanding or questioning the budget, we are setting each other up for a leader who doesn't want us to know where the dollars are going. If you give to any Christian charity (including the Billy Graham Evangelistic Association) and you don't insist on an understandable financial accounting of your gift, you are in danger of falling prey to the horseman who deceives.

Fourth, we are vulnerable at the point of time. Too many of us are so busy that we stumble about in a daze, exhausted, too tired to think, let alone to question. False religious leaders keep their members busy. Exhaustion sets in. Deception follows. At the heart of the Christian calendar is a day of rest. And at the heart of that Sabbath day is God's understanding of His creation. Unless we maintain our physical strength, we will lose our spiritual and psychological stamina as well. At the heart of brainwashing is exhaustion. The rider on the white horse loves to see us too tired to resist. That makes his deception all the easier.

Fifth, we are vulnerable at the point of human relationships. False religious leaders separate family from family and friends from friends. They know that when we are lonely and cut off from each other, we cannot share our questions or raise the issues that would set us free. Modern culture, with its sound and fury (even sometimes within the church), doesn't really honor friendship or the time and energy it takes to maintain those intimate ties with a husband or a wife, a friend or a colleague. So, become active. Commit yourself to a small circle of friends. Honor and build friendship whatever the cost.

Look at Jesus' example. He spent most of His public life with only twelve men and a handful of other friends and family. He often left the crowds to be alone with those closest to Him. He took His close friends to the mountain and to the desert—and to that final place of prayer.

Sometimes the leaders of false religions create environments in which people feel loved. But they also create a climate of fear and suspicion. Cult members meet Christian students in bus stations and airports to woo them away from the Christian community by meeting their needs, offering them food, housing, conversation and entertainment—and by showing them attention. They read the obituary notices and visit recently bereaved widows or widowers. They provide practical help with financial management, balancing the checkbook, upkeep of house and car, a ride to work and a community of friends. Cult members visit hospitals and military bases, prisons and rest homes. They show attention, catering to people's need to be noticed or needed. This is one reason they are so successful. Should not the body of Christ be engaged in the same way?

It is ironic, too, that leaders of false religions insist that their members work hard at helping others. They give twenty-four hours a day and 100 percent of their income to projects aimed at helping others in practical ways so as to entice them to their way of thinking. We Christians talk about demonstrating God's love in our neighborhoods, our cities and in the world. Yet we are satisfied with an occasional special offering for missions or a car-wash benefit for the youth group. We are told to "pick up our cross and follow Christ," and yet we sometimes fail to provide the kinds of strategies

111

of service toward others that the cults provide. So when a false religious leader comes along with an environment of apparent loving that meets people's need and enlists them in a program for helping others, many times we fall prey to the cult.

The horseman who deceives loves to find us alone. But when he finds us surrounded by loyal, loving friends, he finds it all the more difficult to deceive us and lead us off the pathway.

As we look to decrease our vulnerability to those who would take power over our lives, we are preparing spiritual and intellectual muscle for that confrontation with the horseman who deceives when he appears in his final, foreboding form. Much is said about the Antichrist in today's religious and secular literature, music, drama and film. Whatever alias he might assume, by working to reclaim control over our lives now and then by turning over those controls to Christ's own Spirit, we are preparing to face the Antichrist and can be assured that we would not be deceived by him.

The Real Problem—Our Sinfulness

We should be careful not to get confused at this point. What is the cause of our problem? When we are deceived, who is to blame? From one standpoint, the real responsibility rests not with the rider who deceives, but with us. The real problem is our own sinfulness. Do you remember the American television comic, Flip Wilson? He made famous the saying, "The devil made me do it." Geraldine (Flip's remarkable comic impersonation of a woman) had an excuse for everything she did wrong. "The devil made me do it!" she would exclaim. But the beguiling grin and wily wink that followed gave the joke away. Geraldine (or Flip) knew full well that she had done the wrong herself. When a college professor's son was involved in a neighborhood brawl, the housekeeper came to his defense saying, "It is not his fault. He is influenced by the bad boys!" "No," said his father, "I cannot blame the bad boys. I must blame his own 'badness' in his heart!"

I believe in the devil. I have experienced his wiles in my own life. But if and when I sin it is because I yield to temptation. It is my fault. "When tempted," wrote the apostle James (1:13–15), realize that "each one is tempted when, by his own evil desire he is dragged away and enticed. Then, after desire has conceived, it gives birth to sin; and sin, when it is full-grown, gives birth to death." In an early edition of the Anglican Prayer Book one finds a prayer of confession that begins, "By my fault, by my own fault, by my own most grievous fault." And the results of my own error are monumental. As Monsignor Knox translates Genesis 2:17, "thy doom is death."

Three thousand years before Flip Wilson, a Greek comic standing drunk on an ancient marble stage would stagger toward the audience and blame Bacchus, the mythical Greek god of wine and celebration, for his own tipsy condition. But it wasn't Bacchus who drank too much. It was the Greek comic himself who had overindulged. When we sin we like to blame someone or something else for our own act. The four horsemen are God's picture to warn us of our own sinfulness. They do not cause evil. They are a picture of a very human process. We cannot say, "The devil made me do it." We cannot say, "Bacchus made me do it." We use these pictures— especially the four horsemen—to make clear this one fact: evil is an ever-present alternative to doing good. But it is not evil that is to blame for our sins. We ourselves are to blame.

However, there are those around us who work, knowingly or unknowingly, on evil's behalf. They are not evil. They do evil. They are not Satan. They are in league with Satan. The first horseman—the horseman who deceives—rides to warn against deception. At the heart of man's predicament is the daily choice every one of us makes between good and evil—between God and His perfect plan for the world and Satan and his flawed plan. The problem is in knowing the difference between truth and falsehood. That's why the imagery of John's Revelation of Jesus Christ is so remarkably appropriate. The first horseman rides a white horse, wears a crown and looks like a conquering messiah. But he, in fact, stands for all the pretenders who come looking like Christ but are in fact antichrists or opposite Christ in every way but appearances. To be forewarned is to be forearmed. John wrote of ".   . many antichrists. . .   This is how we know it is the last hour" (1 John 2:18).

Fighting the Rider Who Deceives

We have outlined in this chapter some of the ways the rider on the white horse in John's vision deceives and diverts people away from the truth. But how can we be sure we do not fall victim to his devious schemes? What steps can you take to be strengthened spiritually so he will not stand a chance against you? The first step is *daily Bible reading*. Early in my ministry the teaching of Dawson Trotman influenced me to memorize Scripture. He kept stressing, "I have hidden your word in my heart that I might not sin against you" (Psalm 119:11). We have a sword to ward off the temptations of Satan. Jesus, in His hour of temptation, confronted Satan with, "It is written" (Luke 4:8). "Therefore put on the full armor of God, so that when the day of evil comes, you may be able to stand your ground. . . . Take . . . the sword of the Spirit, which is the word of God" (Ephesians 6:13, 17). John in the Revelation of Jesus Christ tells us, "They overcame him by the blood of the Lamb and by the word of their testimony" (12:11). That sword is the Word, the Word of God, and it must be hidden in our hearts. That's why Scripture memorization is so important. It ought to be done when you're young, as much as possible, because as you get older it's harder to memorize. I find it much more difficult to memorize a Scripture and retain it now than I did twenty-five to thirty years ago.

I think of that Scripture, "No temptation has seized you except what is common to man. And God is faithful; he will not let you be tempted beyond what you can bear. But when you are tempted, he will also provide a way out so that you can stand up under it" (1 Corinthians 10:13). I watched a television special on a behaviorist experimenting with a rat. The rat was cornered, but there was one way out—a little hole in the corner where he could escape.

The devil gets us cornered. But we have never, ever, been in a situation where we couldn't get out. There is always a way of escape, but sometimes we may wait until it is too late. And that's the danger of dabbling in sin, letting it get into our minds. We play with it. Most sin is not something impulsive. It is something we've thought about. Our resistance has been crumbling inside. Sinful thoughts work like leaven for a while before we actually commit the act. I'm talking about certain sins now. Of course there are sins in which a person may deliberately tell a lie on the impulse of the moment. But Scripture will give us the way out of sinful traps, whether they are long-term struggles or impulsive sinful acts. Without His Word we are in trouble. With His Word we find a way out of that same troubled state.

Second, the Bible constantly exhorts us to *pray unceasingly*. "Pray continually," wrote Paul to the Thessalonians (1 Thessalonians 5:17). I think that means developing the subconscious in such a way that you're praying all the time. I find myself praying right now, "Lord, help me to think of some things that I should say here."

Ruth and I talk on a lot of subjects, and I will pray during our conversation that we will have the right thoughts. We learned to pray constantly about our family during those years we carried the burden of our children. Each one had his or her own problems during those difficult teenage times. Those years are a very difficult period for parents, too. And I suppose Ruth and I did more praying then than in any period of our married life.

Then, of course, in the third place, there is *being filled with the Holy Spirit*. Actually, the Holy Spirit produces the fruit of the Spirit in us. It's important to remember here that, when our wisdom runs out, the Holy Spirit can be trusted to guide us and to help us discern the difference between truth and lies. (For further reading on the important work of the Holy Spirit in our lives, refer to my book, *The Holy Spirit*.)

What does it mean to be filled with the Holy Spirit? It means to be under His control and guidance. It means that He is helping us and empowering us to do God's will. When we are filled with the Holy Spirit, He also puts the burning searchlight of His truth into the dark corners of our lives, convicting us of sins that hinder our walk with God.

How are we filled with the Spirit? Remember that the Holy Spirit comes to take up residence in you when you come to Christ. But we are filled—controlled and empowered by Him—as we consciously yield our whole lives each day to Christ. Being filled with the Holy Spirit is not necessarily a great emotional experience which happens once or twice and then fades from memory. We can be filled with the Spirit each day as we deliberately seek to walk with Christ and submit our wills to Him.

Fourth, *fellowship with other believers* is extremely important. That is one of the dangers of the television church. I know televised religious services can minister to shut-ins and other people who cannot attend a local church. But for the rest of us the televised worship service must never be a substitute for being an active member and attending a local Christian fellowship.

I am partial to small churches, even though my membership is in one of the largest churches in America. I often join in worship with a small local congregation—it's a wonderfully moving service where we have quiet fellowship. Because of its informality it reminds me of the early church. They gathered in small groups to sing and pray, preach, or listen to the Word. I enjoy a formal liturgical service, so Ruth and I sometimes worship in an Episcopalian or Lutheran service. On other occasions we enjoy an Assembly of God, Christian and Missionary Alliance, or Nazarene service. Actually, God has given me a love for the whole body of Christ. I enjoy whatever type of service I attend. The point is, find a Bible-believing local Christian community and be faithful in it. For in that process of sharing, one finds ways to confront and confound the deceiver as he seeks to mislead and undo us.

Why do we need the church and fellowship with other believers? For one thing, when we go to church we bear testimony to our commitment to Christ. But more importantly, we have the opportunity for worship and instruction. We need to worship God publicly, and we need to be taught the Word of God. Get involved in a church where Christ is preached. Get involved in Bible studies and prayer meetings. We need each other as Christians, and we can help each other grow and encourage each other when we are facing trials or temptations.

In discussion with the head of Scotland Yard's Counterfeit Investigation Division someone asked him if he did not have to spend a great deal of time studying counterfeits. The inspector replied, "Quite to the contrary. I spend my time studying the real."

The best advice against deception that I can give is to urge you to spend your time looking at the real Christ. Then, when a counterfeit appears, you'll have less trouble spotting him.

How Christ Can Deliver Us from Deception (a True Story)

Thousands have mercifully been delivered from satanic power and the occult through faith in Jesus Christ. One example is Ron Baker, who lives in Australia.

Ron was an abused child, beaten almost daily—twice with barbed wire. So he grew up to be an abusive husband and father. He had a terrible stutter, could neither read nor write, was a hopeless drunk, a drug user, and into the occult. He had a wife, Beryl, and two sons, all of whom he treated badly.

In 1959, during the Sydney Crusade, a builder who was doing construction work on their house and who happened to be a Christian, invited Beryl to the meetings. That night I preached on the home. I made the comment, "Every child has the right to a Christian home." Beryl was converted that evening, went home to a drunk husband and said, "I gave my heart to Jesus tonight." He watched her all weekend and noticed the difference in her.

Although Ron could not read, he had learned to make out road signs and had gotten a job as a bus driver. During the Sydney Crusade, he found that sometimes he had to drive busloads of people to the crusade meetings. When this happened he would sit in the bus until the meeting was over—hating every minute of his wait. But one day a fellow bus driver asked if Ron would trade assignments with him; the other driver *wanted* to go to the meeting that night. This meant Ron would have the evening off, so he accepted with pleasure.

Usually, on the way home, Ron's car "automatically" stopped at the pub, where he would have plenty to drink before going home. This night, for some reason, he drove past the pub and arrived home sober—just in time to meet the friendly builder, who was there to invite Ron to go to the meeting with him. Ron heard himself accepting. But he made sure that he sat on the top bleacher, in the farthest seat from the platform he could find.

That evening when I gave the invitation, I did something I don't usually do. I said, "We'll sing one more verse. I've the feeling there's someone sitting on the back row who, if he does not come forward and make his peace with God tonight, will have lost his last chance." And Ron Baker found himself standing down in front of the platform.

When the young counselor opened his Bible to counsel with him, Ron said, "Don't bother, son; I can't read."

So the counselor gave him three verses to go on: "For all have sinned and fall short of the glory of God" (Romans 3:23); "The wages of sin is death" (Romans 6:28); and "If we confess our sins, he is faithful and just and will forgive us our sins" (1 John 1:9).

Ron lived on these three verses for the next two or three years. During that time, he met two Catholic sisters who "tucked him under their wings" and taught him how to read. He was delivered from alcoholism, drug use and the occult. After learning how to read, he worked his way through Bible school by driving a bus, then went through seminary. After seminary he pastored a church for about ten years, but since that time he has been holding evangelistic meetings and is one of Australia's outstanding evangelists.

His two sons became Christians, married Christian wives and have established Christian homes. Just this past spring he welcomed his first little granddaughter.

When his own sons had been born he had been too drunk to go to the hospital to see Beryl. But this time, when his son called and asked him to come over and see his little granddaughter, he drove all the way, thanking God that he was sober enough to drive to welcome her.

Perhaps you, the reader of this book, know someone who is in the grip of a demonic power or entrapped in a monstrous cult. There is hope. There is deliverance. There is forgiveness and restoration. Ron Baker not only was delivered, but he rose from negative living to the positive life and is being used to bring hope and encouragement to thousands through radio and television, and in public meetings. It could happen to you or your acquaintance who may be "caught" in the snares of Satan.

8

The Red Horse and Its Rider

The Rider Who Makes War

Again, somewhere above Patmos, John stands trembling before God's eternal throne. The white horse bearing the rider who deceives has galloped from the scroll and down the parapets of heaven to wreak havoc on the earth. Again the celestial servant of God shouts the command of the Almighty: "Come!" Immediately a second horseman charges from the scroll and reins in before the throne. Does God speak to the rider? All John reports is this: the second rider "was given power to take peace from the earth and to make men slay each other" (Revelation 6:4). Does God Himself hand the rider a Roman sword? John states simply, "To him was given a large sword" (Revelation 6:4). Does the rider lift the sword in salute or simply spur the great heaving flanks of the horse red as blood and plunge from their sight toward the world below?

Remember, God is not the cause of war. God had a far greater plan for His creation—and at first that plan was a reality, with no hint of war or conflict to stain His perfect creation. But man, created free, chose not to obey God, and his resulting fallen nature turned to making war, not peace. This heavenly vision is God's way of showing us our folly and warning us of its consequences. Just as Harry Truman would not obey the warnings before Mount St. Helens erupted, so all of mankind through history has refused to listen to the warnings of God. I have often wondered, while the hoofbeats of that fiery red horse still rang in John's ear, whether he heard other sounds—the clanking of sword against sword, the sound of heavy iron spears piercing flesh and crunching bone, the sound of women screaming and children crying, the groans of the wounded and the gasps of the dying?

Listen! The distant sounds of those same hoofbeats can be heard closing in on the place you now sit reading. Above those noisy hoofbeats arise other sounds—the metallic thud of machine guns, the whistle of flamethrowers and mortar rounds, the crackle of burning schools, homes and churches, the high-pitched shriek of missiles zeroing in with their nuclear warheads, the explosion of fifty-megaton bombs over our cities, the scream of terror and death . . . and the silence of a scorched and desolate earth.

The two scenes I've described above, one ancient and one modern, are no exaggeration. For John the apostle was well aware of the roar and horror of warfare. Just before John's life and ministry, from 67 to 37 B.C., Palestine had been besieged and bloodied by revolution. Without the aid of news teams and television body counts, ancient historians reckoned 100,000 deaths from the conflict. And just before John's exile, in A.D. 61, the Romans crushed another rebellion by Queen Boadicea in the northern empire, with a loss of over 150,000 soldiers and civilians. In the long year between A.D. 68 and 69, Rome had been ruled by four different Caesars. Each brought with him his own unique bloodbath.

War, anarchy, brother against brother, neighbor against neighbor—the complete breakdown of sane human relationships has characterized human history. The rider on the red horse has ridden from the beginning of time, and John's vision was sent as a harbinger of that final holocaust when the Messiah Himself will intervene and crush the allies of evil at Armageddon. Jesus forecast that worst of woes and wars as "unequaled from the beginning of the world until now—and never to be equaled again. If those days had not been cut short, no one would survive" (Matthew 24:21, 22).

It is completely naive and insane for us to ignore the fact that the ominous rider who brings war is, even now, riding recklessly in our direction. Our earth has shrunk into a global village; we are all neighbors. The foreboding sound of the hoofbeats of the red horse pulses like an erratic heartbeat at the center of our beleaguered planet. The current stockpiles of 60,000 hydrogen bombs give the human race the power to destroy the entire earth seventeen times over through nuclear flames reaching 130 million degrees—and all that in one blinding flash.

No longer can we speak of war with a kind of confident detachment. Until 6 August 1945, wars were more or less limited to battlefields and sea-lanes. Supplies had to be transported over vast distances. Oceans, mountainous terrain, snow-covered highways, desert dunes and rivers all created natural barriers to limit war and give combatants at least the illusion of distance and safety. Especially for North Americans, wars have been something fought "over there" on "foreign shores."

But alas, on 6 August 1945, at 8:15 A.M. a warning bell rang in the broadcast department of the Japanese Broadcasting Corporation. A newsman rushed to read the bulletin he had just received from the Chugoku District Army Headquarters: "Three enemy aircraft have been spotted over the Saijo area. . . ." Suddenly there was a blinding blue flash of light over Hiroshima, and in its wake arose an ominous mushroom cloud. This was to be the symbol of the new age for the decades to follow.

The newsman was vaporized and the radio station flattened. The nuclear age had begun. The bombing of Hiroshima and Nagasaki brought an abrupt end to that terrible war. We sometimes forget that it also saved lives. Many Japanese leaders today, even in the two cities that were hit, will tell you that the bomb probably saved millions of Japanese as well as Allied lives because the Japanese would have fought to the last person to save themselves from defeat. But, in that instant, war was redefined for all time to come.

The trouble is, too many of us who were not there that day stubbornly refuse to change our antiquated definitions of war. We refuse to believe the truth about the horrible power we have unleashed. We prefer to remain in our fool's paradise: war is something that happens to someone else.

It is mind-boggling to think that as many as fifteen nations now have nuclear weapons and at least twenty-five more are frantically trying to obtain them. If we add all the nuclear weapons stockpiled by the Soviet Union, the United States, Great Britain, France, India, China and at least ten others, then we get an idea of the massive power of destruction the nations of the world have pointed at one another. No longer is war something that is necessarily limited to "over there." The rider on the red horse has closed the distance. The hoofbeats of the red horse bring a deafening war echo up and down the streets of our towns. What can we do? What can we do to slow his ride?

Before answering that question we need to stop and consider for a moment something that is easy to forget in our contemplation of the horror of a nuclear war. We forget the infinitely greater horror of an eternity apart from God. The horrors of a nuclear war will be transitory as far as eternity is concerned. The horrors that are ahead for all who reject God's offer of mercy, grace and salvation in Christ are far more horrible to contemplate.

We need also to recall that moment just before Jesus' betrayal and crucifixion, as the Master was walking away from the temple in Jerusalem. Then He, too, spoke the warning, "You will hear of wars and rumors of wars, but see to it that you are not alarmed. Such things must happen, but the end is still to come. Nation will rise against nation, and kingdom against kingdom" (Matthew 24:6, 7).

Even while He was uttering these words, the most hideous and horrendous deed in all time and eternity was about to be perpetrated. Man was about to crucify the Prince of Peace. However, it is important for us to remember this: though Christ warned us there will constantly be wars and rumors of war, it does not follow that we should sit silently by while the peoples of the world destroy each other. We must not by our silence give approval to such devastation with weapons of mass destruction. We must warn the nations of the world that they must repent and turn to God while there is yet time. We must also proclaim that there is forgiveness and peace in knowing Jesus Christ as Savior and Lord.

Recently I was in central Europe preaching in East Germany and Czechoslovakia. I could not help but think of all the wars that have been fought across those lands just in the last two centuries—many of them seemingly senseless. One of the great tragedies of history is that the rider on the red horse has ridden, and still rides, throughout the earth, and he always leaves death and destruction in his path.

Some time ago *Newsweek* had as its cover story "Wars Without End" (28 June 1982) "Armageddon." That final tragic triumph of "Evil" over "Good!" That's the direction modern man persists in traveling," suggests Harvard professor of psychiatry Robert Coles in his story, "Psychology and Armageddon" in a recent issue of *Psychology Today* (May 1982). When President Reagan went before the joint Houses of Lords and Commons in England, his address was carried on television throughout much of the world. He said that everywhere "we see around us today the marks of our terrible dilemma—predictions of doomsday." He stated further that as we struggle desperately to coexist, with nuclear weapons beckoning the extinction of mankind, there is the ever-present threat of global war. He then assessed, "No President, no Congress, no Prime Minister, no Parliament, can spend a day entirely free of this threat" (*New York Times*, 9 June 1982).

President Reagan, in a statement to the Third Congress of the International Physicians for Prevention of Nuclear War meeting in Amsterdam in June of 1983, said, "No task has greater significance for us, for our allies, and for the entire world than to work . . . to reverse the growth of nuclear arsenals and to move toward genuine peace." Mr. Olof Palme, the socialist prime minister of Sweden who has often been critical of Mr. Reagan, declared, "If President Reagan has come to the conclusion that you can't win a nuclear war, then he is finally on the right track" (London *Times*, 20 June 1983).

In the middle of 1982, a conference had been called entitled "The United Nations Special Session on Disarmament." It was preceded by a tremendous publicity buildup throughout the world.

But the United Nations Secretary General, Javier Pérez de Cuellar, agonized that the whole affair seemed to be "full of sound and fury signifying nothing." Man, he said, is hellbent on a blind course toward World War III. The President of the United Nations General Assembly, Ismat Kittani, became angry and asked, "What have the governments of the world done to respond to the fervent demands of the peoples of the world that this insane arms race be stopped?" He gave his own reply, "You and I know that answer, but I want to state it for the world to hear—nothing!" Not a single weapon has been destroyed over the past four years. It was calculated that in 1983 over one trillion dollars had been spent on armaments. Few of us argue that man is not arming for Armageddon.

Recently *Time* magazine ran its cover story on the same subject, "Thinking the Unthinkable. Rising Fears About Nuclear War." Peter Newman, editor of *Macleans* magazine, just back from a tour of European capitals, seems to think that war is inevitable. Jonathan Schell, in his *The Fate of the Earth* exhorts, "Those who are indifferent to the threat of terminal war are definitely drowsing toward oblivion." A combined AP/NBC News poll reveals that 68 percent of Americans believe it is likely that the United States will become involved in a war during the next few years. Carroll Allen explains, "Murphy's Law is constant, and what can go wrong, sooner or later will." The *Wall Street Journal* concludes, "There is no protection from the extermination of man from this planet, except the prevention of nuclear war."

We have to ask ourselves: Is this the time of "the end" that the Bible speaks of so graphically in so many places? The Scriptures definitely teach that there is coming an end to human history as we know it. It will not be the end of the world. It will be the end of a world system that has been dominated by evil. The Bible teaches that Satan is actually the prince of this world and the "god" of this world system. As long as he is still at work in this world, in constant conflict with God and doing his deadly work, wars will continue.

The Bible teaches that there will be a number of signs that are easily discernible as we approach the end of the age. All of these signs seem currently to be coming into focus. Jesus said in Matthew 24 there would be famines, pestilences and earthquakes in different parts but, He said, this would only be the beginning. He said people "will betray and hate each other, and many false prophets will appear. . . . Because of the increase of wickedness, the love of most will grow cold." Then He said, "And this gospel of the kingdom will be preached in the whole world as a testimony to all nations, and then the end will come." For example, just in this sign alone we see the possibility through new technologies of reaching the entire world with the gospel before the end of this century. But one of the major signs that He indicated was the increasing intensity of warfare. Turn back to Daniel, whom Jesus quoted as an authority on the final age prior to the coming of His kingdom. The prophet assures us ominously, "War will continue until the end" (Daniel 9:26). Turn to the chapters in Revelation (such as 11, 13 and 16) which indicate the advent of "the Beast" (that is, the Antichrist). He will *make war* (11:7, kjv). And, it is asked, "who can make war against him?" (13:4). The answer is obvious three verses later, "He was given power to make war . . . and to conquer. . . . And he was given authority over every tribe, people, language and nation." (13:7, 8).

The *Los Angeles Times* (2 Sept. 1980) quotes China's Deng Xiaoping on the inevitability of world war: "War will burst sooner or later. And whoever believes the contrary makes a tragic mistake."

At the same time throughout the world *there is a longing for peace*. There has never been a time when there have been more peace conferences, more discussions of peace, more demonstrations for peace. If you took a poll of the world's population, I believe more than 95 percent would vote for peace—almost at any price, especially when they read of the terrifying effects of a nuclear holocaust. Unless the nature of man can be changed, I would have to agree with the pessimistic reasoning of President Reagan: "Man has used every weapon he has ever devised. . . . It takes no crystal ball to perceive that a nuclear war is likely." The President's own contention is, "In a nuclear war, all mankind would lose." Andrei Sakharov, the dissident Soviet scientist, even though a controversial figure, has a brilliant mind, and he warned the world: "I know that pacifist sentiments are very strong. . . . I deeply sympathize with people's yearning for peace. . . This is an extremely important factor, but, I repeat, itself alone does not exclude the possibility of a tragic outcome" (*Newsweek*, 4 July 1983, p. 23).

The late Soviet president and Communist Party chief Leonid Brezhnev once said, "Only he who has decided to commit suicide can start a nuclear war." President Yuri Andropov has declared, "Wherever and however a nuclear whirlwind arises, it will inevitably go out of control and cause a worldwide catastrophe." General Omar Bradley said in an Armistice Day speech in 1948, "We have grasped the mystery of the atom and rejected the Sermon on the Mount. . . . The world has achieved brilliance without conscience. Ours is a world of nuclear giants and ethical infants." One of the dangers we face at the present time is that we can be so taken up with impending doom that we forget to keep our minds on Christ and our eyes on Him. Nothing is going to take Him by surprise.

Jesus said, "But see to it that you are not alarmed. Such things must happen, but the end is still to come" (Matthew 24:6). He indicated that there would be many wars, perhaps thousands, before the last great war—and before His return. In the context of the increasing intensity of warfare, He said, "See to it that you are not alarmed" (Matthew 24:6). For these two thousand years since He spoke those words there have been alternating generations of war and peace—wars big and small, civil and international. But technology has dramatically changed all this. There will likely be only one more great world war because of nuclear, biological and chemical weapons.

Jesus indicated that when this type of war does come to pass (Matthew 24:22), "If those days had not been cut short, no one would survive." This refers to total war, with the annihilation of all mankind as a probable outcome—barring divine intervention. Never before has total cosmocide—world death—been at men's fingertips. There are no precedents in political science or in human history to guide the men who command modern power. Mankind may have always had war, but never on the scale that Jesus predicted in Matthew 24 and Revelation 6. Never before has man had the potential to totally obliterate the human race.

This is the situation, and these are the weapons, of the second horseman of Revelation 6. In verse 4 it is indicated that he has power to take peace from the earth. This likely involves world war, not just local or civil wars or even conventional international conflicts. At this moment, the political and military polarization is taking place. Power blocs have been formed that could eventually clash in the most titanic series of battles in human history. It will be a war so intense and so destructive that, unless God intervenes forcibly to stop it, all of humanity would die. Jeremiah indicated there would come a day when "your towns will lie in ruins without inhabitant" (Jeremiah 4:7).

How many will die? The late Albert Einstein predicted that in a full-scale nuclear exchange at least a third of the population of the world would die. This is the same proportion the Bible indicates: "A third of your people will die of the plague or perish by famine inside you; a third will fall by the sword outside your walls" (Ezekiel 5:12). This is a direct prophecy of how many will die as a result of the sword given to the second horseman. A Soviet scientist recently used almost this exact figure to describe the result of a nuclear exchange.

These are frightening words. But there is no need for true believers in Jesus Christ to be frightened. Jesus said to His followers, "See to it that you are not alarmed" (Matthew 24:6).

Is it possible that we could have a century of peace, or even more? Yes. *War is not necessary.* If the human race would, in true repentance, turn to God from its sins of disobedience, idolatry, pride, greed, and even war itself and all that causes man's wars, the possibility of peace exists. But at the moment I see little indication of widespread world repentance.

As recorded in the book of Exodus, God sent plague after plague upon Pharaoh and the ancient Egyptians so they would let Israel go from the bondage of slavery under which they had suffered for four hundred years. After the plagues, Pharaoh would make promises—but then Exodus 8:19 says, "Pharaoh's heart was hard and he would not listen, just as the Lord had said." Later, in the Book of Revelation (9:20, 21), the author looks forward to a time when God will once again bring judgment on the earth through plagues—and yet, he says, "the rest of mankind that were not killed by these plagues still did not repent of the work of their hands; they did not stop worshiping demons, and idols of gold, silver, bronze, stone and wood—idols that cannot see or hear or walk. Nor did they repent of their murders, their magic arts, their sexual immorality or their thefts." The grace, mercy and goodness of God had not led them to repentance. Neither have His judgments led the people of the world to repentance today. This indicates something of the hardness and coldness of the human heart, apart from God. The second horseman of the Apocalypse will have to help teach man his responsibility to the Creator through the pain of war.

This brings us back to the question: Is there something that we could do about war? Yes, as Christians we have a responsibility. We are to *seek peace* and to *make peace* whenever and wherever we can. Jesus said, "Blessed are the peacemakers, for they will be called sons of God" (Matthew 5:9). We have been commanded by our Lord and Savior to work for a just peace on this earth. When the angels announced His birth they said, "and on earth peace to men on whom his favor rests" (Luke 2:14). Surely as the rider on the red horse came bringing war, Christ came bringing peace.

But there are disturbing passages in the New Testament such as Matthew 10:34–39: "Do not suppose that I have come to bring peace to the earth. I did not come to bring peace, but a sword. For I have come to turn 'a man against his father, a daughter against her mother, a daughter-in-law against her mother-in-law— a man's enemies will be the members of his own household.' Anyone who loves his father or mother more than me is not worthy of me; anyone who loves his son or daughter more than me is not worthy of me; and anyone who does not take his cross and follow me is not worthy of me. Whoever finds his life will lose it, and whoever loses his life for my sake will find it."

While Jesus may not be talking directly about warfare, He is talking about a spiritual warfare that follows both the hearing and the acceptance of the gospel. John Wesley interpreted this type of "sword" to be that of love. He came to spread love on the earth, and this love divides people. Some in the same home can be believers and some nonbelievers. This often brings about misunderstanding, friction, and even division. The gospel is both unifying and divisive.

Peace with God, the peace of God, and peace between nations is possible if we would only repent of our sins, listen to Him, and believe on Him. As servants, followers, brothers and sisters of the Master we are commanded to be His allies in the cause of true and lasting peace. Nowhere does He promise that we will succeed apart from Him. But He calls us to try the best we can to confront the issues of war and peace and to work for peace in spite of seemingly impossible odds. Somewhere in here is the mystery of God's sovereignty and man's free will. We are to expect the coming of Christ at any time, but we are to work as if He will not come for a thousand years.

I remember the great shock I had when the first atomic bomb fell on Japan. I remember the fear I felt. In fact, I shared my fear with a famous American clergyman soon after the bombs were dropped. I confessed to him my feelings about the threat of nuclear warfare and I asked him how he thought the Christian should respond. He did not appear concerned. I pointed out the danger of this new power we had discovered. I had no idea then how far out of control the nuclear arms race would be; still, I had growing intuitive fears that we could destroy the world unless somehow we learned to control the power we had unleashed.

And he answered me in a way I will never forget. "Oh, Billy," he said, "I wouldn't worry about things like that. God is in control. He is sovereign." Already the estimated body count in Hiroshima had passed 100,000 and they were still wading through the ruins. I left that great Christian leader, and I was bewildered by his apparent lack of concern.

He was right—to a point. The uniqueness of Hiroshima was the dramatic concentration of horror. The same people who are frozen in horror by that nightmarish event sometimes do not stop to think that 50,000 people die each year on American highways (25,000 of them as a direct result of alcohol abuse). Nor do we stop to seriously consider the thousands of babies who die at the hands of abortionists every month, and other thousands who suffer and die as a result of drugs and drug-related causes. Of course God is in control of the world. We as believers don't need to be dominated by fear. Christ's triumph over the grave has robbed death of its sting. God has a schedule for Christ's return. We are promised that He will not allow the earth to be destroyed again.

Still, my clergyman friend's apparent unconcern does not seem to reflect the command of Christ. Jesus called us to be peacemakers. When a plague threatens to wipe out an African tribe or an Indian people in South America, we rush doctors and medical support teams into the area in the name of Christ to save those whose lives are threatened. Why, then, would we sit silently by while weapons are created and stockpiled that would not only kill the African tribe or the Indian people but threaten to destroy all the people of the earth and the life systems that support them?

I believed then, as I believe now, that there must be something we can do to control the arms race. To limit the growing threat of nuclear warfare seems perfectly in line with Christ's call to be peacemakers on the earth. Still, in those first years of the nuclear age I did very little in this particular area. I preached the gospel throughout the world which was my primary calling, and I warned people against war in my sermons from the very beginning. I asked people to repent, for sin is the problem that leads to war. I called people to turn to God before His judgment came. But perhaps I should have done more.

In *The Gathering Storm*, the first volume of his memoir on the second world war, Winston Churchill recalled how people laughed in the 1930s when he warned them of the coming war. Like Noah or the prophets, Churchill was mocked, scorned and ridiculed. Still he warned. I wish now that I had taken a much stronger stand against the nuclear arms race at its beginning when there was a chance of stopping it. Even then I was faithful in my primary task of proclaiming the gospel of Christ and calling sinners to repentance. However, as I shall point out later in this chapter, I am *not for unilateral disarmament*—and *I am not a pacifist*. As long as America's security is threatened—and I am not naive about the intentions of those who radically oppose our way of life and our commitment to freedom—we must have strong defenses. But anyone who is sensitive to history can feel that something unique is about to happen in the world.

Jules Masserman, M.D., Honorary Life President of the International Association for Social Psychiatry, has been quoted as saying: "Acknowledged experts in international and military affairs agree [that] unless present trends are reversed, chances are 4 in 5 that a nuclear war will destroy civilization in the next decade." It's up to all of us to try, in the light of a statement like that, to "reverse" the present trends. We cannot go on at this present frantic pace. In Ecclesiastes (9:3) the Old Testament writer says it well: "There is madness in their hearts while they live." A kind of madness has gripped the human race.

What the Nations Must Do for Peace

During the month of May 1982, I went to Moscow to preach the gospel in the churches and to deliver a major address on the subject of peace to an international conference of religious leaders. These were leaders of all religions of the world, not just Jews and Christians. The possibility of a nuclear holocaust had been weighing heavily upon my heart. I felt it was time for me to speak out and bring this issue into a biblical perspective. I began to realize that war has always been primarily a moral and spiritual issue that must concern us all. Many of my Christian brothers and sisters were disappointed that I would speak about peace, especially in Moscow. The world's press was divided. Some scolded me or called me naive, and I was terribly misquoted on occasion. Others, especially the press who traveled with me or carefully covered the events in Moscow, were sympathetic. I want to share with you excerpts from the speech I delivered in Moscow. It states the issue as I see it. For the stakes at hand are the future of our children and their children and all children yet unborn across the earth—if there is such a future. I based my speech entirely on the Bible. I spoke of the cause of war and the three kinds of peace the Bible teaches that we can have. I spoke about human rights and other kindred matters. Read it for yourself as follows:

I speak to you today as a follower of Jesus Christ. . . . declaring that everything I have ever been, or am, or ever hope to be in this life or the future life, I owe to Jesus Christ. In these few minutes, therefore, I would like to present what I believe to be the Christian's responsibility for peace in a nuclear age as it is found in the Bible.

There is a farm in the central part of the United States. On that farm is a monument marking the exact point of the geographical center of the nation. It is a fixed reference point from which, I understand, all other geographical points in the nation can be measured. Each of us has his reference point and, for me as a Christian, the reference point by which I measure my life and thought is the Bible, the Holy Scriptures of the Old and New Testaments.

The whole human race sits under a nuclear sword of Damocles, not knowing when someone will push the button or give the order that will destroy much of the planet.

The possibility of nuclear war, therefore, is not merely a political issue. We must understand, of course, that there are underlying causes and problems that must be removed before the nuclear arms issue will be completely solved, and these issues must be addressed also. These underlying causes have brought about serious political conflicts between nations, and this is not God's intention.

The nuclear arms race is primarily a moral and spiritual issue that must concern us all. I am convinced that political answers alone will not suffice, but that it is now time for us to urge the world to turn to spiritual solutions as well. We need a new breakthrough in how the problem of the nuclear arms race is approached. The vicious cycle of propaganda and counterpropaganda, charge and countercharge, mistrust and more mistrust among nations must somehow be broken. The unending and escalating cycle of relying on deterrents, greater deterrents, and supposedly ultimate deterrents should also be defused. Policies which constantly take nations to the brink of nuclear war must be rejected. We need to turn from our political and ideological conflicts on all sides and moderate them for the sake of the sanctity of human life.

I agree with Albert Einstein, who said, "The unleashed power of the atom has changed everything except our way of thinking.

We shall require a substantially new manner of thinking if mankind is to survive." Perhaps a conference like this, stressing the spiritual nature of man and the need for spiritual answers to the problems we face, can help bring about that new way of thinking.

Pope John Paul II has stated, "Our future on this planet, exposed as it is to nuclear annihilation, depends on one single factor: humanity must make a moral about-face." But the question that confronts us is, How can this happen? Technologically, man has far exceeded his moral ability to control the results of his technology. Man himself must be changed. The Bible teaches that this is possible through spiritual renewal. Jesus Christ taught that man can and must have a spiritual rebirth.

This leads me to some specific comments about a Christian understanding of peace in a nuclear age.

First, the Christian begins with the Bible's affirmation that life is sacred. "In the beginning God created the heavens and the earth," the Bible declares (Genesis 1:1). The world is not here by chance, nor is human life a biological accident. God brought it all into existence. Furthermore, man occupied a very special place in God's creation—man alone was created in the image of God. He had within him the character of God Himself, and one reason for this was so man and God could have fellowship with each other. Human life is sacred not only because God created it, but because He loves us and desires to have a personal relationship with us. Life is a sacred gift of God, and the taking of human life is an offense to God's original design of His creation. The individual person has dignity before God, and this is a fundamental fact that stresses his uniqueness and underlines his value within society.

Second, the Bible also teaches, however, that man, the creature, has turned his back on God, the Creator. Our first parents deliberately chose to rebel against God, and this has caused chaos in God's world ever since. This rebellion against God is what the Bible calls sin. It cuts man off from God, but it also cuts man off from other men and even brings disorder into his own individual life. Hate takes the place of love; greed takes the place of sharing; the lust for power and domination over others takes the place of service and humility. Instead of peace there is war. The first son of Adam and Eve committed the first act of violence by killing his brother.

We live in a world, therefore, that is distorted and warped by sin. We may not fully understand why God—who is all-powerful and loving—permits evil in this world. But whatever else we might say, it must be stressed that man, not God, is guilty of the evil in the world. It is man who bears the responsibility, because man was given the ability to make free moral choices and he chose deliberately to disobey God. The world as it now exists is not the way God intended it to be.

From a biblical perspective, therefore, I am convinced that the basic issue facing us today is not merely political, social, economic, or even moral or humanitarian in nature. The deepest problems of the human race are spiritual in nature. They are rooted in man's refusal to seek God's way for his life. The problem is the human heart, which God alone can change.

During World War II, Albert Einstein helped bring a German photographer to the United States. They became friends, and the photographer took a number of pictures of Einstein. Einstein had never liked photographers, and he had never liked any picture of himself. But one day he looked into the camera and started talking. He spoke about his despair that his formula, $E=mC^2$, and his letter to President Roosevelt had made the atomic bomb possible, and his scientific research had resulted in the death of so many human beings. He grew silent. His eyes had a look of immense sadness. There was a question and a reproach in them.

At that very moment the cameraman released the shutter. Einstein looked up and the cameraman asked him, "So you don't believe that there will ever be peace?"

"No," he answered. "As long as there will be man, there will be wars."

The Bible says, "What causes fights and quarrels among you? Don't they come from your desires that battle within you? You want something but don't get it. You kill and covet, but you cannot have what you want. You quarrel and fight" (James 4:1, 2). Jesus declared, "For from within, out of men's hearts, come evil thoughts . . . murder . . . greed, malice, deceit . . . arrogance and folly" (Mark 7:21, 22).

The Red Horse

I am convinced one of the most vivid and tragic signs of man's rebellion against God's order in our present generation is the possibility of a nuclear war. I include here the whole scope of modern weapons capable of destroying life—conventional, biochemical and nuclear weapons. I know that the issue of legitimate national defense is complex. I am not a pacifist, nor am I for unilateral disarmament. Police and military forces are unfortunately necessary as long as man's nature remains the way it is. But the unchecked production of weapons of mass destruction by the nations of the world is a mindless fever which threatens to consume much of our world and destroy the sacred gift of life.

From a Christian perspective, therefore, the possibility of a nuclear war originates in the greed and covetousness of the human heart. The tendency toward sin is passed on from generation to generation. Therefore, Jesus predicted that there would be wars and rumors of wars till the end of the age. The psalmist said, "In sin did my mother conceive me" (Psalm 51:5, KJV). Thus, there is a tragic and terrible flaw in human nature that must be recognized and dealt with. That is why I have come to see that the nuclear arms race is not God's will, and that as a Christian I have a responsibility to do whatever I can to work for peace and against nuclear war.

I have said that life is sacred because God has made it that way, and that man has perverted the gift of life by rebelling against God's will. But does that mean peace is not possible? No! Peace could be possible if we would humble ourselves and learn again God's way of peace.

That brings me to a third point. The word peace *is used in the Bible in three main ways.*

First, there is spiritual peace. This is peace between man and God.

Second, there is psychological peace, or peace within ourselves.

Third, there is relational peace, or peace among men.

Sin, the Bible says, has destroyed or seriously affected all three of these dimensions of peace. When man was created he was at peace with God, with himself and with his fellow humans. But when he rebelled against God, his fellowship with God was broken.

He was no longer at peace with himself. And he was no longer at peace with others.

Can these dimensions of peace ever be restored? The Bible says yes. It tells us man alone cannot do what is necessary to heal the brokenness in his relationships—but God can, and has.

The Bible teaches that Jesus Christ was God's unique Son, sent into the world to take away our sins by His death on the cross, therefore making it possible for us to be at peace—at peace with God, at peace within ourselves and at peace with each other. That is why Jesus Christ is central to the Christian faith. By His resurrection from the dead, Christ showed once and for all that God is for life, not death. The Orthodox tradition and its Divine Liturgy especially make central this jubilant and glorious event. The Bible states, "For the wages of sin is death, but the gift of God is eternal life in Jesus Christ our Lord" (Romans 6:23). The ultimate sign of man's alienation is death; the ultimate sign of God's reconciling love is life.

Throughout all Christendom you will notice there is one symbol common to all believers—the cross. We believe it was on the cross that the possibility of lasting peace in all of its dimensions has been made. The Bible says about Christ that "God was pleased to have all his fullness dwell in him, and through him to reconcile to himself all things . . . by making peace through his blood, shed on the cross" (Colossians 1:19, 20). The Bible again says, "For he himself is our peace, who has made the two one and has destroyed the barrier, the dividing wall of hostility. He came and preached peace to you who were far away and peace to those who were near" (Ephesians 2:14, 17).

The Christian looks forward to the time when peace will reign over all creation. Christians all over the world pray the prayer Jesus taught His disciples: "Thy kingdom come. Thy will be done in earth, as it is in heaven" (Matthew 6:10, kjv). Only then will the spiritual problem of the human race be fully solved.

Both the Bible and the Christian creeds teach that there will be a universal judgment. Christ will come again, in the words of the ancient Apostles' Creed, "to judge the quick and the dead." But then the kingdom of God will be established, and God will

*intervene to make all things new. That is our great hope for the
future.*

*But in the meantime God is already at work. The kingdom of
God is not only a future hope but a present reality. Wherever men
and women turn to God in repentance and faith and then seek to
do His will on earth as it is done in heaven, there the kingdom of
God is seen. And it is in obedience to Jesus Christ, who is called
in the Bible the Prince of Peace, that Christians are to cooperate
with all who honestly work for peace in our world.*

[If I were preparing this address over again I would probably
expand this point to say: Those who are members of God's kingdom
live in an alien world as pilgrims and strangers. The kingdom is
"already" present in the lives of the believers who glorify Him
by word and deed in the church and in society. But the world is
"not yet" the kingdom for, as we have already seen, the world is
under the rule and reign of the prince of this world—Satan. Nevertheless, King Jesus has conquered Satan and all those who have
received the King and who have been reconciled to God are possessed by the King. He dwells within them by His Spirit. The
crucified King has received all authority and His indwelling Spirit
is greater than Satan and his demon powers: "The one who is in
you is greater than the one who is in the world" (1 John 4:4).
Believers alone have been "rescued . . . from the dominion of
darkness and brought . . . into the kingdom of the Son he loves"
(Colossians 1:13). It is then true that believers bear fruit in every
good work upon the earth but believers cannot change the world
into the kingdom. Only the return of the King to rule upon the
earth can result in His will upon earth as it is in heaven. With
this inward hope and this indwelling power of the kingdom to
come, is it any wonder that the kingdom of the King, the Prince
of Peace, strives to extend the kingdom in the hearts of men and
work to maintain that peace that enables the spread of the gospel
(1 Timothy 2:1–4)? God reigns supreme over the world leading
it providentially toward the day of the kingdom to come (Acts
1:6, 7). This is the day of grace for the world. When Jesus returns
He will establish His kingdom of glory. Mankind now lives between

the times of Christ's ascension to the Father and His return "on the clouds of the sky, with power and great glory" (Matthew 24:30).

Then why should Christians serve the cause of peace? First, because they love the lost of this world. Second, because they love that creation of God which has been cursed and corrupted by sin. Third, because they love those created in the image of God, Who wills that all should come to repentance (2 Peter 3:9).

The signs of the kingdom are not always political, although they always have political implications. Jesus' signs were given to lead people to faith and not only political reform (John 20:30, 31). Jesus' life by the Spirit within believers draws sinners to the Cross and reconciliation. The fruits of righteousness and peace then permeate society.]

When Christ was born, the Bible tells us, the angels said, "Glory to God in the highest, and on earth peace to men" (Luke 2:14). Jesus declared, "Blessed are the peacemakers, for they will be called the sons of God" (Matthew 5:9). The New Testament urges Christians, "Live in harmony with one another. . . . If it is possible, as far as it depends on you, live at peace with everyone. Do not take revenge" (Romans 12:16, 18, 19). We are to pray for peace, and we—both individually and collectively—are to work for peace in whatever ways God would open up for each of us. Christ came to bring peace, and we are to proclaim the possibility of peace, which the Christian believes is found in Christ.

But some people ask pessimistically, "Can anything really be done for international peace? Is it not already too late?" I would suggest that our responsibility in the world is clear no matter what the conditions might be or how late the hour might seem. We must not join with those who stand by and wring their hands, saying all is hopeless. I believe that in spite of the chaos threatening our world there can be hope for our generation and for generations to come. We must be realists, but we must also be optimists. Ancient Nineveh was once on the verge of destruction, but it was saved when the people repented and turned to God.

As a Christian, I have hope—for several reasons. For one thing, as a Christian I believe that God is the Lord of all history. He is sovereign and He is able to intervene in human affairs to accomplish His saving and reconciling purposes, no matter how difficult things may seem. We do not live in a world of blind chance. My confidence is in the living God who remains faithful to His purposes and will ultimately accomplish His will for this world which He has created.

I also have hope, however, because I believe it is still possible for us to turn to God, and to grapple with many of our problems and begin to solve them. We need responsible leaders from every area of life in the international arena—who have the dedication and the vision to provide moral and spiritual leadership for our generation. Yes, human beings often fail, and agreements that are solemnly made in one generation are often broken in the next. But that must not lead us to despair.

One of the horrors of World War I was the development and use of deadly poisonous gases that killed and maimed vast numbers of people. Afterward, the nations of the world agreed to ban such weapons. During World War II the warring nations refrained from using those weapons of mass destruction on the battlefield. Thus it is possible to reach international understandings. And I believe it is the special responsibility of religious leaders who see life as sacred to work toward an international, negotiated treaty to vastly reduce or ban today's weapons of mass destruction.

But what specifically can we do? What are the steps people who consider life as sacred can take to be peacemakers in our world?

It is not my intention to present a comprehensive plan or procedure for disarmament, for I do not consider myself competent to deal with such a highly technical matter. I also know that any specific remarks on this which I or anyone else here might make could easily be misinterpreted as being biased or political in nature. Our purpose is to rise above narrow national interests and to give all of humanity a spiritual vision of the way to peace. All too often religious leaders have accepted war without question as a fact of life by which international disputes are too often settled. In the present nuclear age, however, we must not fall into this psychological trap.

With this in mind, let me suggest five steps that I believe we can and must take if we are to do our part in saving the sacred gift of life from nuclear catastrophe.

1. *Let us call the nations and leaders of our world to repentance.* In addition to personal repentance, which we all need if we are to be accepted by God, we as nations and as individuals need to repent over our past failures—the failure to accept each other, the failure to be concerned about the needs of the poor and starving of the world, the failure to place top priority on peace instead of war, the failure to restrain the international arms race. No nation, large or small, is exempt from blame for the present state of international affairs.

2. *Let us call the nations and leaders of our world to a new and determined commitment to peace and justice.* For the last several decades the world has witnessed an unprecedented arms race. Would it not be wonderful to have a new race among the nations of the world—a disarmament race, one which is equal on both sides, verifiable and leads to at least a few generations of peace?

As a Christian, I believe that lasting peace will only come when the kingdom of God prevails. However, let the leaders of our world face the fact that the overwhelming desire of the peoples of the earth is for peace, not war. Let us urge the leaders of the world to act in accordance with the wishes of the world's people and to set nuclear disarmament as the top priority for the rest of this century.

3. *Let us call the nations and the leaders of the nations to take specific steps that will lead toward peace.* Talk about peace must never become a substitute for actions that will lead to peace.

In connection with this, we should urge all governments to respect the rights of religious believers as outlined in the United Nations Universal Declaration of Human Rights. We must hope that some day all nations (as all those who signed the Final Act of Helsinki declared) "will recognize and respect the freedom of the individual to profess and practice, alone or in community with others, religion or belief acting in accordance with the dictates of his own conscience" (*Final Act of Helsinki*, section VII).

I also feel it is important for the leaders of the world to get to know one another personally.

I would urge the leaders of the world to take specific steps for meaningful negotiations leading to major arms reductions. We should pray for the success of every effort that is made in this direction. We should encourage every initiative that honestly seeks mutual, balanced, verifiable arms reduction among nations. But more than that, we should set before the world the ultimate goal of eliminating all nuclear and biochemical weapons of mass destruction.

Several years ago, when I saw the apparent futility of so many negotiations and conferences about disarmament, I came out for what I have called SALT X—the complete destruction by all nations of the world of all atomic bombs, hydrogen bombs, biochemical weapons, laser weapons and all other weapons of mass destruction. I know this may be impossible to achieve, but it can be our ultimate goal.

4. Let us call the peoples of the world to prayer. If the peoples of the world would turn to God and seek His will in prayer, that prayer would have a tremendous impact on the issues that face us. As God promised through the prophet Jeremiah, "Call unto me, and I will answer thee, and shew thee great and mighty things, which thou knowest not" (Jeremiah 33:3, KJV).

5. Finally, let us who are assembled here today rededicate ourselves personally to the task of being peacemakers in God's world.

I would like to close with this observation. Last Sunday morning His Holiness Patriarch Pimen graciously invited me to attend the Divine Liturgy in the Orthodox Cathedral and to say words of fraternal greeting to the congregation and proclaim the gospel. I could not help but recall in my remarks that the date was May 9, the thirty-seventh anniversary of the unconditional surrender in Berlin of the forces of Nazism to the Soviet Union and its allies—the event which brought World War II to an end. I recalled that the Soviet Union, more than any other nation in that terrible conflict, had experienced death and incredible devastation as a result of that horrible war. I also noted that during the war the great people of the Soviet Union and the United States of America had been allies, fighting side by side against the common enemy of Nazism. We did not agree at that time in our basic ideology, but we united as allies because we faced a common enemy—an enemy so great that our differences faded.

Today I would suggest that we—not only the two great superpowers, the United States and the Soviet Union, but every nation on earth—again face a common enemy. Of course I believe the Bible teaches that sin in the heart is the common enemy faced by all mankind. This is why Christ died on the cross. Our common natural enemy today is the threat of impending destruction. Is it too much to hope and pray that we can unite in a dedicated alliance against this enemy which threatens to destroy us? May all of us, whether we are from large nations or small nations, do all we can to remove this deadly blight from our midst and to save the sacred gift of life from nuclear catastrophe.

What You and I Must Do for Peace

As I made clear in the speech you have just read from my Moscow visit, evangelicals cannot afford to stay isolated in a world where nuclear holocaust threatens to destroy us. We must leave our safe enclaves and journey into the world, standing for what we believe—in love, in strength, in openness and in trust. We don't have to compromise, or give up what we are, to do important business with people who are different or who hold differing views. But we will be criticized. We will be caricatured. We will make enemies. Just remember, the religious leaders of Jesus' day chided Him for His association with publicans and sinners. We must be prepared to be chided as well.

I have spent almost a lifetime proclaiming the gospel of Christ. I do not plan to be a leader in a peace movement or organization. I am an evangelist. But I am a man who is still in process. I would like to say some things informally about this process of my own pilgrimage and my own witness in one or two areas.

My basic commitment as a Christian has not changed, nor has my view of the gospel. But I've come to see in deeper ways some of the implications of my faith and of the message I've been proclaiming.

I was born and reared on a small farm in the southern United States. In my childhood it rarely occurred to me to think about the difficulties, problems and oppressions of black people. In high school I began to question some of the prevalent practices of the society in which I was brought up, but it was not until I had actually committed my life to Christ that I began to realize, that as a Christian, I had to take a stand on the race question. When I attended Wheaton College just west of Chicago it was the first time I had been in school with black people. The school had been founded just before the Civil War as an antislavery school and had a long tradition in working for racial understanding, tolerance and improvement of relations. However, I did not know how to go about it except to love and treat as equals all of those whom I met of the other race. But in 1952 we were holding a series of meetings in a southern city. Ropes had been strung up and black people were to sit behind those ropes. I walked into the auditorium and asked that those ropes be pulled down. Some people, black as well as white, were upset with me at first. But I refused to allow those ropes to go up again. And to this day I have never permitted myself to preach in a segregated crusade any place in the world. That was one of my first public acts of conscience. A short time later I became involved in the Clinton, Tennessee, problem; the Little Rock, Arkansas, problem and the Alabama problems.

I tell that story because it applies now to the issue of peace, the nuclear holocaust and the rider who brings war. I have often spoken on the wonderful story in the tenth chapter of Luke where Jesus tells of the Good Samaritan, teaching us our social responsibilities. From the very beginning, I felt that if I came upon a person who had been beaten and robbed and left for dead, I would do my best to help him. I also felt that this applied to my relatives and friends and immediate neighbors. But I rarely thought of it in terms of corporate responsibility.

It isn't my purpose to suggest ways to influence public policy. But in my own personal spiritual pilgrimage I think I have grown. The Holy Spirit is still changing me, shaping me, teaching me. Thank God, He isn't through with me yet. God's Word still speaks to current situations. In His day Christ Himself stood against injustice—for the widow, the orphan, the powerless and the weak.

In the last years I have read and reread the Bible from Genesis to Revelation. Ruth and I have read volumes together about the current state of the earth. I have had private briefings by top officials in a number of governments. I have frequent meetings with both former and present political leaders. I have learned a great deal. The more I study global issues, particularly the threat of nuclear war, the more I am convinced that Christians have a responsibility to present the biblical view of war and peace, emphasizing that ultimate peace will come to the world only when the Prince of Peace reigns.

As I have said before, for the past number of years I have advocated a plan that I alluded to in my Moscow talk as SALT X, the bilateral, verifiable eradication of all nuclear, biochemical and laser weapons used for mass destruction. Do I honestly think this will happen? Not likely. But does that mean I should cease praying, speaking and working for that day when the people of the earth will unite to remove the ever-present threat of nuclear holocaust? Again, no!

Out of guilt for the part he played in the development of the atomic bomb (a guilt from which he seemed never to be free), Albert Einstein once wrote, "To the village square we must carry the facts [of nuclear war]. From these must come America's voice." Dwight Eisenhower said, "I like to believe that people in the long run are going to do more to promote peace than are governments. Indeed, I think that people want peace so much that one of these days governments had better get out of their way and let them have it."

Every Christian should be praying for peace. I am not saying this merely because it is expected of me but because it is the unmistakable instruction of the Word of God. I am not saying this for last because it is least important, but because as the last point it is the most likely to be remembered. "If my people, who are called by my name, will humble themselves and *pray . . .* then . . ." (2 Chronicles 7:14). How easily we say it. Yet on our knees we are the most powerful force on earth. Only God can bring the world, and in particular this nation, to repentance. Only God's Spirit can lead the world's people and their leaders to their knees.

146

The nuclear problem, like all other major world problems, is ultimately a result of sin. We trust weapons to preserve the peace—but weapons cannot do it alone. The bomb did not make itself, and it will not explode itself. If it ever explodes, and I pray God it will not, then it will be the men and women who built it and use it who will be responsible.

It is time we called the world to pray. The hoofbeats of the red horse are thundering in our direction. The horseman sits high in the saddle, swinging the sword of war in ever-widening arcs of death and destruction. He can bound across the nuclear defenses we have created in an instant, blowing away the walls we have built to hide behind. Only God can intervene. Pray for peace. Prayer is the most powerful weapon we have to end the nuclear threat and bring about God's dream for His creation.

I believe that the Prince of Peace would have us all face the issue of the nuclear threat. Realistically, the issue is not likely to go away, any more than simmering Mt. Saint Helens was likely to subside. This sounds terribly pessimistic, but I base this conclusion on human nature as described in the Bible and as witnessed every day through the news media. We are told in Scripture to await with great anticipation the coming of the Messiah, whom we Christians believe to be the Lord Jesus Christ. He alone will bring peace. But in the meantime, we are to work for peace.

Just as God spared Nineveh for 150 years after its people repented under the preaching of Jonah, so God may give us a generation or several generations of peace if we turn to Him in true repentance! The message is still the same, "Turn away." "Flee the wrath to come." After the people had heard Peter's great sermon at Pentecost, "they were cut to the heart and said to Peter and the other apostles, 'Brothers, what shall we do?' " (Acts 2:37). Then "Peter replied, 'Repent and be baptized, every one of you, in the name of Jesus Christ so that your sins may be forgiven. And you will receive the gift of the Holy Spirit.' " We cannot escape that word *repent.*

9

The Black
Horse
and Its
Rider

The Rider Who Brings Hunger

The Lamb carefully pries open the third seal. The leather scroll gently unrolls. At the same moment, the third of God's servant creatures steps to the center stage of John's vision and gives out God's command, "Come!" (Revelation 6:5). Again into the presence of the Lamb of God, the twenty-four elders and the host of angelic witnesses emerge a horse and rider. This black horse and rider bear yet a third warning to the peoples of our planet—a warning of massive hunger and starvation. "Its rider was holding a pair of scales in his hand. Then I heard what sounded like a voice among the four living creatures, saying, 'A quart of wheat for a day's wages, and three quarts of barley for a day's wages, and do not damage the oil and the wine!'" (Revelation 6:5, 6).

In New York City's Museum of Modern Art, Umberto Boccioni's "The City Rises" depicts the four horsemen of the Apocalypse in a contemporary, urban setting. This huge six-by-nine-foot oil on canvas captures the horror of the third horse and its rider. Boccioni's black horse rises like a tornado, whirling above the other horsemen.

A recent news report showed the incredible havoc of a tornado that devastated several small towns in Texas and the Midwest. Every place it touched to earth, buildings were sucked up into its vortex, pulverized and scattered in ruin across a wide expanse of countryside. Then came the devastating hurricane, Alicia, that hit southern Texas in the summer of 1983. The black horse and rider announce just such a devastation destined for the family of man if we don't repent and turn to God in time.

We read in Lamentations 4:8 and 9 where the blackness of famine haunts the land and kills its victims.

For an instant the black horse and rider stand on parade before John and, through John, before all of us. Just before the rider whirls away on his destructive journey to the earth, we see him in all his prophetic terror. It is easy to picture the horse—black as tar, hooves pounding, flanks heaving, eyes flashing. The rider holds up a balance scale in his hand. Then, John reports, a voice comes from amidst the four apocalyptical beings, announcing: "A quart of wheat for a day's wages" (Revelation 6:6).

John knew well that the denarius was a typical worker's daily pay. It amounted to perhaps twenty cents in our modern currency. In normal times it could buy sixteen quarts of wheat or corn, from which a worker and his family would make bread to nourish and sustain them. In terms of the recent recession that voice was announcing the loss of income in terms of purchasing power to a middle class American worker—for example, a drop from $16,000 to $1,000 a year. Worse yet, for workers in the "less developed" countries of the world who get approximately $560 income per year to feed their families, the rider on the black horse was galloping across the earth to announce, in effect, that their small income would suddenly be reduced in actual value to less than $35 per year. When the voice continued, it said, "three quarts of barley for a day's wages" (Revelation 6:6). In Roman times, barley was the cheaper, less nourishing grain. Even that substituted for wheat or corn would make only a scant three individual meals a day. That might supply the worker a survival diet—probably far less than the 2,600 calories a day he needed—but it would also eliminate food for his wife or family entirely.

Holding up his scale to weigh the tiny amount of grain that will be available to the average working man, the rider on the black horse is a symbol of the desperate plight of the world after the first two horsemen have ridden.

With the advent of this third rider, Jesus is indicating that deception and false religion lead to war, and that war in turn leads to famine and pestilence. Following the white and red horses, famine will prevail upon the earth. Millions will die of hunger. Millions more will suffer malnutrition, and with inadequate diet comes disease, mental and emotional illness, despair and death. The black horse and rider are God's warning of the human suffering that lies ahead if man refuses to obey His commands.

The voice calls out one more instruction to the third horseman, who rides the black horse and carries the scale of judgment. "Do not damage the oil and the wine!" he says (Revelation 6:6). This is a picture of famine coexisting with luxury. Jesus told Peter, Andrew, James and John that, prior to His return, famine would stalk the earth and starve whole peoples in various parts of the world (Matthew 24:7; Mark 13:8; Luke 21:11). But He characterized those in other parts of the world as eating and drinking, apparently to gross excess, implying they could coexist in the same country. He said, "As it was in the days of Noah, so it will be at the coming of the Son of Man. For in the days before the flood, people were eating and drinking, marrying and giving in marriage, up to the day Noah entered the ark" (Matthew 24:37, 38). These two disparate conditions would be parallel and simultaneous. John the apostle later prophesied that there would be societies leading a Babylonian existence—living in the lap of luxury. These are pictures of people surfeiting themselves to the hilt.

Sixty percent of us in Europe and America are overweight. We Americans weigh a billion pounds too much. We spend an annual $15 billion on diet formulas and $22 billion on cosmetics. Those expenditures alone would be the difference between life and death to those who will starve to death worldwide next year.

There is always something radically wrong with a situation in which those who have too much are indifferent to others who have too little. This is often a sign that the society in which it occurs is hastening to its ruin. This is the message of the rider on the black horse—the most exaggerated inequities in the long history of man on the earth.

The rider of the black horse carries a pair of scales that say a worker will work an entire day just to keep himself alive. He will have nothing left to divide with his family. He will watch his children die. (The average parent passing through such an experience would rather be dead himself.)

Then the writer in Revelation adds, don't hurt the oil and the wine. He is stating that alongside the famine-stricken poor there would be the rich who do not suffer famine and pestilence. One of the great problems in our world today is that too often the poor become poorer and the rich become richer. This is one of the basic causes of social unrest in Central America and other parts of the world. And in the future the rich will become fewer in number and the numbers of the poor will increase. The disparity between starvation and riches side by side in the world today will be dwarfed in comparison to that which has been predicted for the future. There is an incomparably blacker day coming.

One of the great problems of the present time is that there is scarcity in the midst of the plenty throughout the world. This situation which will be increased drastically as we approach the end of the age. It is a social maladjustment, a monstrous injustice on a worldwide scale. If the nations do not turn to God but go their own way without Him, that rider on the black horse will swoop closer. The whole surviving human race will suffer the consequences.

A major problem the world community is wrestling with at this moment is food shortage. It is not so much a matter of the total quantity of food, but the problem of *distribution*. Dishonesty among some international relief organizations, indifference of certain governments to the plight of their own people, cheapness with which life is regarded in parts of the world and the terrible fraud in many nations—all complicate the problem. When the anti-Christ system, or its dictator, as the Scriptures predict, takes over for a relatively short time it will, with ruthless regimen, undertake to distribute food to the world from areas that reaped large harvest.

Only three countries in the world annually produce more wheat than they consume: the United States, Australia and Canada. The Soviets have the potential to produce more than any other nation, but because of adverse weather, acknowledged inefficiency, and other reasons they often get only one good crop every four or five years. It was only a few years ago that a newspaper editorial in Chicago said, "By modern methods of agriculture we have solved the question of famine. We can produce any amount of grain we decide to produce. Science has triumphed over the constant dread of less enlightened communities." Not only was this contrary to the predictions of the Bible, but it was premature and at variance with the facts. The Scriptures teach that famine and pestilence will continue and intensify until Christ comes back as Prince of Peace and world Ruler.

As bad as things are now, the most fearful days of famine this world has ever seen lie ahead, according to the Scriptures. Lester Brown, described by the *Washington Post* as one of the world's most influential thinkers, is president of Worldwatch Institute, one of "the most respected and independent think tanks in the world." Ross Howard's critique of Brown's newest study suggests that we'd better "forget about using the word *crisis* when talking about world production of food. Crisis suggests a severe and temporary shortage. The correct word now is *climax*, meaning a final and irreversible shortage. The earth is no longer a sustainable society." And that strong language is nothing compared to what is up ahead!

At the 1981 Rome conference of the United Nations Food and Agriculture Organization recently the Pope addressed the peril of mass death and famines. The Pope, expressing concern, spoke of "the persistence of . . . degrading poverty, and especially a lack of the absolutely basic minimum of food, as the scandal of the modern world."

The black horse and his rider thunder in our direction. The hoofbeats of warning are the cries of children dying of starvation and disease. The flashing scales that have been weighing out bread in crumbs to the people of less developed nations of the world are now hanging above our heads like a vastly oversized sword of Damocles. We have grown immune to the warnings, having seen too many television specials on world hunger. We have found too many third-class letters in our mailboxes requesting funds for the starving children with their bloated bellies. The graphic photos enclosed in such appeals no longer shock us. There are so many hungry. There are so many dying.

To protect our sanity we often stop our ears and close our eyes— our senses have become satiated. We give our contributions but the problem escalates. We write checks, put money in offerings, pledge extra gifts and work at a host of money-raising projects. In spite of all the criticism to the contrary Americans are probably the most generous people in the world. But we have also become a bit cynical because of fraud and corruption in administration of aid. And no matter what we do, there seems to be no diminishing of the suffering. So, to protect ourselves, we try not to think about it. But we must not grow weary of the warning of the rider on the black horse, for the warning is addressed to us—and to the whole world.

The Problem of Famine

Biblical writers have promised us that the four horsemen ride to awaken us before the final judgment of God arrives and we find it forever too late to repent or to heed their warnings. Since the beginning of time there has been famine on the face of the earth. But with the population explosion and the complexity of modern society, the problem of the hungry has greatly increased.

No one knows how many die of starvation each year. Many underdeveloped countries keep few—if any—statistics, particularly concerning the deaths of infants and children. In addition, countless people die not from starvation directly but from indirect causes, such as illnesses which ravage people because their resistance to disease has been lowered by malnutrition.

The Mennonite Central Committee reports that an estimated twelve million newborn infants die of the effects of malnutrition every year in the developing countries. The World Bank reports that "half of the people in absolute poverty live in South Asia, mainly in India and Bangladesh. A sixth live in East and Southeast Asia. Another sixth are in sub-Saharan Africa. The rest are divided among Latin America, North Africa and the Middle East." The United Nations estimates that at least 100 million children go to bed each night hungry.

But the problem of hunger and malnutrition is not limited to developing countries. Recently the Congressional Office of the Budget announced that many of America's children, too, suffer greatly from malnutrition. Millions in North America live below the poverty line. (Of course the poverty line is set very high compared to developing nations, and what would be considered poor in America could be considered middle class or even wealthy in many countries of the world. If you have even a pair of shoes, or water to drink, or a few morsels of food to eat, you are considered rich in some areas of the world today.)

"Bread for the World" researchers recently set out to discover "who are the hungry in the USA." These are their findings: the hungry are "the young mothers rearing children alone; families of workers who have lost jobs as a result of the recession or plant closings; young people who lack training required by today's industry; jobless minorities crowded into city and rural slums; elderly poor people struggling to survive on small Social Security or assistance checks; native Americans and low-paid migrant farm workers." They say that five million children are among the nearly thirty million people living below the official poverty line. (Again, of course, by world standards this poverty line is relatively high. It should also be noted that many of these people are illegal immigrants. However, they too are people God loves and for whom we have a responsibility.)

As bad as poverty is, however, there is another important truth about the human spirit that needs to be emphasized. Out of poverty have come some of the greatest men of history. John Wanamaker, the great merchant of Philadelphia, started business on a salary of $1.25 a week. Andrew Carnegie began life on a weekly salary of $3.00. Abraham Lincoln was a miserably poor farmer's son. Andrew Johnson was a tailor's apprentice boy and learned to read after he was married. Columbus used to beg bread for his hungry child and died in utter poverty, but he gave the world that which was better than gold—a new continent. Our Lord Himself had neither gold nor silver. He supported Himself as a carpenter and often ate the bread of a beggar, but He changed the world.

This indicates to me that there is a spiritual possibility very deep in the heart of people—that in the midst of poverty they can rise above their circumstances and do great things for God and the world in which they live. At the same time, this is no excuse for our complacency about poverty and its effects on its victims. Yes, some have risen above the disadvantages of their poverty—but how many more would have made a wide impact on society if they had not been held back by their circumstances?

The Rider Who Brings Disease

Famine and disease ride as one on the back of the black horse. Jesus put them together in Matthew 24. With malnutrition comes mental, emotional and physical illness. With hunger comes weakness. Immunological systems break down. People, especially children, can no longer fight off the germs, viruses and bacteria that infect them. We cannot understand the problem of famine without understanding the problem of disease as well.

In 1981 it was estimated that, out of 125 million children born that year, twelve million would die before their first birthday. The weapons of the rider astride the black horse who brings famine and disease include these six child-killers—measles, whooping cough, tetanus, polio, tuberculosis and diptheria—and many more.

Only a small percentage of the world's children receive protection from these crippling diseases through immunization shots or vaccination. Five million children a year will die from them. Five million more will be permanently disabled. As Christians we need to look upon these killers as harbingers of judgment. We need to try to understand that the spread of these diseases, easily prevented with modest, inexpensive doses of preventive and curative vaccine, should be adequate warning of our insensitivity to God's laws. As Christians we should not sleep easily in our beds until we have endeavored to reduce or even eliminate these diseases in the name of the innocent children of the world.

I would also have to add to this list the killing of unborn fetuses by the millions. The Bible does not support the indiscriminate practice of abortion. Many of the great characters of the Bible, such as Jeremiah or John the Baptist, were chosen by God before they were born. Many people feel that an exception might be made in the case of incest, rape or when the mother's life is in danger. I think in these instances the decisions must be based on individual cases and the serious moral and spiritual implications must be carefully considered. For example, some of the greatest people whom I have ever met were born as a result of rape. I am thinking, for example, of Ethel Waters, who did more than almost any other person to pave the way in Hollywood and New York for black people to be in show business. She was the queen of black stars. Later, when she gave her life wholly to Christ, she joined our Team. Ethel stayed with us for many years and was loved by people all over the world. Suppose her thirteen-year-old mother, who had been raped, had chosen abortion? The world would never have known Ethel Waters. And I could name many like her.

It is also a horrifying fact that in so-called civilized America thousands of children are abused each year by their parents, many even to the point of death.

Remember that moment two thousand years ago when Jesus interrupted an important teaching seminar with His disciples? Perhaps the neighborhood children of Capernaum had interrupted Jesus' session with a loud game of tag. Perhaps they were playing nearby when a tossed toy landed at Jesus' feet, and the children burst in to retrieve it. Whatever happened, Jesus stopped His teachings, took the children in His arms, and said to the assembled throng, "But if anyone causes one of these little ones who believe in me to sin, it would be better for him to have a large millstone hung around his neck and to be drowned in the depths of the sea" (Matthew 18:6).

Just preceding that ancient biblical account is another deeply moving story which illustrates Jesus' compassion for the children. A distressed father rushed into Jesus' presence begging Him to heal his lunatic son. "I brought him to your disciples," he cried, "but they could not heal him" (Matthew 17:16). I imagine Jesus' eyes flashed as He turned to His disciples and said: "O unbelieving and perverse generation, . . . how long shall I stay with you? How long shall I put up with you? Bring the boy here to me" (Matthew 17:17). Jesus cast out the child's demon and the child was cured from that hour.

The distressed parents of millions of children hold up the bodies of their dying infants to us who are Christians. We have the wherewithal to at least make a big dent in this problem, but we are not doing nearly enough. Jesus turns to us and says, "O unbelieving and perverse generation, how long shall I put up with you?" That is the message of the rider on the black horse who brings famine and pestilence. That is the warning we must hear before we are judged and found guilty of neglecting the world's children.

We should repent of our neglect, ask God's forgiveness and do what we can. We can't do it all—but we can do something! And both by His actions and by His command, Christ calls us to do all we can to heal the sick, feed the hungry, and help those who are suffering. Christ's great mission was to bring redemption to humanity through His death on the cross, and when He faced the cross He could say that He had finished the work His Father had given Him to do (John 17:4). But that did not mean He neglected the suffering and hunger of those around Him—quite the opposite. So you and I are called not only to proclaim the Good News of Christ's salvation but to demonstrate His love for those who are in need.

It is difficult to picture the vast chasm of difference between health care in our Western nations and health care in the developing nations of the world. For example, in Europe and North America there is one doctor for every 572 people. In East Asia there is one doctor for every 2,106 people. In Southeast Asia there is one doctor for every 14,956 people. In East Africa there is one doctor for every 17,480 people! The shortage of nurses and midwives is similarly grim. In Europe and North America there is a nurse for every 194 people. In Central America there are 1,245 people for every nurse. And in South Central Asia there is just one nurse for every 4,031 people!

158

Preventing the Problem

Incomparably more crucial than curing the ill, is the prevention of illness.

There's the matter of *nutrition.* One child in three of those who survive birth in the poor countries is unhealthy because of inadequate nutrition. We looked at the problem of hunger as we began this chapter, but here, again, we need to be reminded how hunger and disease ride hand in hand on the black horse. Every time we eat a balanced meal we should pause, not only to thank God for the food before us, but to ask forgiveness for not making a greater effort to help feed the hundreds of millions of the world's children who never once have had a nutritious meal in their entire lifetime. That fact itself should serve as a warning that one day all the thousands of balanced meals we have eaten thoughtlessly will be spread before us in judgment. And it should act as a signpost pointing us in the direction we could best invest our lives, our creative energies and our means.

You who are young and looking for a purpose in life, why not consider the world's children? You who are old and looking for a way to serve out your retirement years, why not dream big dreams? I cannot say precisely how you yourself can best assist in helping to feed the hungry children of the world, but there is someone out there who can direct you. Call your church about the problem of hunger in your town or neighborhood. Call your denomination or a large Christian service organization and volunteer. If no one has a plan, create one. We have an Emergency Relief Fund in our organization. We never take one penny for administration. All of it goes one hundred percent to the place of need. If you are interested in helping in any of these areas of need through us, write to me, Billy Graham, Minneapolis, Minnesota, and we will see that you get some literature.

Recently my son, Franklin, while on a visit to the Central Highlands of Guatemala, saw a family that had walked several days through the jungles to government-controlled territory to escape their area which was overrun by guerrillas. They brought with them their children, who were so malnourished that they could not even sit up by themselves. When Franklin looked at these children, it was almost like looking at skeletons covered with a layer of skin. All the children could do was quietly sob—no expression or joy—just a constant low sob. The doctor who examined them was not even sure whether the children would live. As in the illness known as anorexia nervosa, there is a point in starvation where a person's vital organs begin to break down and the damage that has been done cannot be repaired.

Second, there's the matter of *water and sanitation* in the developing countries. Four children out of every five in the rural areas of the developing world do not have a safe water supply or adequate sanitation. In Africa ninety out of every one hundred people have no piped water and, worse, the great rivers of Africa carry the germs of infection. A. T. B. N'diaye calls African waterways "the waters of misfortune" and points out the desperate need to create water-purifying and delivery systems similar to the water programs we take for granted in towns and cities.

I saw a young girl in India with a five-gallon empty water drum on her head. She was walking from her home village to a dirty water hole several kilometers away. And I have watched older women return bent under the strain of that unbelievably heavy load. The water sources near their homes had dried up from a prolonged drought. As I stood watching, I knew that girl's spiritual thirst was more important than her physical thirst, but I couldn't force myself easily to separate the two. Like the woman at the well at Sychar in Samaria to whom Jesus ministered, there was a person who needed, physically and spiritually, the water of life. Our loving witness for a lost soul must go hand in hand with our loving concern for a dying body. We are called by God to bring the water of life for both soul and body. God created them both, and His purpose is to redeem them both. The death of Jesus Christ on the cross demonstrates God's concern for the eternal salvation of our souls. The resurrection of Jesus Christ from the dead—and the promise we have that our bodies will someday share in His glorious resurrection—demonstrates God's concern for our bodies. Man is not just another animal whose life and death has little meaning. Man is created in the image of God and even though that image is scarred and torn by sin, he still is God's creation. If we are believers we will have not only a new heart as a result of the new birth, but someday we will have a new glorified body made very similar to the risen body of Jesus Christ.

Therefore God is concerned about those who suffer, no matter who they are or where they are found. And those of us who claim to seek God's will for our lives must be concerned also. The rider on the black horse draws closer to us in judgment and in warning when we fail in that task.

Third, there is the crisis need for *health care* in the Third World. Seven children out of every ten born in the less privileged parts of the world are never seen by health workers who can prevent the childhood diseases that cripple and kill. There can be no visits to a dentist when there is no dentist. And if there were dentists within a hundred miles, there would be no way to make the journey or pay the dentists' bills. There are so few doctors, so few nurses, and virtually no public health clinics. There is literally nothing between hundreds of millions of children and their desperate, helpless parents but us Christians and our compassionate concern.

Several years ago Dr. Ernie Steury, the surgeon at Tenwek Hospital in Kenya, East Africa, told of an incident that had happened to him a few months earlier. A woman out in the bush had been in labor for about two days. The family had sent for the witch doctors, but of course the witch doctors were not able to do anything to help her. Finally, in desperation, the family decided to take this woman to the mission hospital in Tenwek. They had to carry her several hours down a narrow jungle trail before they reached the road. Once they got to the road, they had to wait more hours before a bus came. Then there was another delay of several hours before they reached the hospital. It was late evening when she arrived and was brought immediately to the emergency room. The nurse sent for Dr. Steury. He came and examined the woman. She was already dead.

The husband was standing in the corridor waiting anxiously for the doctor's report. Dr. Steury went over to him and told him that it was too late; his wife had already died. The man broke into tears, crying out, "Oh, but please sir, isn't there anything you can do? Isn't there anything at all you can do?" Dr. Steury explained that he could do nothing.

Dr. Steury remembered later, "I turned, and what crushed me more than anything else was not the fact that she had died, but that she died never once having heard the gospel message. Thousands of people die every day, and they die never having heard about Jesus. This is what compels me to stay as a volunteer missionary doctor in Africa. This is what drives me to keep on. Last year we had over 8,000 in-patients. Each one of those patients heard the gospel. Over 5,000 made decisions to accept Jesus Christ as their Lord and Savior. We can't reach them all, but we can reach some. I have been told to go with this gospel message and go into all the world, and I am going to do my part." It wasn't so much the physical death that disturbed Dr. Steury, because we are all going to die. It was the spiritual death that saddened him.

The Red and the Black Horsemen Ride Together

While famine and disease stalk much of the Third World, nearly all countries, even the smallest ones, are arming to the teeth. To me, this is one of the most pathetic developments taking place in our world. The problem illustrates the precise contemporary relevance of ancient biblical truth. The rider on the red horse (who brings war) appropriately precedes and paves the way for this rider on the black horse (who brings famine, disease and starvation). Our world seems obsessed with war. The trillion or more dollars spent annually on armaments would feed, adequately clothe and amply house the world's famishing family of a billion. The annual income of an average family in Bangladesh is $94, which is less than a steel worker or an auto worker makes in *one* day here in America.

Even small developing nations are spending more on armaments than they are on anything else. Many of them do not need these armaments. But people suffer the lack of the necessities of life in order to feed the building military power of the nations of the world. I certainly do not have the answer to this because man is a fighting creature. He has been fighting wars ever since Cain killed Abel. Jealousy, greed and hate still stalk the world. It seems that satanic forces are now on a rampage. While I do not have the answers, I can certainly take the privilege of asking questions based upon the Bible.

Again I would like to emphasize, as I did in my speech in Moscow, that I am not for unilateral disarmament. I do not believe that America should lay down its weapons while other countries continue to arm. The problem is so complex that it staggers the imagination.

The Pope summed up the matter succinctly: "The arms race kills without firing a shot." Willem Boichel wrote some time ago, "The human family must ask itself the profound question: WHY? Why the fatal order of priorities and why is technology not being preponderantly used to improve the welfare of humanity?"

Too often, we in the United States have a feeling of guilt, and we should feel guilty. But there is a tendency in much of the world to blame the United States alone. The acceleration of the arms race is greater proportionately in many other countries than in the United States. There are some countries where people are practically starving and most of the national budget is being spent on armaments. There are two areas of genuine blame. One is the work of Satan, and the second is man's human nature in rebellion against God.

In 1982 former Prime Minister Malcolm Fraser of Australia hosted the world leaders in a North-South dialogue. In a part of the Melbourne Declaration (as it has come to be known), it was stated that "the protracted assault on human dignity and the deprivation from which many millions in developing countries suffer must inevitably lead to political turmoil." "Such turmoil," Fraser added, would be used "to extend the realm of dictatorship in the world." He is right—only a world government can solve it. The Antichrist and his satanic forces will attempt it, but will fail. Only Christ is going to set up His kingdom at some future date that will solve these problems.

The American president was similarly advised in the *Global 2000 Report* that there is simply no arguing that the current shrinking resources and soaring populations will lead to a world in which the widening gap between rich and poor nations will inevitably "lead to economic disasters and open conflict."

Former World Bank president Robert McNamara agrees: "Many of the poorest countries of the world are . . . doomed to economic and political chaos in the decade ahead."

As the world rushes madly toward these climactic events, we cannot but agree with Nikita Khrushchev when he said, "The survivors will envy the dead."

The world's situation has reached a climactic point and it is going to continue to grow worse and reach some sort of a climax which the Bible graphically describes in both the Old and New Testaments. But it is not enough for Christians to stand glibly by and applaud the impending Apocalypse. It is up to us to pray and work. As one individual I can do very little. I only have one bucket of water to throw on the fire, but I am going to throw it with all my might, asking God to use it as He did the five loaves and two fishes.

Our Response to Hunger and Disease

The sound of the hoofbeats of the black horse and its rider thunder ever louder in our ears. Biblical prophecy is being fulfilled before our eyes. All around us we see the human tragedy of destitution and disease. Starving people grub in garbage heaps and ditches for a few paltry crumbs to deaden their chronic hunger pangs. Now, how do we respond? By my reading of Scripture I am convinced that we are called to action, not apathy—to involvement, not detachment.

When Sargent Shriver was head of the poverty program in the United States he asked me to help him, and I did. We made a motion picture together on poverty in Appalachia. I addressed about two hundred members of the United States Congress and gave to each of them scores of Scriptures about our responsibility to the poor. Here are just a few of them:

Do not go over your vineyard a second time or pick up the grapes that have fallen. Leave them for the poor (Leviticus 19:10).

164

There will always be poor people in the land. Therefore I command you to be openhanded toward your brothers and toward the poor and needy in your land (Deuteronomy 15:11). [Jesus emphasized the same point when He said, "The poor you will always have with you" (Mark 14:7)]

Blessed is he who is kind to the needy (Proverbs 14:21).

He who is kind to the poor lends to the Lord, and he will reward him for what he has done (Proverbs 19:17).

The righteous care about justice for the poor, but the wicked have no such concern (Proverbs 29:7).

Learn to do right! Seek justice, encourage the oppressed. Defend the cause of the fatherless, plead the case of the widow (Isaiah 1:17).

One of the great judgments of Scripture was the judgment that God rained upon Sodom, and one of the great sins of Sodom was the neglect of the poor and the needy: "Now this was the sin of your sister Sodom: She and her daughters were arrogant, overfed and unconcerned; they did not help the poor and needy" (Ezekiel 16:49).

Jesus made it very plain in Matthew 25 what our responsibilities are: "For I was hungry and you gave me something to eat, I was thirsty and you gave me something to drink, I was a stranger and you invited me in, I needed clothes and you clothed me, I was sick and you looked after me, I was in prison and you came to visit me." Even though this passage may have a double meaning, its implications to us are very clear concerning our practical responsibility. He also warned of severe judgment if we fail in our duties.

The apostle Paul struck the same theme in Romans 12:20 and 1 Corinthians 13:13: "If your enemy is hungry, feed him; if he is thirsty, give him something to drink. In doing this, you will heap burning coals on his head." "If I give all I possess to the poor and surrender my body to the flames, but have not love, I gain nothing."

James approached it in a slightly different way, yet with the same meaning: "Has not God chosen those who are poor in the eyes of the world to be rich in faith and to inherit the kingdom he promised those who love him?" (James 2:5). "If you really keep the royal law found in Scripture, 'Love your neighbor as yourself,' you are doing right" (v. 8).

As I have already pointed out, however, there are one or two passages that do not have easy explanations, for example where Jesus said, "The poor you will always have with you" (Matthew 26:11). Jesus, however, was only pointing out the fact that poverty will never be eliminated until His kingdom is established; in the meantime, we should do all we can to help those who suffer.

Our modern tendency is to lay the blame on the wrong party or circumstance. The criminal is "the victim of his environment." Yet the earth's first crime was committed in a perfect environment. Today, statistics prove that many of our crimes are committed in upper-middle class or affluent environments. Poverty is no excuse for crime any more than the girl from a socially prominent family could be excused for murder because "she had too much of everything but what was important."

God created man with the power to choose. And each will ultimately be held responsible for how he chose.

"Do not follow the crowd in doing wrong. When you give testimony in a lawsuit, do not pervert justice by siding with the crowd, and do not show favoritism to a poor man in his lawsuit" (Exodus 23:2, 3), or as the RSV version puts it, "Nor shall you be partial to a poor man in his suit." Provision: Yes; Protection: Yes; Partiality: No. Leviticus 19:15 says, "Do not pervert justice; do not show partiality to the poor or favoritism to the great, but judge your neighbor fairly."

I am persuaded that the very threat of the coming horsemen is not just to warn or judge, but to awaken. They come not merely to move the people of that day (or our day) emotionally, but to motivate the people to do something—to point them in the direction that God Himself would have them go. I am convinced that we are to work against hunger and disease with all the power and energy at our command. And I am equally convinced that we can make a big difference. Whether our efforts will feed all the hungry or heal all the diseased is not the issue. It is always better to do something than to do nothing. To paraphrase James Kelley, "It is better to light one little candle than to curse the darkness." God calls us to act. The rest is in His hands.

In 1982 the General Convention of the Episcopal Church adopted a resolution on the church's response to the problem of hunger. It urged "all individuals and congregations . . . to deepen their commitment to the hungry." The resolution indicated five avenues such commitment could take.

The first of these is *"becoming familiar with local needs for food and assisting in establishing programs such as food pantries, food banks, cooperative programs on life style assessment."*

Many local churches have established donated or budget-purchased emergency food supplies in a storage area of the church or in a building or rental unit near the church. People in need of food can simply stop by the emergency food center, state their need and be supplied by the Christian volunteers manning the center. One church in Los Angeles established a store in the inner city where there are many suffering refugees—legal and illegal. They sell food supplies and clothing to the needy at cost. I've noticed another commendable trend. Some local churches are examining their life styles to see where money can be saved from personal food bills so that they can share more with the poor and hungry in their neighborhoods.

Second, the Resolution strongly urges *"each member of the Church to pledge at least one hour per week of volunteer time to direct service to those in need, and each congregation to provide facilities, food and money to meet those needs."*

I know a church that has a "People Mover" program, a system for keeping volunteers available, trained and useful in Christian service organizations established by the church or by others in the community. This "talent bank" offers weekly opportunities for members, young and old, actually to contribute to the needs of the community with their time and energy. One pastor asks for his people to volunteer one-tenth of their work time to the work of the kingdom in that town. Others limit volunteers to an easily manageable amount of volunteer time each week. It is important not to demand too much of any one individual in time or money.

The struggle to help the destitute and oppressed in our towns should not lead to the destruction of a volunteer's vocational, spiritual or family-life commitments.

I know of one family who has found it a tremendous blessing to give anonymously as they have heard of those in need in their area. Together the family decided on the projects, worked, prayed, and sometimes had to struggle to see them through to completion. The poor, hungry, or needy people helped either directly or through the church never knew where these gifts came from, and the family found the Scripture true which says it is more blessed to give than to receive. Perhaps your family would want to try to do what it can to help those around you.

Third, the Resolution constrains us to pray *"for greater awareness and sensitivity among all citizens to the problems of hunger and malnutrition,"* and to work toward such awareness *"by distributing materials for educational programs."*

Again, prayer is central to the problems of privation and human hunger, but prayer also goes hand in hand with action. Charles Schulz's cartoon series, "Peanuts," has an unforgettable strip in which Snoopy, the tragicomic beagle, is lying shivering on top of his doghouse in a terrible snowstorm. It is suppertime, and Linus and Lucy are enjoying the warmth of their fire. Lucy looks out the window at the cold and hungry dog and shouts: "Pray, be ye warmed and fed, Snoopy." So many times prayer without works is hypocrisy, and works without prayer is futile and short-lived. But together, praying and working for the hungry will make a tremendous difference and provide the community with an example of Christian love that leads to the most effective kind of Christian witness.

Sometimes there are no materials printed on the needs of the impoverished in a town or neighborhood. A pastor friend of mine in California knew that there were many needy people in the blocks surrounding his church. But he didn't know the statistics and wasn't sure how to obtain them. He telephoned city hall for a population graph and found that the city could provide a complete demographic study on his neighborhood. From the demographics it was easy to discover the needs of the people who lived within walking distance of that parish church. To his shock and chagrin, the data showed that 70 percent of the people living within ten blocks of his church were refugees who had escaped the war zones of Central America. They were often talented, professional people without hope of reestablishing their lives in the United States. Many were illegal aliens. They were hungry, unemployed, lonely and afraid. Just finding out who lived nearby opened an entirely new ministry to that Evangelical Covenant church. The pastor organized a team of volunteers, who reached out in love to the needy around them. Eventually they hired a Spanish-speaking volunteer coordinator, began worship services in Spanish and offered various programs to aid the needy or to refer them to organizations that could help.

Fourth, the Resolution counsels *"joining forces with other individuals and Christian organizations."*

There are, of course, many denominational and parachurch organizations that could be recommended, such as the Salvation Army or World Vision. One of the best of the small relief organizations in the world is Samaritan's Purse of Boone, North Carolina. As I mentioned earlier in this book we have our own emergency relief arm of the Billy Graham Evangelistic Association.

After investigating these organizations and the work they do, decide on one or two groups you want to support. Once you have determined the denomination and/or parachurch organization that you feel is truly trustworthy and effective, work to support that group in its local, national and international ministries.

Still, there is no way for any group or groups really to serve the entire world and its needs. There are plenty of needy areas—beginning in the houses around your home. Start in your own community. Serve your neighbors while reaching out to minister to the hungry and the needy around the globe. Remember charity always begins at home—and from there, around home.

Fifth, the Resolution urges *"policymakers and the entire community to call for increased use of our national resources to meet basic human needs."*

Our public officials appreciate a person's honest and informed concern. As we have seen, Christ called us to care for the widows and the orphans. In no uncertain terms, He commanded us to feed the hungry and to clothe the naked. Our taxes support national, state and local service programs. It is our interest in those programs that keeps them effective. Our attention to their results will keep their executives honest and on target. Why should only nonbelievers work to influence the way our tax monies are spent? Why shouldn't we?

During the 1950s, especially, it was my privilege to be a friend of Dwight D. Eisenhower—both before and after he was elected President of the United States. I hope I had some influence on him, and certainly he had a strong impact on my thinking. The statement of his that had a great influence on me was one he made to the American Society of Newspaper Editors in April 1953. It reads: "Every gun that is made, every warship launched, every rocket fired signifies—in a final sense—a theft from those who hunger and are not fed, those who are cold and are not clothed. This world in arms is not spending money alone. It is spending the sweat of its laborers, the genius of its scientists, the hopes of its children. . . . This is not a way of life at all in any true sense. Under the threatening cloud of war, it is humanity hanging on a cross of iron."

That proclaimed position by our Chief Executive was part of what prompted me and some of my colleagues in 1956 to make a tour of the developing countries. Before, I had seen few people dying from starvation, and I had never experienced firsthand the horror of an almost entirely poverty-stricken nation gripped by hunger. Destitute people wearing hand-me-downs—or nearly nothing at all—were evident everywhere. In some places, beggars seemed to be omnipresent, draped in filth, and the fumes of rotting odors emanated to meet every drawn breath. Such situations would leave even the most insensitive sick in the pit of their stomachs. When I returned to the United States it seemed that everyone looked like an affluent Dives or an opulent King Midas by comparison. I went directly to the White House and shared my feelings with President Eisenhower. He listened intently, then he asked me to share my impressions with the Secretary of State, John Foster Dulles. Dulles was a churchman. He had been president of the Federal Council of Churches before his appointment by the Eisenhower administration.

Mr. Dulles was very cordial. He asked that I visit him at home rather than in his State Department office. We talked at length about the hungry people I had seen. I was emphatic about the needs there and insisted that we should do something about them. "What about this nation's surplus wheat?" I asked. "Why can't it be used to help meet at least some of the basic needs of those around the globe who are dying because they have no grain to make bread?"

I feel even more strongly today about the social responsibility of the rich nations sharing their surpluses with the poor—even if it involves altering our thinking about how it can be done. There must be a way to shift grain and dairy products such as cheese from the storerooms of the rich nations to the empty huts and hovels of those who are dying from hunger around the earth. It is time we put our best Judeo-Christian brains to work on this problem to solve it, for there is no reason why so many people, especially the children of the world, should suffer and die from hunger while we are so well fed. You can't read the Epistles of either James or John and draw any other conclusion about where our responsibility lies.

In traveling through approximately sixty countries of the world I have found that there exists a false impression of America. Millions of people have an idea that almost everyone in America is a millionaire. They look on Americans as super-rich. They do not realize that there are several countries that have a per-capita income much higher than the United States.

There is no way they could be aware that America, for some years, has been broke and getting in more financial trouble all the time with an incredible, mind-boggling federal deficit. The Americans of this generation are already spending their great-grand-children's money. A financial judgment day is going to come to the United States before the end of this century unless the budget can be balanced and we start paying back what we owe.

At the moment this does not seem likely. Items that were luxuries when I was a boy have come to seem like necessities to many people. Our total standard of living is far too high. We as a nation are living far above our means, yet America is often blamed for many of the economic problems in other countries. The blame should be shared with other parts of the world. For example, Middle Eastern countries with huge reserves should be asked to do far more.

It is true that in my early life and ministry I spent less time thinking about our corporate responsibility as Christians. I had less consciousness of the fact that millions of people throughout the world lived on the knife-edge of starvation—and that the Bible was so specific about the obligations of believers to do something about it. As I traveled throughout the Third World and studied the Bible on this theme, especially the many New Testament verses that speak of our responsibility to the poor and hungry, the conviction regarding our corporate responsibility as Christians deepened.

I am fortunate enough to be a citizen of the United States, a nation that has been blessed in many ways beyond any other nation in the world. But I must not take these blessings for granted. We are stewards of what God has allowed America to have. As long as we have something more than our neighbors, Christ calls us to share with those in need around the world, especially of the household of faith. If we fail Christ, we will be judged for that failure. The rider on the black horse carrying the scales rides to warn us that we can no longer escape our responsibility to the hungry in spite of all the barriers which stand in our way. And there are formidable barriers.

Summary

Why is there hunger in the world? Why do millions die from starvation and the effects of malnutrition every year? Let's summarize. The National Academy of Engineering, the Institute of Medicine and the National Research Council agree on these four major reasons for world hunger. I have given a good deal of thought to these recently.

First, there is an *insufficient supply of the right food where and when it is needed.* There is the problem of inadequate production and low crop yield in the areas where people are starving. This is complicated by the inadequate transportation systems for getting foodstuff to the hungry. Faulty distribution systems fail to get the food into hungry hands. Antiquated storage methods and facilities fail to keep the food in edible condition when and if it arrives in the targeted areas of greatest need. The need for Christians with the technical know-how and the creative commitment to follow Christ into administering these programs is second only to the need for those ministering the gospel. God loves the children of the world. He calls us to work on behalf of their physical as well as their spiritual salvation.

Second, there is *poverty*—grinding, dehumanizing, emaciating, abject poverty. According to the World Bank, there are approximately 800 million people living in "absolute poverty." That is almost 40 percent of the total population of the world's developing nations. When we see the comparison between the per-capita gross national product for the affluent nations over against the poor nations, the ever-sharpening polarization and inequity is staggering. We Christians should be working much harder to correct these monstrous inequities. We should be working much more arduously on behalf of the poor and their future in a world where every year the gap widens between the rich who grow richer and the poor who die of hunger.

Third, there is the *population* explosion in the countries of the Third World. It is ironic that, due to the advances of science in the control of modern diseases, the human population of the earth has grown so rapidly in the twentieth century. The *Rand McNally New International Atlas* reports that in 1900 there were about 1.6 billion people on the earth; today there are 4.5 billion and, at current rates of growth, there are projected to be some 6 billion by the year 2000. And we must not minimize the efforts of the Third World nations to slow population growth. While the percentage of natural increase in the United States is currently 0.6 percent per year, India has managed to decrease its rate of natural increase over the past decade to two percent.

Yet there are moral and ethical questions here. For example, we have read recently in our newspapers of one country that does not encourage families to have more than one child. In that particular country it is the boy who is revered and wanted. Thus, sometimes the moment a little baby girl is born she is killed. This practice has reached epidemic proportions in that country.

But there is no doubt that where the population explosion is the sharpest, the hunger is the most acute. The human family is adding ninety million per year. Ninety percent of this increase will take place in the poorest countries of Asia, Africa and Latin America. China reached one billion in 1982. Of course, one of the pathetic outcomes of the population boom is, as Major Eva Den Hartog reports after returning from her Third World trek, "Fifty million children die annually in the world from starvation." Naturally the estimates vary. No one even counts the bodies of the children who die. There are too many.

I don't know fully how concerned and intelligent Christians can help in the worldwide population control. The issue is extremely complex. But we must do what we can and use our God-given creative resources to work with all our ingenuity to alleviate the population problems that lead to hunger and premature death.

Fourth, there is the *unstable food supply* throughout the world—erratic surpluses and shortages that sometimes defy the imagination. Some of the root causes of unstable food supplies include pests—both animal and insects. Then there are the irregular water sources; 600 million people live in marginal desert areas, and only one out of ten people in the world can turn on the tap for immediate water in their home or even in their village. Add to these problems unpredictable weather (such as has been devastating many areas of the Southern Hemisphere), poor soil, agribusiness and wars. In addition, unfavorable government policies order raw material to be grown for export at the expense of foodstuff that could feed the domestic hungry in the nation concerned.

These, then, are the main reasons for hunger which many observers find in the world. But I would suggest there is also another reason for hunger in the world today—a reason which is at the root of many of the other reasons.

This fifth reason is human selfishness and greed. Why do we not take more deliberate, sacrificial action to build adequate distribution systems for food or combat the grinding poverty of so many nations? Why do we not take the steps that are necessary to root out corruption or overturn political policies which chronically favor the few at the expense of the many? The reason is human greed and selfishness—and that is why hunger and disease and poverty are moral and spiritual issues as well. It is why political and social answers alone will not suffice. Our hearts must be changed before we will really be burdened about the spiritual and physical plight of others. Only when we yield our lives to Christ and seek above all else to see our world as God sees it will we really be willing to come to the aid of those in need without reserve. I am encouraged that Christians are doing this on an increasing scale today.

Traditionally Christians have seen missionaries as those who preach, teach, translate or engage in ministries of healing. We must in addition train and equip our best brains, young and old, to serve Christ in the world also through pest control, agricultural science, engineering, farm and soil management and weather research. I congratulate the mission boards who are already working to train the new generation of missionary engineers and technicians, scientists and managers who will in turn join other Christian servants, at home and abroad, to exercise their skill in ministry and in witness—never forgetting their priority of preaching and living Christ.

World Vision's Information and Resource Center suggests we need to increase our assistance to the peoples of the world in several crucial areas to diminish hunger and reduce dramatically the needless waste of lives through starvation. We need to increasingly volunteer our expertise to help nations design plans for storage of grain reserves, so that this stored grain can efficiently and expeditiously be distributed whenever and wherever a food crisis suddenly develops. This is precisely what God revealed to Joseph in Egypt. As a result not only Egypt, but also, eventually, Israel, was saved from famine and starvation. We must help find, create and distribute appropriate technology for agriculture challenges wherever the need arises. And it is imperative that we assist nations to develop arable land by demonstrating to them how to fertilize and irrigate what otherwise would remain unclaimed desert.

As I write this my son, Franklin, is in war-torn Lebanon, building homes for those left homeless by the many wars. In spite of their long-term dedication and concern Christian missionaries have had minimal impact on Moslem populations anywhere in the world. Lebanon is no exception. Now Franklin and his associates in Samaritan's Purse are building homes for Moslems made homeless by the bombings, out of concern for their needs, but also in hopes that their acts of Christian charity will make a difference in the attitudes of Moslems toward Christians.

Their efforts are making a difference. As the Moslems watch Christians sacrifice to help them in the rebuilding of their city, they see a kind of Christian witness that is different from what they have known before. They applaud Franklin and his friends as they pass by in the street. They even approach to embrace them with tears in their eyes, expressing their gratitude in every way they can. And when they ask, "Why do you do this?" they answer, "We do this because we love you and because God loves you. We do this in the name of Jesus Christ."

Many Christians working around the world are earning the right to be heard. They are backing their message with compassion. Of course it isn't a new idea. Missionaries, lay and clergy alike, have been on the field for generations earning the right to be heard and backing their message with compassionate acts. They stand up before the rider on the black horse.

We should never, with our modern technology, criticize or despise the methods of those brave missionaries who paid a price during the last 200 years to carry the gospel to the entire world. My father-in-law, Dr. Nelson Bell, was one of those great missionaries to China. He left a successful professional baseball career, studied medicine, and in 1916 went to China to help build a hospital. He combined medicine and the proclamation of the gospel. Jesus said to the disciples, "I sent you to reap what you have not worked for. Others have done the hard work, and you have reaped the benefits of their labor" (John 4:38). The tremendous evangelical surge around the world today came because faithful men and women of God paid a price in blood, sweat, tears and death to lay a foundation upon which we are building.

My priorities are in the same order they've been since I first became a clergyman. The salvation of lost souls was, is and always will be my number-one task. As I pointed out earlier, Jesus didn't heal everybody. He didn't feed everybody. His greater mission was the salvation of our souls. When the paralytic was brought to Him, the first thing Jesus said was, "Your sins are forgiven" (Matthew 9:2). Jesus knew that man needed first to understand God's forgiveness, but then Jesus reached out and met the physical needs of the man as well.

It is the duty of Christians to go all out to do what they can to feed, medicate, house and clothe the poor of the world. Jesus had compassion on all those He met who were in need. So must we. God has given each of us different gifts, talents and abilities. We are different parts of the same body. The carpenter (Jesus was a carpenter before He was a minister to the public), the engineer, the architect, the weekend volunteer, the pastor and the evangelist should all stand shoulder to shoulder to slow down the advent of the black horse.

Does that mean we are all called to give away everything we have, or that there is something wrong or immoral about having wealth? Not necessarily—although some may be called of God to give away much and make great sacrifices. Wealth, however, can be a stewardship given by God. Wealth can be used selfishly and sinfully—or it can be used for the glory of God. The Christian businessman, for example, who uses the resources God has given him to build a business that will give jobs to the poor can be making an important contribution. We all have been given different talents and opportunities. The real question is, are we using them for the glory of God and the physical and spiritual betterment of others?

Listen! Hear the sound of the distant hoofbeats. Hunger and disease are closing in on us. Day by day the black horse and rider draw nearer. We are called by our Lord and Savior to proclaim the gospel and serve our fellowman in his psychological, physical, moral and spiritual needs. It will require spiritual muscle for each of us to place our body on the defensive line of scrimmage. Before we rush to volunteer our lives in the cause of the hungry and diseased of the world, we must rush to the Cross for forgiveness and for strength.

This is a spiritual battle. Children are dying because evil rules the hearts and the pocketbooks of men. To feed and care for the world will require a spiritual revolution. As men and women turn to God in Christ they will be liberated to give up the false hope that weapons alone will save us from our enemies. They can reach out in love and share, for every possession we have is a gift of God. Remember, we are only stewards of the world's resources. They are not ours; they are God's. And until we trust Him to take care of us we will clutch our possessions and hold them selfishly. But when we find our security in Him we can give generously of what God has entrusted to us, and then perhaps the hoofbeats of the black horse will not sound quite as loud.

10

The Pale
Horse
and Its
Rider

The Rider Who Brings Pestilence and Death

Three horses had galloped into John's vision and, bearing their riders of judgment, had ridden toward the earth. Again, the Lamb moved to break a fourth seal holding the pages of God's great scroll in place. As before, one of God's appointed emissaries stepped forward to command. "Come!" he exclaimed. And another page was thrown back to reveal a fourth horse and rider.

What did John see in that flashing moment? And what did it mean to him and through him to all of us? In the biblical text John writes, "I looked, and there before me was a pale horse!" (Revelation 6:8). The word in Greek is *chloros*. The horse trembling there, rearing high in anger, was the yellow-green color of sickly grass. Goodspeed translates *chloros* as the "color of ashes." Barclay calls it the color of a face "blanched with terror." Moffatt paints the horse as livid, the bloodless color of a corpse. We use the root of that ancient Greek word when we describe the color of chlorine gas that seeps from a wrecked tanker car and mists its poisonous way across the landscape, lethally levelling all life—plants and people alike—in its wake.

At that moment John's eyes were confronted with a consummately terrifying sight. Seated on the pale horse was a rider "named Death, and Hades was following close behind him" (Revelation 6:8). In the Victoria and Albert Museum in London there is a painted reproduction of a series of seven tapestries woven in the fourteenth century. Some 472 feet long, it depicts John's vision of the Apocalypse. Six hundred years ago the artists-weavers read the sixth chapter of Revelation and artistically interpreted the rider as a skull wrapped in graveclothes sitting upon the pale horse and carrying the Roman broadsword in preparation for the carnage he would inflict.

In the fifteenth century, Albrecht Dürer depicted John's vision in fifteen large, carefully cut wood blocks. Death rides the pale horse in the more traditional form of Father Time, an emaciated, bearded harbinger of judgment carrying a three-pronged spear and riding at full gallop toward men whose faces are upturned in defenseless horror.

Of all the dozens of artistic interpretations of the four horsemen the most graphic for me is the nightmare vision of a modern Japanese artist, Fujita, who painted the fourth horseman as a full skeleton grinning fiendishly, riding on the full skeleton of a horse across a battlefield strewn with skeletons. The entire charnel scene is framed in a chlorine green cloud of death. With Hiroshima and Nagasaki being etched into the Japanese psyche, who could better portray the pale horse than a Fujita?

The little phrase, "and Hades was following close behind him," has puzzled scholars over the centuries. Was there a second rider on the pale horse riding tandem with Death? Or was there a fifth horseman of the Apocalypse? Hades is the place where departed spirits reside between death and the resurrection, the transitional abode of the dead. This is the place that for a time swallows up the spirits of those who die outside of Christ. In the vision, John sees Death and Hades in all too ordinary terms of a man cleaning up refuse along a public road, spearing a bit of trash and dumping it into the trash bag he lugs along.

Speaking this time of Death and Hades, John uses the mysterious phrase, "They were given power . . ." (Revelation 6:8). Did God speak an order to the fourth horseman of the Apocalypse? Did one of God's creature servants give the rider a scroll with a divine commission enclosed? However it was delivered, in that awful instant when horse and riders paused, something transpired between God and Death giving him power to kill one of every four people living on earth.

By the end of the next decade it is estimated world population will pass the six billion mark. That means if this harbinger of judgment were given divine permission to kill one-fourth of the world's population at that time, one and one-half billion people would be slain. That is more people than currently live in Europe, South America and North America combined.

Why would God allow such suffering to take place? John's vision is consistent with ancient biblical pictures describing what happens when God sends His wrath upon men who disobey Him. William Barclay, the late great Scottish professor at Glasgow University, warned that "at the back of it all there is the permanent truth that no man and no nation can escape the consequences of their sin" (*The Revelation of John*, Vol. 2, p. 12). And Lynn Howard Hough explains that Death, here, does not bring meaningless destruction "but destruction which serves the purposes of the justice of God. [Death] is a part of the divine administration. A fourth of the earth feels his power that the rest may see and have the opportunity to repent" (*The Interpreter's Bible*, Vol. 12, p. 414).

We were all horrified at the Holocaust, in which Hitler coldbloodedly sent some six million Jews (as well as hundreds of thousands of non-Jews) to the gas chambers. No one was more grieved than God. It breaks His heart when His own children die. It was not God's intent that any should perish, but man defiantly refused God's plan, the consequence of his disobedience being that he followed the way of death. Now, Death as the rider on the pale horse is only taking his due as he has done throughout history—very few people ever reach the age of 100! Still, in this vision, God reaches out in love. He illustrated His great love by giving His Son to die on the cross—the most horrible death a person can die. God hopes that through this evidence of love and this warning of the fourth horseman before the final judgment that the rest of the world might see the wages of sin, turn from their sinfulness, seek God's forgiveness, and be saved from the jaws of hell.

We should not be horrified at what God is doing. We should be grateful. Physical death is actually a blessing to the human race because of the evil tendencies within man that produce the Hitlers of almost every generation. This world would have been turned into hell had they lived forever. But man not only dies physically, he is spiritually dead while he is physically alive until he finds new life in Christ. The Bible also speaks of the second death, or eternal death. This refers to hell. God, through this rider, hopes to cheat hell of the billions who have by their own sinfulness chosen death over life. If the love He offers is accepted, and the warning He gives is heeded, then billions will be saved.

But the order is even more specific. The weapons of death are clearly described: sword, famine, plague and wild beasts are named. These New Testament instruments of "holocaust" are taken directly from the Old Testament texts. The vision of John has roots in a vision of Moses almost thirteen hundred years before John's island vision. Again it is Barclay who reminds us that in Leviticus (26:21–26) Moses described the judgment God will send upon His people because of their disobedience. Barclay says, "*Wild beasts* will rob them of their children, and destroy their cattle, and make them few in number. The *sword* will avenge their breaches of the covenant. When they are gathered in their cities the *pestilence* will be among them. He will break the staff of bread and they *will eat and not be satisfied*" (*The Revelation of John*, Vol. 2, pp. 11–12). Later, the prophet Ezekiel heard the sovereign Lord say, "How much worse will it be when I send against Jerusalem my four dreadful judgments—sword and famine and wild beasts and plague—to kill its men and their animals!" (Ezekiel 14:21). But even these promises of horror bring hope. God assures Ezekiel that "there will be some survivors" and those survivors will console the prophet when he sees "their conduct and their actions, for you will know that I [God] have done nothing in it without cause" (Ezekiel 14:22, 23).

Hoofbeats of the Fourth Horseman

Throughout the centuries the fourth horseman has ridden in warning to effect positive change. And again his hoofbeats echo in our brains. Scan this morning's television news for signs of his destructive presence. Listen to the radio news as you drive along the freeway. Just open tonight's newspaper. Add up the victims. It doesn't take a science fiction writer to imagine the modern forms that these ancient instruments of death now take in our time.

Count the bodies slain by the *sword:* a terrorist attack in Rome, a bombing in Beirut, a burst of machine gun fire in Belfast, another massacre in Africa, an earthquake in Iran. Before World War II this passage (and many others) throughout the Scripture would have boggled our minds. They would have been totally beyond man's comprehension. That was why the Bible was derided or ignored by many scientists a half a century ago. It is reckoned worldwide that today twice the percentage of scientists believe in a personal God (and His accurate revelation through the Scriptures) as was the case early in this century. And what is even more encouraging: it was stated by a lecturer at Harvard in April 1983, that 41 percent of the high schoolers in America are daily reading a portion from the Bible. However, when the first atomic bomb was dropped, the general orientation of scholars was to scoff, especially at the apocalyptic passages of Scripture. But in August 1945 the laughter turned to trembling. Now, with the advent of new and more awesome weapons it is an entirely different story.

The devil has always had a desire to kill. In John 8:44 Jesus said that "he is a liar and the father of lies" and his desire to kill is also seen in the same verse. "He was a murderer from the beginning, not holding to the truth, for there is no truth in him." Here in Revelation 6:8, he is given permission to go forth to kill hordes of humans with his sword—a holocaustic one-quarter of the population of the earth. "One quarter of the population of the earth" is precisely the prediction that a Soviet scientist said (in May 1983) would perish in the first major nuclear exchange between the superpowers. On the other hand, the Bible teaches that God, too, has swords. "The sword of the Lord, and of Gideon" (Judges 7:20, kjv) is the one with which the ancient Israelites destroyed the invading Midianites. And in the New Testament we read of the Lord's "sword of the Spirit, which is the word of God" (Ephesians 6:17). The weapon of Satan is, of course, counterfeit. It would represent "the spiritual Lie" as opposed to the truth of God. Second

Thessalonians 2:7–12 says: "For the secret power of lawlessness is already at work; but the one who now holds it back will continue to do so till he is taken out of the way. And then the lawless one will be revealed, whom the Lord Jesus will overthrow with the breath of his mouth and destroy by the splendor of his coming. The coming of the lawless one will be in accordance with the work of Satan displayed in all kinds of counterfeit miracles, signs and wonders, and in every sort of evil that deceives those who are perishing. They perish because they refused to love the truth and so be saved. For this reason God sends them a powerful delusion so that they will believe the lie and so that all will be condemned who have not believed the truth but have delighted in wickedness." In some translations, the word "lie" in the eleventh verse is capitalized. Thus we see that God's truth makes us spiritually alive, but Satan's "Lie" kills.

The passage in Revelation 6 concerning the pale horse probably has a double interpretation. One is literal, the other is spiritual. The Bible teaches in the last days there will be a famine of the Word of God (Amos 8:11). Spiritual death follows spiritual starvation.

Concerning physical death, we have already discussed the lifeless forms of the 40,000 children who died from *hunger and disease* in the short time you were sleeping. Count up the Third World victims of plague and pestilence that now sweep the famine and drought-ravaged towns and villages of the earth. The *Amplified Bible* translates Deuteronomy 28:15, 21, 22, 27, 28: "If you will not obey the voice of the Lord your God. . . . The Lord will make the pestilence cling to you until He has consumed you from off the land, which you go to possess. The Lord will smite you with consumption [wasting, degenerative diseases?], with fever, and inflammation [communicable diseases?]. . . . and the tumors [cancer?], the scurvy [deficiency diseases?] and the itch, of which you cannot be healed [such as VD, herpes simplex II, and AIDS?]. The Lord will smite you with madness [mental illness?] and blindness [birth defects?] and dismay of [mind and] heart [emotional traumas?]." The parenthetical questions in the above quotation are inserted to stimulate your own thoughts on this descriptive passage. This is only a short list of what pestilence will inflict the population when the rider on the pale horse traverses the earth.

Then to be counted are those slain by *wild beasts*. Moses, Ezekiel and John lived in a world where wild beasts frequently stalked wayfarers as they trudged the primitive roads and capriciously invaded the unwalled villages, terrorizing and dismembering their inhabitants. Now, in most civilized cultures today wild beasts are locked away in zoos or traveling circuses. But like the evolution from sword to nuclear missile, so wild beasts have evolved into modern killers that stalk us everywhere we are or go. Oh, there is still the very real threat of actual wild beasts sweeping down into modern cities in search of food and water like the coyotes of southern California or herds of wild boar that recently ravaged a Third World village. But there are new wild beasts that threaten us all.

We do not know exactly how the wild beasts are going to arise or in what form they are to come. The Bible says man also will be killed "by the wild beasts of the earth" (Revelation 6:8). This could refer to the animal and insect-borne epidemics. It could refer to the vicious beasts we read about later on in the book of Revelation that are going to roam the earth unrestrained, torturing and killing their human prey. For example, when the bottomless pit is opened in Revelation 9 there are going to issue forth locusts with faces and hair like humans which indicates that they are intelligent beings. They do not necessarily kill, but the torment unleashed on the human family is to be so devastating that men will beg for death only to find that death eludes them. Apparently, these hideous, heinous and ferocious creatures are demonic in nature with supernatural power. Many of our horror movies today are depicting such events. Jesus prophesied clearly that a part of the "distress of those days" (Matthew 24:29) will be that "wherever there is a carcass, there the vultures will gather" (v. 28). Perhaps they are men who will live like wild beasts.

The Warning of Pestilence

Also in Matthew 24:7 (kjv) after Jesus had warned about counterfeit religion, the maddening escalation in wars, and the raging famines, He pointed to rampaging pestilences. This word pestilence can be translated as "death," a word meaning any infectious malady which is fatal. There have been virulent wars, famines and plagues during the long history of man, but nothing comparable to this event which is still future. Its fury is depicted in its devastation of all before it, killing a large part of the earth's population. To quote Jesus again, "those will be days of distress unequaled from the beginning, when God created the world." Yes, "and never to be equaled again. If the Lord had not cut short those days, no one would survive" (Mark 13:19, 20). Thus, under the fourth seal we see Death and Hades given authority over the fourth part of the earth to kill with God's four judgments listed in Ezekiel 14:21— sword, famine, pestilence and wild beasts.

Suddenly all of man's programs for bringing peace, plenty and longevity through science and technology will be eclipsed by a cataclysmic apocalypse and overturned in appalling brevity—*unless in the meantime man turns to God.* This is one of the reasons I feel compelled to continue my preaching all over the world. Medical science has made such quantum leaps to bring to the brink of paradise whole peoples who a short century ago were living at primitive subsistence levels in the jungle. And science continues to make incredible breakthroughs for which we are all by light-years the more convenienced. But pestilence is coming! Many are saying, "Peace, Peace," where, despite our best efforts, there will be no permanent peace because we have ignored the Prince of Peace. We have rejected God's commandments that would have helped us live in peace. Thus the sword is coming. There are those who are promising prosperity and plenty if we adopt their particular programs, regime or ideology. But ultimately the worst famine ever to strike our world is coming.

The fourth horseman on the pale horse kills men and women with the sword, famine, pestilence and wild beasts. It is not so much an empire of man which is to be feared, as the one who controls the activities of this savage horseman. Over against the grossest political injustice is put the justice of a God of love. As we examine the fourth horseman we must not forget that he comes not only at the permissive will of God, but also at the command of the One who opens the seals—Jesus Christ. The Bible teaches that the devil is the one who has the power of death (Hebrews 2:14), but he can only act by God's permission, for as Jesus Christ had said to John five chapters earlier, "I am the Living One; I was dead, and behold I am alive for ever and ever! And I hold the keys of death and Hades" (Revelation 1:18). In the Old Testament we see Satan using this permission to kill the family of Job. There's a *mystery* here that none of us can really comprehend. This is the mystery of iniquity that we do not yet fully understand. It involves all the great attributes of God including His righteousness, holiness and justice. It also includes the cleverness, the subtlety and the power of Satan—and also includes man's yielding to Satan's temptation, and defying God, and how this sin was passed on from generation to generation.

I have been re-reading Jonathan Schell's *Fate of the Earth*. The cultural community of this country called his best seller "the new bible of the nuclear holocaust age." It has a section on "the second death." For Schell, "the second death" is the death of the earth when ecosystems are destroyed by nuclear war and its aftermath. In theological terms, "the second death" is referred to in Jude 12 as "twice dead"; and in Revelation 21:8 as "the fiery lake" which is the destiny of all unbelievers. "This is the second death." It is what occurs to the human spirit after the body dies. It is what comes after death that is so terrifying. If we were two-dimensional beings who had total mortality, but no immortality, death would simply end our earthly existence. But to borrow and redefine Schell's "second death" phrase, the Bible says that "the second death" is separation from God.

I used to have a medical doctor friend in Glasgow, Scotland, Dr. J. Brown Henry. One day he went to see a dying patient and happened to ask him, "Are you afraid to die?" The dying man raised himself up on his elbows and said, "No, doctor, I'm not afraid of death but I'm afraid of what comes after death. Terribly afraid."

Anne Frank, four months before being discovered and deported to concentration camps by the Nazis, wrote in her now famous diary: "I want to go on living even after my death" (Introduction, *The Diary of Anne Frank*, p. 6).

Simon Wiesenthal, the famous Nazi hunter who brought some 11,000 war criminals to justice during his extraordinary thirty-six-year stint, when learning that he had serious heart trouble, said, "I cannot fight against the calendar. . . . As for the Nazis, we are rapidly reaching a biological solution. As I die, so will they" (*The Mail*, 26 June 1983, "Weekend People"). Thus, death is universal and total in every generation. The generation in which we are now living, that is struggling with the problems of the world, will soon be dead and another generation will follow to wrestle and try to cope with similar problems. For many intellectual unbelievers, life is meaningless and hopeless. They do not know where they came from, why they are here, or where they are going. They stumble on in the cosmic darkness. Those of us who have put our trust and faith in Christ know where we have come from, the purpose of our existence, and the glorious future toward which we are headed. This makes life more than worth living. It gives us a sense of optimism.

I cannot help but think of the statement that Paul made as a great comfort to all of those who believe in Jesus Christ. He said, "Christ Jesus . . . brought life and immortality to light through the gospel" (2 Timothy 1:10). That is a wonderful comfort to those of us who believe. But it's one of the most terrifying verses in all the Bible for the unbeliever because it means that if you have never repented of your sins and received Christ by faith you are stuck—with a lost immortality. You can commit suicide physically, but you can't "self-destruct" your soul. You are going to live forever whether you like it or not.

The fourth horseman rides to warn us. He warns us first of all of *physical death*—the death of both man and our planet—and what we must do if it is to be delayed. The fourth horseman warns us also of the *spiritual death* of humanity (eternal separation from God) and what Christ has done to save us from this "second death," which is far more serious.

Another Chance for Lost Mankind

Almost every headline, almost every television news flash, almost every radio bulletin proclaims one truth: the rider who brings death is on his way and hell is close behind. But there is still reason to rejoice nevertheless: for in this harbinger of judgment man is given yet another chance, his last chance to repent, to abandon the foolish ways of sin and disobedience, and to receive God's love and mercy. These headlines are God's warning. The television news flashes are a shadow of His loving hand at work for the world's redemption. The radio bulletins are one more reminder that in spite of our obsessive determination to ruin the earth and destroy God's program of salvation, He has not given up on us. Until that fixed day when God's final judgment affixes each of us into place for eternity He offers us the chance to begin again, as Jesus put it, to be born again.

To his eternal peril, may man not miss the primary purpose of this fourth rider to dramatically bring God's warning of future judgment. We are called to hear the approaching hoofbeats and to humble ourselves before God while there is yet time.

Jesus repeatedly warned us to fear him who is able to cast men into hell, and instead be saved by faith in Christ. Sydney Harris, the eminent syndicated newspaper writer, in his column for 6 January 1983, remonstrated: "Neither Heaven nor Hell has been presented by 'today's preachers' to make the former attractive or the latter credible, so that the mass of people are moved to yearn for the one or fear the other." Paul soberly solemnized that knowing the terror of "the Lord, we try to persuade men" (2 Corinthians 5:11) with every facility at our command.

The great Methodist preacher, author and missionary of the past generation, Dr. E. Stanley Jones, described how he was once addressing an Indian university on the verities of eternity. When he sat down, the thoughtful Hindu president stood up and sonorously solemnized, "If what this man says is not true, then it doesn't matter. But if what he says is true, then nothing else matters." I feel strongly that my love for Christ and love for people demands of me, as it did of the ancient John the Baptist, to warn people to "flee from the coming wrath" (Matthew 3:7) by putting their faith in Jesus Christ. "Since, then, we know what it is to fear the Lord, we try to persuade men. For Christ's love compels us" (2 Corinthians 5:11, 14).

The sword therefore in the hand of the rider on the pale horse should arouse us to call people to repentance and faith in Christ and thereby be saved from the second death. It also points us to all jobs yet undone relevant to the uplift of our fellowman. The famine and plagues point to the responsibilities God has given us to help Him preserve life on earth and witness the Judgment Day further in the distance. It also points us to the millions who have never heard the name of Christ. According to Matthew 24:14, God has tied the second coming of Christ with the success of world evangelization, "And this gospel of the kingdom will be preached in the whole world as a testimony to all nations, and then the end will come." For the first time in history we now have the technology and the capability of reaching the entire human race with the gospel of Christ in this century. While the Bible teaches only a minority will accept and the vast majority of humanity will reject God's offer of mercy, yet God has spared many nations and cities because of a dedicated minority. The wild beasts in their modern forms are red lights to stop our perilous journey away from God and His design—and turn us back into His loving, ever-lasting arms.

The Physical Death of Mankind

The fourth horseman of the Apocalypse is the rider who brings death. To achieve his goals, the horseman on the pale horse is armed, as we have seen, with four deadly weapons: the sword, famine, plagues and wild beasts. Let us take a closer look at these four weapons and their designated role in the physical death of one-quarter of the world's population.

First, the rider carries the sword—the symbol of warfare. I already mentioned earlier the interesting story about a young man named Damocles who used flattery to endear himself to Dionysius, tyrant ruler of ancient Syracuse. To instruct and warn the ambitious youth, Dionysius invited the flatterer to a banquet and seated him under a sword suspended over his head by a single hair. This graphic lesson was designed to illustrate the perilous nature of one's happiness. We are one broken hair away from death. The sword of Damocles is a graphic figure of speech understood by everyone who hears it alluded to, and an apt analogy of the state of the world now that the fourth rider closes in on us, sword in hand.

We North Americans and Europeans (in comparison to much of the world's population) still sit at that banquet of pleasure. By the world's standards we are still feasting in relative luxury, while we forget that just above our heads hangs the Damoclean sword of our own design. At any moment the hair could break, the sword fall and the luxuries and pleasures of this world could evaporate for millions. In John's time the sword of the fourth rider *was* actually a sword. In those ancient cultures when a man's weapon could be broken across the knee of a conqueror, there was hope of containing warfare. Now, the sword of the fourth rider is no longer easily sheathed. There are monstrous machines of war that may or may not be controllable. No ancient swordsman could kill millions of the world's people. But currently one "rider" is capable of pushing a button that could set off a chain reaction of death.

Without reference to the Bible, or certainly these passages in the book of Revelation, the world's scientists are saying many of the same things.

The *New York Times* labels Isaac Asimov as today's most widely respected science writer. It was hard science Asimov was writing when he published his best-seller, *A Choice of Catastrophes.* He expects man to destroy himself sooner or later, probably sooner—and he presents several worldwide scenarios as to how it will happen.

As we have seen, the nuclear weapon is only one of the whole arsenal of weapons that have been created by modern science, such as chemical, laser and biological weapons.

Now, the fourth horseman rides on that potent pale steed in our direction waving his sword about. How should we respond? I am convinced that Jesus spoke the truth. If we trust only our armaments to save us, we will die. The Scripture warned ancient Israel, "Woe to those who go down to Egypt for help, who rely on horses, who trust in the multitude of their chariots and in the great strength of their horsemen, but do not look to the Holy One of Israel, or seek help from the Lord" (Isaiah 31:1). The psalmist wrote, "Some trust in chariots and some in horses, but we trust in the name of the Lord our God" (Psalm 20:7).

To me, one of the most amazing passages on this theme in the whole Bible is 2 Peter 3:9, 10. Verse 10 says: "The day of the Lord will come like a thief. The heavens will disappear with a roar; the elements will be destroyed by fire, and the earth and everything in it." But despite this inevitability, Peter says we are to reflect Christ who is "not wanting anyone to perish, but everyone to come to repentance" (v. 9). The Christian is always—and with every passion and persuasion at his command—to be for the eternal salvation of the souls of men. Also, if possible, he is to be for the salvation of society from mass holocaust, even though it seems hopeless.

The second weapon used by the fourth horseman is famine. We have discussed the problem of hunger in the world under the black horse and of its obvious connections with disease. I have suggested that every person who is a follower of Christ is responsible to do something for the hungry and the sick in the world. Doing something, even if it feels hopeless or seems insignificant, is better than doing nothing. We must never forget that Jesus made Himself one with the poor saying, "When you feed one of the least of these, you are feeding me." Yet there is a mystery here. As I pointed out earlier, Jesus had the power and the ability to feed every hungry person in the world of His day. As a matter of fact, this was one of the temptations of Satan: if Jesus would turn stones into bread and feed the hungry then He would not have to go to the Cross to redeem the world. But Jesus refused this temptation. There is a danger that we can get away from man's need of eternal salvation by overemphasizing the need for satisfying physical appetites. The Cross and its eternal, redemptive power is primary, but as disciples of Christ we are called upon to follow Him in obedience in helping the hungry and sick of this world.

Third, in John's vision we are warned of death through plague and pestilence. Jesus also warned of pestilences. Our Lord prophesied the period of Apocalypse in Luke 21. He warned us there would be plagues. In the Living Bible it is translated "epidemics." We are being warned by scientists today about bacteria, viruses and insects that are highly resistant to radiation, antibiotics or insecticides. Some feel the tilt of nature has already been affected by modern chemicals. One scientist said: "If the meek don't inherit the earth, the cockroaches will." As we read on in the book of Revelation, many things that we read are highly symbolic, but some are literal. One of the judgments referred to in Revelation 9:3 indicates "locusts came down upon the earth." Recently in Florida millions of toads overran whole counties. We have been warned in many articles of the possibility that insects could take over the earth before the end of this century. They have become resistant to many of the insecticides. Recently, one of our most reputable national news magazines carried as its cover story: "The Insects Are Coming." It was a frightening article to read, especially for those who do not know the Bible. And it reminds us of what happened in Egypt when Pharaoh refused to let the ancient Israelites leave.

Among the "plagues" that we are reading most about today is the shifting climate patterns throughout the world. Val Sears points out, "There is something awesome happening to the weather. Those rolling cold snaps one behind the other" have brought on what serious meteorologists are calling "little ice age number two." The National Academy of Science in the United States calls it a "serious worldwide cooling: with profound social and economic implications" (*Toronto Star*, 18 January 1982). The Canadians are especially worried because, as *The Toronto Globe and Mail* warns, if the average annual temperature in western Canada dropped by one degree Celsius it would no longer be possible to grow wheat there (15 March 1982). On the other hand, these assessments would seem to be contradicted by the devastating drought that America has known since the "Dust Bowl" days fifty years ago.

There is another plague sweeping America called "herpes simplex II." Millions of people are being forced to alter their sexual habits to avoid infection. *Life* magazine said, "For better or worse, herpes is the disease of the year" (1982) and those unlucky enough to catch it may find that prejudice is its most painful symptom. One girl who was infected the first time she had sex experience at the age of sixteen said, "Now I have sexual leprosy."

If herpes was the scare of 1982 (and *Time* declared its cover story on this sordid theme to have evoked the most interest of any of its features for the whole year), the scare story of 1983 and 1984 is "AIDS" (Acquired Immune Deficiency Syndrome). To the homosexual and prostitution communities, as one expert says, it's the worst news since cancer. In fact, its scourge resembles cancer in many ways. And who any longer can deny that with the diagnosed epidemic of herpes and AIDS following each other so rapidly into the headlines, God is saying in love and warning, it's time to call a halt to sexual permissiveness and promiscuity!

All of these noxious plagues, destroyer diseases and famines should arouse the world to repent of their sins and turn to God while there is time. The fourth horseman rides. These scourging plagues afflict for one reason. They are to awaken man to obedience. The Bible teaches that peoples and nations will have brought this pain upon themselves by humanistic religion and man-made war. God has chosen to allow man to reap what he sows to help him learn the bitter lesson that sin brings pain. God does not infect people with herpes simplex II, AIDS and other diseases.

That is the nature of the horsemen. They ride in part to warn us. They ride to point the world back to God and His way. God's love is forever! There is nothing that can separate us from Him but our own continuing disobedience. Even then, God loves and pursues us even through our self-inflicted ailments. But these warnings can help us turn to God.

Just off Wilshire Boulevard in Los Angeles are the La Brea tar pits. In the nearby museum thousands of animal skeletons have been reclaimed from the primordial ooze. A mural depicts the landscape thousands of years ago, when animals ruled the area that is now the city of Los Angeles. A recent Los Angeles magazine cover ominously suggested a future time when wild beasts would again rule the spot where this great city stands. The cover was an artist's imaginative projection of what downtown Los Angeles would look like after a nuclear holocaust. In the picture coyotes prowl among the dusty rubble, and vultures hover over the dying megalopis, looking for any possible survivors. *I think the fourth weapon of the fourth horseman—the wild beasts—is a similar pic-ture. It is John's picture of the earth after warfare has claimed its dead, after hunger and disease have struck down their victims, and after the plagues have decimated those who remain. The wild beasts will then attack those who are unfortunate enough to survive the other instruments of death.

For the past twenty years a rather controversial group of men and women known as ecologists has been warning us about the depletion of the earth's limited resources. They talk about reckless waste, about nuclear and chemical pollutions, about indiscriminate killing of wildlife, about cementing over the forests with freeways and slicing through neighborhoods with on-and-off ramps that feed those ribbons of concrete crisscrossing our country. They warn us about acid rain belching from industrial smokestacks to descend on nature and defoliate God's beautiful creation.

Ecology is that science that deals with organisms and their environments. Ecologists study people, animals and plants in their own unique living spaces. They raise warnings when those living places are being damaged and destroyed. They have been the watchmen and watchwomen on the gates warning of the enemy within. They've been ridiculed and threatened, tolerated and lauded. But now with the sound of the fourth horseman's hoofbeats approaching, perhaps it is time we saw them in the light of Genesis and Revelation and took their warnings more seriously. Of course, as in every movement, there are the extremists and the publicity seekers who bring a bad name to the whole movement.

But I find myself becoming more and more an advocate of the true ecologists where their recommendations are realistic. Many of these people have done us an essential service in helping us preserve and protect our green zones and our cities, our water and our air. A case in point is what has been done to restore Lake Michigan. Everyone hated to see the death of that most southerly of the Great Lakes, but the ecologists had the courage of their convictions. Now the lake is coming back to life. The same is true of its sister Lake Erie. And in this small way God's commission in Genesis to "rule . . . over all the earth" (Genesis 1:26) has been obeyed and the fourth horseman of Revelation has been slowed in his destructive ride.

When I was a boy growing up near Charlotte, North Carolina, I remember the creek that ran through the middle of my father's farm. It was a fairly big creek. I loved Sugar Creek; but what should have been a thing of beauty, a swimming hole for hot summer afternoons, a source of nourishment and growth for my father's cattle, a deliverer of nutrients to the land, was, instead, a cause for grief, even death. One morning we found a Holstein cow lying dead and swollen on Sugar Creek's polluted bank. A mill upstream somewhere was dumping poison into the stream. Sugar Creek died and carried death wherever it went.

We couldn't do anything then. There were no laws to which my father could appeal to have Sugar Creek cleaned and restored. People were not restricted to the extent they are today in their dumping of anything they wanted to dispose of in the flowing water. All we could do was build a fence around the stream to protect the cattle.

In the award-winning Saul Bass film, "Why Men Create," there is an animated history of the world. In the last scene, a man, representative of us all, climbs to the top of a huge pile of junked civilization. The scene ends with the man clinging to the refuse, coughing. It is humorous on first viewing, but the growing possibility of our destroying ourselves and the world with our own neglect and excess is tragic and very real.

How Shall We Respond?

We cannot simply mourn the fate of the earth. We cannot go on pretending that someone else is guilty for its current disastrous state. We cannot act as though we are helpless to work for the world's renewal. We must do what we can, even though we know that God's ultimate plan is the making of a new earth and a new heaven. Signs indicate that the end of the age is near, yet there is no certainty. It may be several generations from now.

Stories of Caring People

One of the people of the world today most identified with Christian compassion and service is Mother Teresa of Calcutta. There are thousands of unknown servants of Christ who are similarly and with comparable sacrifice investing their lives in feeding, clothing and caring for the poor. But Mother Teresa has become a kind of representative of them all. I remember the first time I met this tiny, wrinkled, radiant lady. An American consul in Calcutta offered to drive me to Mother Teresa's compound in the heart of that sprawling megalopolis. When I was introduced to her, she was ministering to a dying person, holding him in her arms. I waited while she helped him face death. When he died, she prayed quietly, gently lowered him to his bed and turned to greet me.

We talked till dusk that day. I was surprised to learn how much she knew about me and about our crusades. In her lilting, broken English she asked if I would like to hear some of her experiences with the hungry and the dying. Very simply, she explained her calling to me. Mother Teresa looks past the physical features of every needy man, woman or child and sees the face of Jesus staring up at her through them. In every starving child she feeds, she sees Jesus. Around every sick and frightened woman she cares for, she sees Jesus. Surrounding every lonely, dying man she cradles in her arms is Jesus. When she ministers to anyone, she is ministering to her Savior and Lord.

I also recall the story from my son's book, *Bob Pierce: This One Thing I Do*, about a missionary who ministered to the lepers in China. Through sheer hard work and her own ingenuity, Beth Albert supported the lepers outside Kunming. She was "the merry heart that doeth good like medicine." She loved these people and they loved her. This was the first time these lepers ever had anybody do anything for them, and they all became Christians because of Beth's love. When they asked Beth, "Why are you doing this?" she replied, "Because I love Jesus and He loves you. He loves you so much He sent me to help you. You are precious to God and He sent His Son to earth to die for you so that you might be saved and be in heaven with Him and have a wonderful body. He sent me to show you that He loves you, and I love you" (pp. 68–71).

Until the day the new government gave the edict that every missionary had until sundown to get out of the area, Beth helped her patients in every way she could—she gave sulphatone injections to treat their leprosy, she showed them how to grow some of their own food, and she helped them beautify their surroundings with flowers.

The debate which existed in the church between "the liberals" who supposedly minister "to the body" and "the evangelicals" who supposedly minister "to the soul" is about over. The evangelicals have often come to see that the Bible teaches we must be concerned about both the soul and the body; some liberals, on the other hand, have begun to realize that social action without the proclamation of the biblical gospel is futile. We are called to minister to human bodies and human spirits simultaneously. The two are inseparable. We are commissioned to follow our Lord onto the streets, trails and byways of the world and minister to the whole person, whoever he or she may be. As a Christian I am called to minister to the soul and body. But the Lausanne Covenant makes it clear that the priority must always be spiritual. For example, when Jesus was in Capernaum a great crowd came to hear Him preach, and four men brought a man sick of the palsy. But they couldn't get in the house the normal way, so they went up on the roof and broke it up and let down the bed in front of Jesus. The Scripture says, "When Jesus saw their faith, he said to the paralytic, 'Son, your sins are forgiven' " (Mark 2:5). Jesus' first concern was with the man's sins, then later He healed him of the palsy. I have visited places in the world where I felt I must help meet these physical needs before I could preach the gospel to them. And yet I have always known that their deepest need was spiritual, and that they needed the Water of Life and the Bread of Life more than anything else in the world. Yet I must follow the example of Jesus and have compassion on suffering humanity.

In one Third World city I have seen dilapidated lorries at sunrise rumbling up and down the streets picking up the corpses of those who had died in the night. When I reflect on those heartrending scenes, I think of Death riding up and down those same streets with Hades close behind. Men and women in the Salvation Army, Mother Teresa and thousands like them have thrown their lives into the path of the fourth horseman. They are reluctant to let anyone within their reach starve to death unprovided for, or die unattended. They stand in Christ's name squarely in the path of the pale horse of death as he thunders in their direction. The odds on beating him are ultimately hopeless. Still they stand, solitary and strong. People call them naive, do-gooders, fanatics. Yet they stand. And on and on the fourth horseman rides. And this very day, you and I, like the Good Samaritan, must do what we can to help in a torn, bleeding world. Evangelical Christians have built hospitals, nursing homes, clinics, and sent doctors and nurses by the thousands wherever there was need. But still it is only a drop in the bucket—much more is needed.

Do you remember that moment in Jesus' life when a rich young man came up to Him to ask, "What must I do to inherit eternal life?" Jesus answered, "You know the commandments." And the young man answered, "All these I have kept since I was a boy." It was quite a claim. Jesus must have looked carefully at the young man. He must have seen that this seeker was telling the truth. The rich man was sincere, a struggler, a lover of truth. So Jesus answered him, "Sell everything you have and give to the poor. Then come, follow me." The young man couldn't do it. It would have cost him too much. So "he became very sad" (Luke 18:18–23). He missed the chance of a lifetime. He asked for life and missed it. He clung to the standards of living to which he had become accustomed, to his security—and he lost everything. We must not let this happen to us.

As I have said earlier, that does not mean Jesus necessarily calls every one of us to renounce all wealth. God may entrust wealth to some individuals who are to use it for His glory. But the rich young ruler's problem was not that he was wealthy, but that his wealth came before his commitment to Christ. Is there anything in your life that is keeping you from Him? If so, there is no shortcut—you must loosen your grip on it before you can reach out to Christ.

In a baccalaureate address at a theological seminary, a visiting minister looked down on a large graduating class. He knew firsthand the struggle every student would have at making enough money to live in the vocation of the Christian ministry. So, instead of a formal sermon he used an offering plate and passed out a newly minted dollar bill to each member of the class. Then, to this startled crowd who had never taken from an offering plate before, he told the story of the rich young man. Because of this power of the dollar in his life, he missed the priceless opportunity. "Frame this dollar," the baccalaureate speaker suggested. "Hang it up in your office or home. And write across the face of it, 'Remember the rich young man.' "

That speaker knew the power for good or evil that money could be in our lives. Once we really discover that all our resources are His, then we are free to spend them on others. They are God's gift to us. They are simply tools God has given us to aid Him in proclaiming His love and mercy.

The rich young man clung to God's resources believing they were his, and in clinging he lost his way to life eternal. If only he had shared his possessions; if he had trusted God for his future, he would have found life everlasting.

As the fourth horseman rides we must not forget the rich young man, for if ever a nation could be compared to him, it is the Western world at this time. By continuing on in waste and self-indulgence and rejecting God's plan of salvation, we risk losing not just our homes and the earth, but for millions the "life everlasting" in heaven, which Christ has gone to make ready for those who have been born again. Meanwhile, Jesus taught those who are His: "Give, and it will be given to you. A good measure, pressed down, shaken together and running over, will be poured into your lap. For with the measure you use, it will be measured to you" (Luke 6:38).

Physical and Spiritual Death—and Hell

In Revelation we learn that the rider who brings death will strike down one-fourth of the world's population. In the preceding section, I have examined the instruments of death he holds in his hands. Whether we die from one of these terrible judgments that God is going to allow to fall upon the earth really is not the question.

When Isaac was an old man he told his children, "I am now an old man and don't know the day of my death" (Genesis 27:2).

None of us knows the day of our death. We do not know exactly how we will die. But we do know one thing: we are all sentenced to death, and we are all going to have to face the judgment. The writer of Ecclesiastes said, "There is . . . a time to be born and a time to die" (Ecclesiastes 3:1, 2). Achilles' mother was told if she dipped him in a river, he would be invulnerable to all wounds. She dipped him in the river, holding him by the heel. He won many battles. Finally he died of an arrow wound which had struck his heel. That story says to us that we all try to find ways to escape the many dangers of life and death itself, but one day each of us will die.

Newsweek recently ran a cover story entitled, "Living with Death." At the moment there's a rash of best sellers on death. Death is tragic because of its finality—the terror of separation, the breaking of ties, the loss of and severance from things we love. We do not like to leave family and friends behind. Death ushers in so much uncertainty, terror and fear of the unknown. People never like to be unprepared. Many are anxious about the future. Thus we want to soften the reality of death. We don't want to talk about it. We don't want to think about it. Millions are spent on cosmetics, face-lifts and a frantic search for the mythical fountain of youth. The apostle Paul calls death "an enemy." Death was the penalty for sin. God said: If you break my moral law, "you will surely die." Man broke the Law and the judgment after man's rebellion was "dust you are and to dust you will return" (Genesis 3:19).

The Scripture emphatically teaches that all humans carry in themselves a death sentence: but that's not the end. "Man is destined to die once, and after that to face judgment" (Hebrews 9:27). Here we have a picture of physical death and after that the judgment. Here is the pale horse with Hades riding just behind him. Because of Adam and Eve's sin in the Garden of Eden, man suffers three deaths: *physical, spiritual* and *eternal.* In 1 Corinthians 15:21, 22, 26, 55–57 we read: "For since death came through a man, the resurrection of the dead comes also through a man. For as in Adam all die, so in Christ all will be made alive. . . . The last enemy to be destroyed is death. . . . 'Where, O death, is your victory? Where, O death, is your sting?' The sting of death is sin, and the power of sin is the law. But thanks be to God! He gives us the victory through our Lord Jesus Christ."

Jesus Christ came for the purpose of abolishing death, suffering, social injustice and oppression from this earth. He came to forgive us our sins and to give us the assurance of eternal life. At this very moment He is preparing a place for us who know Him (John 14:1–3). Meanwhile He bequeaths the gift of everlasting life which "has now been revealed through the appearing of our Savior, Christ Jesus, who has destroyed death and has brought life and immortality to light through the gospel" (2 Timothy 1:10). In Hebrews 2:14, 15 we are assured "that by his death he might destroy him who holds the power of death [that is, the devil] and free those who all their lives were held in slavery by their fear of death." Not only is He going to eliminate death, He is going to remove forever the devil who is the cause of suffering and death.

Thank God, the power of this great enemy of mankind, "death," has been broken. The last enemy to be destroyed or nullified is death (1 Corinthians 15:26). That is what Jesus Christ did on the cross. God raised Him from the dead. Now those of us who put our faith in Him can say with Saint Francis of Assisi, "Oh thou most kind and gentle death." Paul exclaimed: "Where, O death, is your victory? Where, O death, is your sting?" (1 Corinthians 15:55). By the death and resurrection of Christ we can read with joy and certainty, "I am the Living One; I was dead, and behold I am alive for ever and ever! And I hold the keys of death and Hades" (Revelation 1:18).

For the unbeliever, death is solemn and terrible. The unbeliever goes immediately to await the Great-White-Throne Judgment. One cannot read the Bible and miss the references to hell. They are unmistakable in the teachings of Christ Himself. For every time He spoke of heaven, He spoke of hell several times. To be in hell is to be out of the presence of God.

Three words are used by Jesus to describe hell. First, *fire*. "For our God is a consuming fire" (Hebrews 12:29). Jesus used this symbol over and over. I believe that it means a thirst for God that is never quenched. The second word that is used is *darkness*.

The Scripture teaches that God is light (1 John 1:5). Hell will be the opposite: "but the subjects of the kingdom will be thrown outside, into the darkness" (Matthew 8:12). Those who have rejected Christ will be separated from this light and subsist in eternal darkness. The third word is *death*. God is life. Therefore hell is separation from the life of God. "Then death and Hades were thrown into the lake of fire. The lake of fire is the second death" (Revelation 20:14). God takes no delight in people going to hell. He never meant that anyone would ever go to hell. He created hell for the devil and his angels.

But if we persist in going the devil's way and obeying the devil instead of God, we are going to end up there. The Scripture says that God's desire is that all men should be saved. The death of Christ was a judgment. God laid on Him the iniquity of us all (Isaiah 53:6). He bore our judgment. He bore our hell. In that brief span of time, He endured hell for every person who ever lived. All we have to do is put our trust and confidence in Him.

But we have a responsibility to accept His free gift of salvation. We are not automatically saved just because Christ died for us; the Bible does not support universalism (the idea that all people will be saved). You personally must make your decision for Christ, and if you refuse to do so you are, in a sense, already making a decision—the decision to reject Him and turn your back on His salvation.

For the true believer in Christ, one who has repented of sin and has been born from above, the judgment is past. There will be no hell. There will be no eternal death. Christ died for our sins and by His death He destroyed death. In Christ, we no longer regard death as the king of terrors. Paul wrote, "I desire to depart and be with Christ, which is better by far" (Philippians 1:23). Why? Was it because he worked so hard for Christ and had suffered so much? No! He was ready because half a lifetime earlier he had met Christ on the Damascus road. In 1 John 3:14 we read that we have already "passed from death to life." You can have eternal life *now*. The conquest of death is the ultimate goal of Christianity. Physical death is a mere transition from life on earth with Christ to eternal life in heaven with Christ. For Christians there is such a thing as the shadow of death. Death casts a shadow over those who are left behind.

Dr. Donald Grey Barnhouse was a prince among American Presbyterian clergymen. I knew him well. He died a few years ago. His first wife had died from cancer while still in her thirties. All three of his children were under twelve. He had such victory that he decided to preach the funeral sermon himself. En route to the funeral they were overtaken by a large truck which, as it passed them, cast a large shadow over their car. He asked one of his children, "Would you rather be run over by that truck or its shadow?" "By the shadow, of course!" replied the twelve-year-old daughter. "A shadow can't hurt you." With that answer, Dr. Barnhouse said to his three motherless little children, "Your mother has been overrun not by death, but by the shadow of death." At the funeral he spoke on Psalm 23: "Even though I walk through the valley of the shadow of death, I will fear no evil, for you are with me."

An unbeliever only sees a hopeless end to life. But the Christian sees an endless hope. In a network television program Malcolm Muggeridge reflected that a true Christian "is longing for the termination of life in time as one longs for the end of a long and arduous three-week sea voyage when one is in the last three days. I look forward to the time when my life will partake of eternity with near irrepressible eagerness."

Perhaps these words of Malcolm Muggeridge do not describe your feelings about death. Perhaps you are afraid of death and don't relate to the quiet confidence this famous British journalist and TV personality feels. The torturing, tormenting fear of death is a condition that is perfectly normal for any who have never come to Christ. Death is an experience from which people instinctively shrink. Yet for the Christian the fear is removed. He has the assurance that the sins for which he would be judged at death have been dealt with, whereas the non-Christian has no such assurance. I do not look forward to the prospect of dying—but I do look forward to death itself. It will be a glorious release. It will be the fulfillment of everything I have ever longed for. The Scripture says, "In thy presence is fulness of joy; at thy right hand there are pleasures for evermore" (Psalm 16:11, KJV).

Many non-Christians try to convince themselves that they believe neither in the supernatural, nor in the hereafter. Try as they will, there lingers the nagging, irrepressible realization that we have not been created just for time. We instinctively know that justice alone demands some judgment day. Unless we have knowingly settled the question of our sinful guilt, we are chronically beset by this fear. Until you acknowledge this fact, your fears will worsen. If you admit the possibility of the supernatural and acknowledge the facts of the gospel as they apply to your own life, you would find the fear of death removed and the glorious peace of believing a part of your life.

Lord Byron, who early in life abandoned himself to the pursuit of pleasure, a year before he died wrote, "My days are in the yellow leaf;/The flowers and fruits of love are gone;/The worm, the canker, and the grief/Are mine alone." I cannot help but contrast him with Adam Clarke, whose commentaries on the Bible are used throughout the world. At age eighty-four he said, "I have passed through the springtime of my life. I have withstood the heat of the summer. I have culled the fruits of the fall. I am even now enduring the rigors of its winter, but at no great distance I see the approach of a new eternal springtime. Hallelujah!"

Death will be a wonderful and glorious adventure for those who are prepared for it, but not for all. The fear of death is a fear that many have, but they suppress their fear by refusing to think or speak about it. Consequently, they never solve the problem. The Bible clearly warns us to "prepare to meet your God" (Amos 4:12), and that means to meet Him in judgment. It is because one is not prepared that he has fears. The Bible says that "the sting of death is sin" (1 Corinthians 15:56), and until we settle the sin problem, death remains something to be properly feared. The Bible answer to that is to repent of sin and receive Christ as Savior and Lord. With the sin problem settled, death will have no sting and most of its fears will be gone.

You can have peace in your heart and the personal and perennial assurance of salvation if you will humbly acknowledge yourself as a sinner in God's sight, ask for His forgiveness and cleansing by the blood of Christ shed on the cross, and trust in Jesus, God's Son, as your Savior and Lord. Christ died to do all this. Let me urge you to get a Bible and read, or ask someone to help you read the following verses: Romans 3:12, Romans 3:23, 2 Timothy 3:5, Romans 3:19, Ephesians 2:8, Luke 19:10, Romans 5:8, Hebrews 7:25, Romans 10:13 and Romans 10:9, 10. These are not magic verses. They simply tell us about our need and how to find that need met in Jesus Christ. You do not have to do some wonderful thing to be saved. All you have to do is to accept the wonderful thing Christ has done for you. After you have this assurance in your heart, tell other people about it. Also, show by your daily life that Christ has changed you for His own glory.

The fourth horseman, Death and Hades, rides across our horizons even while you read this page. How will you respond? Will you hear the hoofbeats in time? Will you vote for life or will you give in to death? The pale horse and its riders are God's warning to you, to give your life to Christ—and then to give your life to help others spiritually and physically.

11

Hope
in the
Holocaust

Suddenly, somewhere in the heaven above Patmos, the vision changes. The Lamb opens the fifth seal and John witnesses a spectacle of such poignant grandeur that it has staggered readers of Revelation for almost 2,000 years. Picture it. The four horsemen have ridden past John on their journey of warning across the planet. As the fifth seal is severed, the sound of countless voices is heard.

John must have gasped at the sight God then revealed to him. In a place the writer calls simply "under the altar," he saw "the souls of those who had been slain because of the word of God and the testimony they had maintained" (Revelation 6:9). They are crying out their loud complaint in one voice! "How long, Sovereign Lord, holy and true, until you judge the inhabitants of the earth and avenge our blood?" (Revelation 6:10).

Westminster Abby in London and St. Peter's Basilica in Rome have great altars with marble crypts beneath them. Imagine such a church at midnight. All is quiet. The tombs of the saints and martyrs lie sealed as they have for centuries. Suddenly, coffins spring open, seals break, stones roll away and hundreds, maybe thousands, of spirits pour into the cathedral, all crying out with one voice, "How long, Sovereign Lord? How long until we are avenged?" John was witness to just such a vision. Now the scene was packed with the souls of men and women who had died because they were faithful. They were asking the obvious question. When would justice be done? When would they be relieved? When would their faith be rewarded?

It is the question everyone asks; yet no one but God Himself can answer it. Then, as now, God was silent. If John could have seen God's face at that instant, what would he have seen? What happened in the eyes of the saints and martyrs in that awful pause when the question hung on the air waiting for an answer? We do not know. It would not be appropriate to guess. All we do know for certain is this: When the commotion was subdued, each martyr was given a white robe and "they were told to wait a little longer, until the number of their fellow servants and brothers who were to be killed as they had been was completed" (Revelation 6:11).

We learn two important facts from this mysterious moment. First, there will be a point at the end of time when God will judge the inhabitants of the earth. Second, before that moment can come, other men and women equally dedicated to God and His kingdom will be martyred for the Word of God and for the testimony they will maintain.

Where Are We Going?

"What is the world coming to?" is another way the question has been asked. It is the question haunting people everywhere today. People pick up their morning newspapers, read the headlines and ask, "What is the world coming to?" Let them read John for God's reply. The 1960s were called "the decade of activism," the '70s "the 'me' decade." The '80s have been called "the decade of survival." As we have seen, many experts project that man will not live to see 2000. Millions of people all over the world are desperate to know what the future holds. There's a phenomenal rise in the sale of crystal balls and ouija boards. People everywhere eagerly study the signs of the zodiac. Spiritual mediums are prospering.

Computers are being used on a massive scale to try to predict the future.

But there is only one authoritative book in the world that *accurately predicts* what is going to happen in the future—and *that is the Bible*. This short vision in Revelation summarizes the Bible's promise of the future and how we are to prepare for it.

The Promise of the Future

Let me remind you of the promise. In the midst of the pessimism, gloom and frustration of this present hour there is one hope—the promise of Christ: "If I go and prepare a place for you, I will come back . . ." (John 14:3). He died on the cross for our sins; He was raised again; He ascended to heaven; then the Bible predicts that someday in the future He's going to return in triumph.

One day after His resurrection, He was talking to His disciples. "They asked him, 'Lord, are you at this time going to restore the kingdom to Israel?' He said to them: 'It is not for you to know the times or dates the Father has set by his own authority. But you will receive power when the Holy Spirit comes on you; and you will be my witnesses in Jerusalem, and in all Judea and Samaria, and to the ends of the earth'" (Acts 1:6–8). After He had said that, He was taken up from them. They watched His ascent and a cloud enveloped Him beyond their sight. I imagine that the disciples had tears streaming down their cheeks. Their faith was still small, and some of them probably had those nagging doubts that they would never see Him again in spite of His promises. They must have been looking intently into the sky, with a sense of loss and sadness as He was ascending. Then there appeared beside them two men dressed in white. " 'Men of Galilee,' they said, 'why do you stand here looking into the sky? This same Jesus, who has been taken from you into heaven, will come back in the same way you have seen him go into heaven'" (Acts 1:11).

The time of His return, Jesus had assured them, was a secret known only to His Father. However, indications as to when it will happen are foretold in various books of the Bible. In the ninth chapter of Daniel we are told that an angel brought the word to the prophet that God had appointed seventy weeks to His people and their holy city. There have been scores of books written about these seventy weeks, and I do not intend to spend time here discussing what they mean. I can only meditate, think and interpret as best I can. There are some things I believe we can know for certain about this and other prophetic passages; there are other passages where we must be more cautious, and sincere Bible scholars may disagree on some details where God has chosen not to speak as clearly concerning the future. But virtually everything has been fulfilled that was prophesied in the Scriptures leading up to the coming of Christ. We know His coming is near!

What needs to be noted here is that the angel did say something to Daniel that relates to the four horsemen: "War will continue until the end, and desolations have been decreed" (Daniel 9:26). This gives us a clear clue to the whole history not only of the Middle East, but of the past several thousand years of the human race. It has been a great battleground and a scene of unfulfilled dreams, dashed hopes, broken hearts, mutilated bodies—thousands of battlefields on which hundreds of millions have died.

The Hope of His Coming

The promised coming of the Lord has been the great hope of true believers down through the centuries. Emil Brunner once said, "What oxygen is to the lungs, such is hope to the meaning of life." Some years ago in a Telstar discussion, Lord Montgomery asked General Eisenhower, "Can you give any hope?" Mr. Eisenhower prescribed a way out, "which if man misses," he said, "would lead to Armageddon." Winston Churchill's favorite American song was, "The Battle Hymn of the Republic," which begins with the stirring phrase, "Mine eyes have seen the glory of the coming of the Lord."

The great creeds of the church teach that Christ is coming back. The Nicene Creed states that "He shall come again with glory to judge both the living and the dead." Charles Wesley wrote 7,000 hymns, and in 5,000 he mentioned the coming of Christ. When Queen Elizabeth II was crowned by the Archbishop of Canterbury, he laid the crown on her head with the sure pronouncement, "I give thee, O sovereign lady, this crown to wear until He who reserves the right to wear it shall return."

But till that time, one of America's best-known columnists summed it up when he said, "For us all, the world is disorderly and dangerous; ungoverned, and apparently ungovernable." The question arises: Who will restore order? Who can counter the danger of the nuclear holocaust? Who alone can govern the world? The answer is Jesus Christ!

A Promise for This Planet

The psalmist asked centuries earlier: "Why do the nations rage and the peoples plot in vain? The kings of the earth take their stand and the rulers gather together against the Lord and against his Anointed One. 'Let us break their chains,' they say, 'and throw off their fetters.' The One enthroned in heaven laughs; the Lord scoffs at them. Then he rebukes them in his anger and terrifies them in his wrath, saying, 'I have installed my King'" (Psalm 2:1–6). He promises the Anointed One, "I will make the nations your inheritance, the ends of the earth your possession. You will rule them with an iron scepter. . . . Therefore, you kings, be wise; be warned, you rulers of the earth. Serve the Lord with fear and rejoice with trembling" (Psalm 2:8–11). Then He advises the whole earth, "Blessed are all who take refuge in him" (v. 12).

Yes, God has promised this planet to His Son, Jesus Christ, and someday it will be His. He will bring an end to all the injustice, the oppression, the wars, the crime, the terrorism that dominate our newspapers and television screens today. *But before that time comes,* four horsemen are going to gallop across the pages of history.

For the Christian believer, the return of Christ is comforting, for at last men and women of faith will be exonerated. They will be avenged. The nonbeliever will see and understand why true Christians marched to the sound of another drum. But for the sinful unbeliever, the triumphant return of Christ will prove disastrous—for Christ's return ensures final judgment.

211

The Final Judgment

Consider what happened next in John's vision above Patmos that day. In it you will get a feeling for the absolute horror of this final judgment for those who do not believe. Picture it. Carefully the Lamb opens the sixth seal (Revelation 6:12–17). Suddenly, chaos grips the universe. An earthquake shakes the entire world, no Richter scale could measure its fury. There is a complete eclipse of the sun. In fact, reports John, "the sun turned black . . . the whole moon turned blood red, and the stars in the sky fell to earth, as late figs drop from a fig tree when shaken by a strong wind" (Revelation 6:12, 13).

The world is trembling with terror. The great cities collapse. John sees kings, princes, generals; the rich, the mighty, slave and free—every human being left on the earth running to escape the horror of God's final judgment. They flee to mountain caves. They cower behind rocks and boulders. But there is no escape. Desperately they cry out, "Hide us from the face of him who sits on the throne and from the wrath of the Lamb! For the great day of their wrath has come, and who can stand?" (Revelation 6:16, 17).

There will be a day of reckoning when God closes His books on time and judges every creature, living and dead. This vision of the judgments leading to the final judgment permeates the sixty-six books of the Holy Scripture. Before John's vision it was called the "day of wrath" (Zephaniah 1:15, Romans 2:5). Amos, the Old Testament prophet, called it "the day of the Lord" (Amos 5:18), as did Jesus' own disciple, Peter (2 Peter 3:10). Paul, again and again, called it "the day of our Lord Jesus Christ" (1 Corinthians 1:8, Philippians 1:6). It is often referred to as the Great Tribulation.

All through history there have been days of judgment. The first judgment of God fell on Adam and Eve at the beginning of time (Genesis 3:16–19). Their original sin brought God's "day of wrath" and a permanent curse on all who followed. God judged Cain. God judged the descendants of Cain with the flood that Noah escaped. Other judgments include the confusing of tongues at Babel, the fiery destruction of Sodom and Gomorrah, the captivity and dispersion of the Israelites.

The New Testament record makes the final judgment clear. In the wilderness outside Jerusalem, John the Baptist warned of the coming judgment. He instructed those who would hear that true repentance is the only way to escape the Judgment Day. Then came Jesus Himself. He, too, spoke of the final judgment—often in the language of fields and harvest. "At that time," our Lord warned, "I will tell the harvesters: First collect the weeds and tie them in bundles to be burned, then gather the wheat and bring it into my barn" (Matthew 13:30).

At another place, Jesus met a Jewish teacher and explained the judgment to him. "For God did not send his Son into the world to condemn the world," Jesus informed the man, "but to save the world through him" (John 3:17). Then He made perfectly clear how one can be saved from the wrath of God's judgment. "Whoever believes in him is not condemned, but whoever does not believe stands condemned already because he has not believed in the name of God's one and only Son" (John 3:18). The man who does not believe dooms himself to the judgment.

My wife and I are parents. When our children disobeyed our family rules, it was necessary to correct them. Where there is no judgment, there is no justice. We didn't like reprimanding the children. To the contrary, we hated it. We loved them, and it hurt us to see them suffer. But simply to allow them to get by with those acts which were destructive to them in the long run would not have been good parenting. It would have been soft, uncaring parenting. We threatened judgment for their own good. We carried out the judgment for the same cause.

I know a wealthy family whose oldest son was exposed to the drug culture during his senior year of high school. At a party the boy snorted lines of cocaine with his rich friends. The father found out and confronted his son. Carefully he explained the risks of drug use, especially cocaine. He took the boy to the library periodical files and they read together the stories of lives ruined by drug habits begun at similar high-school parties. But the teenager laughed at his father's "old-fashioned" ideas. So, hoping to prevent his son from further experiments with cocaine, the father threatened the boy with a day of judgment. "If you try it again," he warned, "you will be grounded and your car will be parked in the garage."

Still the boy disobeyed. The father discovered his son's disobedience and called a day of judgment. The son was grounded. His car was taken from him. All this was motivated by a desire to help the son—to save him from the horror of drug addiction. But nothing worked; the son continued using cocaine in college. Knowing of the son's growing addiction, his parents refused to supply funds to maintain the habit. Instead, they worked and prayed and telephoned. They poured out love to their son. They begged him to come home for treatment and offered to pay all the expenses for a drug rehabilitation program in a local hospital. The son ridiculed their fears and ignored their warnings. He began to steal to pay for the expensive drugs. Then, one Saturday night, he was shot and killed in the attempted robbery of an all-night liquor store.

That young man brought judgment on himself. Like God, the parents threatened judgment not to condemn him but to save him. Still, the son's disobedience frustrated the purposes of the father and brought even worse judgment on himself. Death came, not because of the father, but through the son's disobedience.

As God, our loving Father, looks on, we, His disobedient children, continue to disobey. It would not be *just* for Him to let our sins go unpunished. Justice requires judgment. But God loves us and works to save us from the results of our own disobedience. In His Word, God has repeatedly warned us of the coming judgment. He has offered us the way of escape through repentance of sin and faith in Christ His Son. He has sent harbingers like the four horsemen to sound the alarm, to awaken us from our deadly sleep, to point us in the right direction, to get us on the trail again. There is a final judgment coming, but God hates that day and continues to postpone it that the world might be saved.

A God of Mercy and Justice

But we fool ourselves if we think our God will hold back His judgment forever. He will not. God *is* a God of love. We sing, "Jesus loves me; this I know, for the Bible tells me so," when we are children. We sing, "Love lifted me," as adults. And we must never forget that God loves us more than we can ever begin to realize—God is a God of mercy. But we must remember as well that He is also a God of justice. He is a consuming fire. Nothing we have ever seen or heard compares to the holiness of God. He is absolutely pure. Our purest thoughts are ugly in the sight of God compared to His purity. Like the woman in clean, white clothing who looks gray and faded when standing in the new-fallen snow, man's attempts at holiness are as filthy rags compared to God's purity. He can never change. He cannot look upon evil. Evil is the enemy, and those who ignore God's warning and continue to be allied with evil will be judged.

Still He has done and continues to do everything He can to save us from that Judgment Day. We have already referred to Jonah, who preached to the people of Nineveh—a very idolatrous and wicked people. Like the four horsemen, this reluctant prophet warned the people of God's day of judgment. And the king and all the people obeyed; they repented in sackcloth and ashes. Estimates of the number of those who confessed their sins through Jonah's preaching range from 300,000 to 2½ million souls. It was probably the largest spiritual awakening in history.

The Result of Repentance

Because Nineveh repented, God changed His mind. He spared them, withheld His hand of judgment. In fact, judgment did not fall on Nineveh for 150 years. In other words, the judgment was slowed down for several generations until the people became wicked again. Then Nineveh was destroyed by invading armies. Then came God's day of judgment.

Huldah, the prophetess, was told by the Lord to send a message to the people of Judah that judgment was going to fall, "This is what the Lord says: I am going to bring disaster on this place and its people . . ." (2 Kings 22:16). However, the message to the king himself was different (v. 19, 20), "Because your heart was responsive and you humbled yourself before the Lord when you heard what I have spoken against this place and its people, that they would become accursed and laid waste, and because you tore your robes and wept in my presence, I have heard you, declares the Lord. Therefore I will gather you to your fathers, and you will be buried in peace. Your eyes will not see all the disaster I am going to bring on this place."

I believe the judgment of God can be withheld for a period of time. It doesn't even take the repentance of a whole city to delay God's judgment plans. Abraham was granted a delay if he could find a mere ten righteous men in Sodom. Still, the Judgment Day is coming. The distant sounds of the four horsemen grow louder every day. How long will God postpone the judgment? We do not know. But we do know from this wonderful vision of John what we believers must do in the meantime. Those who have died in Christ must patiently wait for that day. Those of us still alive in Christ must continue working as God's allies in the salvation of the lost and in social justice.

Again, remember John's vision. The saints "under the altar" were instructed to wait longer until their brothers and sisters in the faith "who were to be killed" would join them. The martyrs and the saints had been killed because of the Word of God and the testimony they had faithfully maintained. When we hold up the Word of God, when we maintain our testimony faithfully, we too will suffer. Some of us will die.

We must not be content with easy answers. The call to follow Christ is not easy. It is easy to receive salvation—but there can never be "cheap grace." Our redemption by the Cross of Jesus was costly to God. So also we must be willing to deny self and take up a cross and follow Christ. It is not easy to follow Him. It is not easy to decide what tasks you can do and what tasks you must leave for others. It is not easy to take a stand when issues are complex and two-sided. It is not always easy to witness for Him. It is not easy to work against evil that judgment might be postponed, but it is the task to which we all are called.

Listen! It is the distant sound of horsemen. They ride in our direction. As Christians, we must maintain our testimony. We must take our stand and be God's people—even unto death.

This is why the Bible's prophecies are in such stark contrast with the synthetic predictions of the computer. The Bible takes human nature into account. The Bible prophesies a swift descent into lawlessness and world chaos so shocking that only God Himself can intervene and save the human race. With his mind illuminated by the Holy Spirit, the apostle Paul predicted that "the final age of this world is to be a time of troubles. Men will love nothing but money and self; they will be arrogant, boastful, and abusive; with no respect for parents, no gratitude, no piety, no natural affection; they will be implacable in their hatreds, scandal-mongers, intemperate and fierce, strangers to all goodness, traitors, adventurers, swollen with self-importance" (2 Timothy 3:1-4, NEB).

Such people, he said, will not long enjoy the fruits of their scientific attainments, however marvelous. He predicted in 2 Thessalonians 2:10, "Destroyed they shall be, because they did not open their minds to love of the truth, so as to find salvation" (NEB).

When Christ was asked by His disciples, "What will be the sign of your coming and of the end of the age?" He replied along the same line. Instead of picturing a future filled with scientific achievements amid an era of perpetual peace, He foretold an endless sequence of disorder and tragedy until He, Himself would return to bring it to an end. He said, "Nation will rise against nation, and kingdom against kingdom. There will be great earthquakes, famines and pestilences in various places" (Luke 21:10, 11). The Bible teaches that there will be no break in the chain of sorrows and disasters that will afflict the human race until they see "the Son of Man coming in a cloud with power and great glory" (Luke 21:27).

Warning Before Culmination

Before judgment falls, however, God always warns. He warned the people of Sodom before destruction came. He warned the people of Nineveh before judgment came. He warned the people of Jerusalem before destruction came. And He warned the people of Noah's day before destruction came.

Now what happened in Noah's day will be repeated at the end of history. We have the word of Jesus who said, "As it was in the days of Noah, so it will be at the coming of the Son of Man" (Matthew 24:37). The two experiences will run parallel in many important aspects—not only in the vast extent of lawlessness and the universality of catastrophe, but also in the earnestness of warning and the provision of a way of escape. At God's bidding, Noah preached for 120 years. During that time he warned the people to repent of their sins and turn to God, but the people laughed and sneered. Then, as time ran out, astonishing things began to happen. Clouds appeared in the sky for the first time. Animals began to gather. The rain came. Jesus said, "The flood came and destroyed them all" (Luke 17:27).

Something just as devastating and just as global in its effects is going to happen again, unless man repents.

The apostle Peter wrote, "In the last days mockers will undoubtedly come—men whose only guide in life is what they want for themselves—and they will say: 'What has happened to his promised coming? Since the first Christians fell asleep, everything remains exactly as it was since the beginning of creation!' " (2 Peter 3:3, 4, Phillips).

But Peter warned, "The day of the Lord will come as suddenly and unexpectedly as a thief. In that day the heavens will disappear in a terrific tearing blast; the very elements will disintegrate in heat and the earth and all that is in it will be burned up to nothing" (v. 10).

Before all of these terrifying things take place, the Bible indicates there will be a turning away from the true faith on the part of many who profess Christ, as well as much social and political unrest all over the world.

Global Preaching

However, Jesus also said another interesting thing that I have already elaborated on. He said this: "This gospel of the kingdom will be preached in the whole world as a testimony to all nations, and then the end will come" (Matthew 24:14). Today, for the first time in history, we are witnessing the preaching of the gospel on a global scale such as the world has never known—using radio, the printed page, television. It's one of the signs that we are to look for as we approach the end of history. The Bible teaches that there is deliverance from the things that are about to come upon the world for those who put their faith and trust in Jesus Christ.

Not by chemicals, but by Christ. Not by swallowing psychedelic drugs on a piece of sugar, but by bringing the mind and heart into harmony with God through submission to His will and accepting His forgiveness as offered from the cross. In Christ alone there is deliverance from man's tortured thoughts, healing for his weakened mind and body, and freedom from the sordid, ridiculous habits which are destroying many people.

But more important, there is hope for the future. The Bible teaches that God has planned utopia. There *is* a glorious new social order coming, but it is going to be brought by Jesus Christ Himself when He comes back. Jesus said, "So you also must be ready, because the Son of Man will come at an hour when you do not expect him" (Matthew 24:44). Are you ready?

12

The Grand
Finale

There is definitely a "mystery of iniquity" attached to the four horses in chapter 6 of Revelation. We may not fully understand everything that will happen when they come upon the earth. But Revelation does not end with chapter 6! For John points us in chapter 19 to another horse and rider—One who rides to bring the kingdom of God in all its fullness to earth. Like the first horse in chapter 6, this horse is white. But there the resemblance ends, for the rider of this horse is Jesus Christ Himself, coming in glory and power to the earth.

Let us see what the aged apostle is trying to tell us in the account of the rider on the white horse in Revelation 19. Chapters 7 to 18 deal with that catastrophic saga of history, perhaps just ahead, about which Jesus insisted we are to make no mistake, when "there will be great distress, unequaled from the beginning of the world until now—and never to be equaled again. If those days had not been cut short, no one would survive, but for the sake of the elect those days will be shortened" (Matthew 24:21, 22). It will be a time of nuclear conflagrations, biological holocausts and chemical apocalypses rolling over the earth, bringing man to the edge of the precipice. History will "bottom out" in the battle of Armageddon. We already see its shadow creeping over the earth.

Will man exterminate himself? He *almost* will, as Jesus stated. But just before man does so, Christ will come back! The demonized leaders "of the whole world" will have mobilized both as antagonists and protagonists of that coming world anti-God system—probably headed by the Antichrist. They'll be "gathered," we're told, "together to the place that in Hebrew is called Armageddon" (Revelation 16:16).

Franklin D. Roosevelt spoke of "the war to end all wars," and now Ellen Goodman, the columnist, speaks of a possible ominous war ahead, "to end all life." *It won't happen.* God has other plans for the human race! Life is not going to be brought to a catastrophic end. God's intervention will see to that.

Everywhere I go, people ask, "Are you an optimist or a pessimist?" My reply is that I'm an unswerving optimist. In the words of Robert Browning, "The best is yet to be." I believe that, too, and in the final pages of this book I want to explain why.

It is estimated that forty wars are going on somewhere in the world at any given time. Any one of them could be the beginning of "the beginning of the end!"

So we have to ask: Can paradise be restored? Is there light at the end of the tunnel? As the late Sir Winston Churchill asked a young American clergyman thirty years ago, "Young man, can you give me any hope?"

Back to the Bible

For the answer to Churchill's question, I take you into the future by going back to the Bible.

In Revelation 19:10–13 the ancient apostle writes, " 'The testimony of Jesus is the spirit of prophecy.' I saw heaven standing open and there before me was a white horse, whose rider is called Faithful and True. With justice he judges and makes war. His eyes are like blazing fire, and on his head are many crowns. He has a name written on him that no one but he himself knows. He is dressed in a robe dipped in blood, and his name is the Word of God."

So the four horses of the Apocalypse of Revelation 6 have gone on before. Other judgments have fallen. Now God is about to make His final move. The identity of the rider on the white horse in Revelation 19 is the Lord Jesus Christ, Israel's Messiah, head of the church, the King of Kings and Lord of Lords. The white horse of deception in Revelation 6 darkens into a dirty gray in comparison to the impeccable, immaculate white horse here in Revelation 19. Whereas the red horse in Revelation 6 inflicts war to kill and defoliate, this white horse, with the mounted "King of Kings" draped in a robe dipped in blood, declares war on the killers—to establish His kingdom of salvation and peace. Whereas the black horse of Revelation 6 carries famine and disease, the white horse of Revelation 19 brings healing and the Bread of Life. And whereas the pale horse of Revelation 6 brings death and hell, the white horse of chapter 19 brings life and heaven to all who place their faith in Him.

When will the Man on the white horse, as outlined in Revelation 19, appear? The clear teaching of the Word of God is that He will come when man has sunk to his lowest and most perilous point in all history—the time when the four horses of the Apocalypse, with their mounted riders, have run their course and pushed man to the very edge of the precipice. There is an eerie feeling throughout society today that concurs with the late Dr. Albert Schweitzer, who lamented, "Man has lost the capacity to foresee and to forestall. He will end by destroying the earth." Left to himself, that is precisely what man would do. Barbra Streisand put her finger on the problem; she is reported in *Esquire* as having said, "I do believe the world is coming to an end. I just feel that science, technology and the mind have surpassed the soul—the heart. There is no balance in terms of feeling and love for fellow-man."

Who is better qualified to make a statement on this theme than the dean of behaviorists, Harvard's B. F. Skinner? At 78, Skinner shocked the American Psychological Association Convention (1982) by asking in understandable anger and anguish, "Why are we not acting to save the world? Is there to be much more history at all?" Asked afterward, "Has the observer of social conditioning lost his optimism?" his reply was, "I have. . . . When I wrote *Beyond Freedom and Dignity*, I was optimistic about the future. A decade ago there was hope, but today the world is fatally ill. . . . It is a very depressing way to end one's life. . . . The argument that we have always solved our problems in the past and shall, therefore, solve this one is like reassuring a dying man by pointing out that he has always recovered from his illness" (*Philadelphia Inquirer*, 25 September 1982).

Of War and Peace

In his article on "Psychology and Armageddon" in *Psychology Today* (May 1982) Harvard Professor of Psychiatry Dr. Robert Coles describes a prevailing feeling worldwide that mankind is heading for its final Armageddon. The gamble that man will have taken will be the worst in all history. The Antichrist or system will be a monstrous impostor, the incarnation of iniquity. And all people the world over will think and say, "We've been had!" As I wrote earlier in this book, there is coming a time in the future—whether near or far I do not know (since Jesus warned us not to speculate on dates), when a counterfeit world system or ruler will establish a false utopia for an extremely short time. The economic and political problems of the world will seem to be solved. But after a brief rule the whole thing will come apart. During this demonic reign tensions will mount, and once again the world will begin to explode with a ferocity involving conflict on an unparalleled scale. Even the grip of the world leaders will be unable to prevent it. This massive upheaval will be the world's last war—the battle of Armageddon.

According to secular and scientific writers, there is an inevitability to man's date with Armageddon. "Everybody who's anybody believes that global war is imminent," reckons Phil Surguy of *Today*.

Arming for Armageddon

If I were not a believer in Christ, I might at this point in history succumb to total pessimism. On 10 August 1982 Ellen Goodman wrote in her column that with "Armageddon perhaps around the corner, what are intelligent people to do? Wrap ourselves in mourning sheets and wait for the end?" Are we to stare up at that intimidating nuclear sword of Damocles that "has hung over us like some apocalypse without the promise of redemption?"

Emphatically not! Jesus urged that when universal holocaust begins "to take place, stand up and lift up your heads, because your redemption is drawing near" (Luke 21:28). Rather than pulling mourning sheets around us, we are to look for redemption in Christ. We are also to work as if these events are far in the future. Jesus promised a blessing on those who would be found working when their Lord returns.

I will not here deal with the who, what, why, how or when of Armageddon. But I know from a vast number of scriptures that Armageddon will be interrupted by the return of Jesus Christ on the white horse leading the armies of heaven, as clearly prophesied in many Bible passages. In no place is it more definitively or dramatically described than in Revelation 19. When John foresaw "heaven standing open and there before me was a white horse, whose rider is called Faithful and True," he went on to describe the rider as "the Word of God" followed by the armies of heaven "riding on white horses and dressed in fine linen, white and clean." Turning his focus back on the coming Messiah, John saw that "out of his mouth comes a sharp sword with which to strike down the nations. 'He will rule them with an iron scepter' " (Revelation 19:11–15). And in case anyone gets confused as to His identity or authority, John makes it unmistakably plain, "On his robe and on his thigh he has this name written: KING OF KINGS AND LORD OF LORDS" (Revelation 19:16).

The Man on the White Horse

What does the Man on the white horse do? John makes clear that He and His army from heaven are faced with the Antichrist and the military forces gathered together to make war not only against each other but against the armies of heaven. But the Antichrist is "captured, and with him the false prophet who had performed the miraculous signs on his behalf. With these signs he had deluded those who had received the mark of the beast and worshiped his image. The two of them were thrown alive into the fiery lake of burning sulfur" (Revelation 19:20). The Antichrist's collaborators and colleagues are all conquered by Jesus Christ.

Adolf Hitler's grandiose notion of Nazism was that he would aggrandize an imperialist empire over the entire earth, and that it would "last a thousand years." It didn't happen! *Time* (4 January 1982) points back to Mao Tse-tung's global "export of revolution" as an obsessive vision "to hasten the Communist millennium." Mao's aegis is gone, his vision already radically altered.

People may ask: Is John the only one who in this way made Christ's second coming to this earth so plain? No, the oldest extant quotation from all literature, to a Bible believer, has to be Jude 14 and 15. Jude cited "Enoch, the seventh from Adam, who prophesied that the Lord is coming with thousands upon .thousands of his holy ones to judge everyone" alive, including "all the ungodly." And the ungodliest man or system ever will be the Antichrist. Paul wrote to the Thessalonians, "The Lord Jesus will overthrow [that lawless one] with the breath of his mouth and destroy [him] by the splendor of his coming" (2 Thessalonians 2:8).

The Return of Jesus Christ

The return of Jesus Christ is the great assurance for the Christian. Seymour Siegel has commented, "The central problem of Christianity is: If the Messiah has come, why is the world so evil? For Judaism, the problem is: If the world is so evil, why does the Messiah not come?" The Messiah is coming to solve both dilemmas, and perhaps soon! Every devout orthodox Jewish worshiper prays every day, "I believe with complete faith in the coming of the Messiah. Even though He tarry, yet I will wait for Him every coming day."

The Scripture says, "The government will be on his shoulders. And he will be called Wonderful Counselor, Mighty God, Everlasting Father, Prince of Peace. Of the increase of his government and peace there will be no end. He will reign on David's throne and over his kingdom, establishing and upholding it with justice and righteousness from that time on and forever." (Isaiah 9:6, 7).

The late Arnold Toynbee of Cambridge foresaw that "only a world government can save mankind from annihilation by nuclear weapons." That's right! And Jesus Christ will be the King over all the earth in His theocratic world government.

Jonathan Schell's book *The Fate of the Earth* (which I have quoted several times in this book), envisages a day when "existing institutions must give way to some sort of transcendent sovereignty and security, presumably by a government that embraces all mankind," in fact "world government" (*Time*, 19 April 1982). That will happen when Christ returns.

What Happens to the Nuclear Monster?

And when Jesus Christ really does return to this earth with His saints to set up His kingdom, where He'll rule as King of Kings and Lord of Lords, what will happen to what remains of the uncounted weapons of mass destruction, such as nuclear weapons and the biological, chemical, laser and outer-space weaponry that is today increasingly stockpiled around the world? As I mentioned earlier, on a statue across from the United Nations building in New York is the inscription, "They will beat their swords into plowshares." Where did that quotation come from? From the Bible! In Micah 4, only one of many scriptural prophecies which deal with this catastrophic question, we read that the world's "nations will come and say, 'Come, let us go up to the mountain of the Lord, to the house [of the true God who] . . . will teach us his ways.' " As King of the world "He will judge between many peoples and will settle disputes for strong nations far and wide. They will beat their swords into plowshares and their spears into pruning hooks. Nation will not take up sword against nation, nor will they train for war any more. Every man will sit under his own vine and under his own fig tree, and no one will make them afraid, for the Lord Almighty has spoken" (vv. 2–4).

But in the long run the beating of our "swords into plowshares" is something Jesus Christ Himself, as King over all the earth, will effectively enact.

The King Is Coming!

As Bill and Gloria Gaither lyricized for the world to sing, indeed "The King Is Coming!" What was future tense for Isaac Watts will be present tense then—"Jesus shall reign, where'er the sun/doth his successive journeys run;/His kingdom spread from shore to shore;/till moons shall wax and wane no more." That precious promise makes life here exciting every moment, regardless of the circumstances.

The New Catholic Encyclopedia points out that the result of Christ's triumph over Antichrist and the forces of evil will be a reign of Jesus Christ and His saints of all the ages over an earth that will know unprecedented prosperity and peace. From time immemorial, man has longed for a combination of true law and order, of peace and prosperity, of freedom and fulfillment, of health and happiness, of godliness and longevity on this earth. It will happen when Christ comes again to set up His kingdom.

A New World Coming

There can be no new world under present conditions. Something dramatic has to happen to alter man and his world. That leaves us with only one absolute certainty about the future: Christ as the Prince of Peace, with the government upon His shoulders. The utopian dreams and schemes of the Platos, the Bellamys, the Owens and similar philosophers and idealists throughout history will all be fulfilled through His rule. That's the message of the God-Man on the white horse coming down out of heaven, which the apostle John foresaw and recorded in Revelation 19.

John Milton yearned for "Paradise Restored." I'm sure that for nearly a thousand years Adam longed to get back into the Garden of Eden, from which he was driven because of his sin. But he couldn't! Professor John Walvoord puts it concisely, "The longing for perfect government, righteousness, equity, economic prosperity, and deliverance from insecurity and fears which plague the modern world finds its answer in the Return of Christ and the establishment of His kingdom."

The Scriptures have a great deal to teach us about the world of the coming Christ. The Messiah will take complete charge of the peoples of the entire earth. He "will stand as a banner for the peoples; the nations will rally to him, and his place of rest will be glorious," assures Isaiah. "The Spirit of the Lord will rest on him—the Spirit of wisdom and of understanding, the Spirit of counsel and of power, the Spirit of knowledge and of the fear of the Lord." Throughout the world today people crave a society of peace and provision, but also one of goodness and justice. The Messiah Christ will implement all these, as "with righteousness he will judge the needy, with justice he will give decisions for the poor of the earth," as "righteousness will be his belt and faithfulness the sash around his waist." Will it work? Yes: "they will neither harm nor destroy . . . for the earth will be full of the knowledge of the Lord as the waters cover the sea" (Isaiah 11:10, 2–5, 9).

So transformed will the prevailing order be that even the animal world will be completely tamed: "The wolf will live with the lamb, the leopard will lie down with the goat, the calf and the lion and the yearling together; and a little child will lead them. The cow will feed with the bear, their young will lie down together, and the lion will eat straw like the ox. The infant will play near the hole of the cobra, and the young child put his hand into the viper's nest. They will neither harm nor destroy" is the promise of the coming King (Isaiah 11:6–9). This will be in complete contrast to the savage beasts, scavenger birds, devouring insects and raging diseases that have been among the most ferocious foes of primitive and civilized man from the Adamic to the atomic ages.

A Message from the Messiah

This leads me to contemplate from the Scriptures that future era under the reign of the Messiah. Sickness will be remedied by Christ, the great healer of nations. And He will remove all deformities and handicaps. At that time there'll be no designated spots on parking lots, or graduated ramps on buildings, for the handicapped. There will be no blindness, deafness, muteness, paralysis—no need for eyeglasses, hearing aids, speech therapy, wheelchairs, crutches, or white canes. "No one living," assures Isaiah (33:24), "will say, 'I am ill.'" "I will restore you to health and heal your wounds, declares the Lord" through Jeremiah (30:17). "Declares the Sovereign Lord" through Ezekiel (34:15, 16), "I will bind up the injured." "Be strong, do not fear; your God will come," prophesies Isaiah, and "then will the eyes of the blind be opened and the ears of the deaf unstopped. Then will the lame leap like a deer, and the tongue of the dumb shout for joy. Water will gush forth in the wilderness and streams in the desert. The burning sand will become a pool, the thirsty ground bubbling springs. In the haunts where jackals once lay, grass and reed and papyrus will grow. And a highway will be there; it will be called the Way of Holiness" (Isaiah 35:4-8).

"Surely the day is coming" prophesied Malachi (4:1, 2) in the last chapter of the Old Testament, when the peoples of the world will finally "revere my name, the sun of righteousness will rise with healing in its wings." And in the last chapter of the New Testament, we read that there will stand in that era "the tree of life, bearing twelve crops of fruit, yielding its fruit every month. And the leaves of the tree are for the healing of the nations. No longer will there be any curse." (Revelation 22:2, 3). "He will wipe every tear from their eyes. There will be no more death or mourning or crying or pain, for the old order of things has passed away" (Revelation 21:4).

Currently, as Paul wrote to the Romans (8:22, 18-21), "the whole creation has been groaning as in the pains of childbirth right up to the present time." But these "our present sufferings are not worth comparing with the glory that will be revealed," for the whole "creation waits in eager expectation for the sons of God to be revealed. For the creation was subjected to frustration, not by its own choice, but by the will of the one who subjected it, in hope that the creation itself will be liberated from its bondage to decay and brought into the glorious freedom of the children of God."

Our Vanishing Problems

We've had enormous controversies in and beyond the church, throughout the world, on birth control, abortion and euthanasia. These problems will all vanish as the curse on the earth is removed, and in place of thorns and thistles, drought and deserts, will be fruits and vegetables, fountains and fertility.

Rabbi Dr. Harvey Fields was so right recently to exclaim, partly from exasperation but mostly from expectation, "Without the Messiah, the human enterprise would crash into darkness forever." But thank God, the Messiah is coming. He saves individuals today. In the great tomorrow, He will remake all creation.

One day it *will* happen. The prophet Isaiah predicted, "The desert and the parched land will be glad; the wilderness will rejoice and blossom. Like the crocus, it will burst into bloom; it will rejoice greatly and shout for joy." Yes, the world will be like the "splendor of Carmel and Sharon; they will see the glory of the Lord, the splendor of our God" (Isaiah 35:1, 2).

A Pointed Invitation

With that kind of future ahead for believers, and beyond that in eternity with Christ and the believers of all the ages in a new heaven as well as a new earth, I could not finish a book like this without another pointed invitation to you as a reader to be absolutely sure that you are Christ's. And in feeling this way so strongly, I am only reflecting exactly the way the ancient apostle John felt. He simply could not conclude the Revelation of Jesus Christ without making the last six verses of his book one of the most compelling invitations to repent of sin and receive Jesus Christ as Savior and Lord to be found anywhere in the entire Bible.

"I, Jesus, have sent my angel to give you this testimony for the churches," is what we read in Revelation 22:16. Jesus Christ Himself wants John to make no mistake about it. After envisaging a panorama of scenes covering the past, the present and the future; after peering deep into the heavens, the earth and hell; after being introduced to God, to man all the way from his best to his worst

231

and to Satan himself—Jesus wants the last word! Why? Because, as we read in chapter 1 (v. 5), He is the one above all others "who loves us and has freed us from our sins by his blood" shed on the cross for our sins to purchase our pardon and peace. And He is, therefore, the One to whom we are ultimately as well as immediately answerable. Later in that first chapter (vv. 17, 18) He assured, "I am the First and the Last. I am the Living One, I was dead and behold I am alive forever and ever! And I hold the keys of death and Hades"—of hell itself!

In chapter 3 (v. 20) Jesus comes a step closer and declares, "Here I am! I stand at the door and knock. If anyone hears my voice and opens the door, I will go in and eat with him, and he with me." Jesus is saying to you, right now, that if you have never admitted Him as Savior and Lord into your life, you not only vitally *need* to do so now, you *can* do so now! Many say, "There is no need." But the goodness of God should lead to repentance. When, however, difficulties and heartaches come into your life, God can use those "hard knocks" to show you your need of Christ in every circumstance. It may be a business disappointment, a reverse in your love life, a broken marriage, a tragic bereavement, a hopelessly severed or even strained relationship between you and a parent or child. It could be the gradual or rapid deterioration of your own health. Whatever your disappointment, it's His appointment!

So He's knocking at your heart's door, just as when there's a knock on the door of your home. You may open the door and invite the individual on the threshold in to share in your hospitality and friendship. Or you may indeed simply ignore the knock. It's that way with Jesus knocking at your heart's door. Right now, you can bow your head on an airplane, in a jail—in an office, in a hotel, in a hospital, or in your home, and you can open your heart to Christ by a simple prayer of faith.

So we have this good news made possible in the past by Christ's everlasting love and death on the cross for us. And we have His knocking at our heart's door in the present, seeking possession of our lives, not only for our eternal benefit, but—incredibly—for His also. He wants to "show us off" to the rest of the universe as an example of what His grace can do. Then, in chapter four (v. 1) we are shown the future, invited through John's eyes to look ahead: "And there before me was a door standing open in heaven. And the voice I had first heard speaking to me like a trumpet said, 'Come up here, and I will show you what must take place after this.'" And Jesus gives us a preview of the heaven He has gone to prepare for us.

You ask: What if I reject Jesus Christ and choose instead the way of sin? He is also loving and caring enough to warn you of the peril of that route. In Revelation 21 He makes unmistakably clear that "the cowardly, the unbelieving, the vile, the murderers, the sexually immoral, those who practice magic arts, the idolaters, and all liars—their place will be in the fiery lake of burning sulfur." Then He assures, "This is the second death" (Revelation 21:8), so "I, Jesus," initiate this final biblical invitation. "I, Jesus . . . give you this testimony" (Revelation 22:16).

Accompanying Christ's testimony is the powerful voice of the Holy Spirit who says, "Come!" (Revelation 22:17). It would be completely futile for me to preach the gospel, as I have done to many people every year for the past generation, if the Holy Spirit were not convicting the hearers of their sin and prompting them to open their hearts to Christ. And your reading of this book is entirely in vain, if through doing so, the Holy Spirit has not inspired you to spiritual growth or, if you are not a believer, issued an unmistakable call to you to give your life to Jesus Christ. Right now, the Holy Spirit is saying one thing to you, "Come!" Come to Christ! Open your life to His salvation and to His control.

In verse 17 we read that "The Spirit and the bride say, Come!" The bride of Christ is His church. It is made up of those who have received Him as Lord and Savior. Doing so, we take His name and are thereafter known as Christians. We love Him and we live with Him as our Lord, to the exclusion of all others. He has promised to provide for all of our needs. So, we're the bride! He is the bridegroom!

Then again, Jesus invites, "Let him who hears say, 'Come!'" (v. 17). We're told that "faith comes from hearing the message, and the message is heard through the word of Christ" (Romans

10:17). One of the verses I have used most frequently to lead people into a saving experience with Jesus Christ is John 5:24. It is Jesus speaking, "I tell you the truth, whoever hears my word and believes him who sent me, has eternal life and will not be condemned; he has crossed over from death to life." That's one of the clearest promises in all of the Bible as to how to come to Christ. Then, when we come to Christ, we'll urge others to come to Christ. When we confess Jesus as Lord of our lives, we'll want to confess Him before others.

"Whoever is thirsty, let him come" (Revelation 22:17), testifies Jesus! So many are chronically thirsty but can't put a finger on what that thirst is or a handle on how to quench it. Pascal, the great French physicist and philosopher of the seventeenth century, noted that all humans have in their hearts a God-shaped void that only Jesus Christ can fill. John had already written in his Gospel years before what Jesus said to a morally mixed-up woman at the Samaritan well: "Everyone who drinks this water will be thirsty again, but whoever drinks the water I give him will never thirst. Indeed, the water I give him will become in him a spring of water welling up to eternal life" (John 4:13, 14).

Do you have that thirst deep down in your soul which has characterized all people who have ever lived, but especially many of the great men and women of history? Riches cannot quench that thirst! Knowledge cannot quench that thirst! Alcohol cannot quench that thirst! Drugs cannot quench that thirst! Sex or romance cannot quench that thirst! But Christ can! And He asks you right now, wherever you are, to come to Him. Believe in Him! Tell Him that you do! Call upon Him to save your soul, to satisfy your thirst with the water of eternal life.

Again, in Revelation 22:17, Jesus repeats the invitation one final time with the strongest and most inclusive call of all: "And whoever wishes, let him take the free gift of the water of life." By this, Jesus is saying that—from our human viewpoint—a decision for Christ is entirely a matter of the will. God has done everything possible to bring you salvation; you can add nothing to what He has done. If you wish to be saved and go to heaven, you can, by believing in the Lord Jesus Christ as your Savior. If you wish not to be saved and therefore to be lost forever, that also is your privilege. Insofar as Jesus is concerned, He "wants all men to be saved and to come to a knowledge of the truth" (1 Timothy 2:4).

Peter, writing the closing chapter of his two letters, pleads that Christ is certainly "not wanting anyone to perish, but everyone to come to repentance" (2 Peter 3:9). I cannot think of how God could open the door wider for you to enter into the household of faith! And to be sure that no one thinks salvation is something we buy, contribute to, or earn, He clarifies, "Take the free gift."

Jesus Christ rose from the dead to be alive forever. And because He is alive, and because He can be everywhere at once, He is right there where you're reading. All you have to do is take Him, receive Him, accept Him personally into your heart as your Lord and Savior.

You might reply, "But I've received people into my life before, in relationships that didn't last and I'm wondering, will Jesus Christ love me and leave me? Will He take me and then forsake me, even perhaps forget that I exist?" No! In the next to the last verse in the Bible, Jesus "testifies" to you, "Yes, I am coming soon." The old apostle is so happy about that reassurance that he replies, "Come, Lord Jesus!" When you really mean your commitment to Christ not just as a momentary, but as an ongoing relationship, you will have Jesus Christ as your Lord and Savior forever. You can choose to "be with the Lord forever" (1 Thessalonians 4:17).

You may have one final hesitation. You may ask, "But could I live the Christian life on my own?" No, you couldn't! But you will not be on your own. Christ gives you day by day and moment by moment His unmerited favors. He strengthens, energizes and directs your life. The last verse in the Bible, Revelation 22:21, promises, "The grace of the Lord Jesus be with God's people. Amen." What more could you desire, ask, or ever hope for than that the grace of our Lord Jesus Christ be with you forever?

> You asked me how I gave my heart to Christ,
>   I do not know;
> There came a yearning for Him in my soul
>   So long ago;

I found earth's flowers would fade and die,
I wept for something that would satisfy
And then, and then, somehow I seemed
   To dare
To lift my broken heart to God in prayer.
I do not know, I cannot tell you how;
I only know He is my Saviour now.

                      Anonymous

Let me offer you a final suggestion. I have led tens of thousands who have come forward to make decisions for Christ in every part of the world in this simple prayer: "O God, I am a sinner. I'm sorry for my sins. I'm willing to turn from my sins. I receive Christ as Savior. I confess Him as Lord. From this moment on I want to follow Him and serve Him in the fellowship of His church. In Christ's name. Amen."

If you prayed this prayer, write to me and tell me about it. Write to Billy Graham, Minneapolis, Minnesota 55403, USA. We will reply with a letter and some literature that will help you to renew, or to begin, in the Christian way. God bless you.

Bibliography

Adams, Ruth, and Cullen, Sue. *The Final Epidemic: Physicians and Scientists on Nuclear War*. Chicago: Educational Foundation for Nuclear Science, 1981.

Aldridge, Robert C. *The Counterforce Syndrome: A Guide to U.S. Nuclear Weapons and Strategic Doctrine*. rev. ed. Washington, D.C.: Institute for Policy Studies, 1979.

Augustine, Saint. *Confessions of Saint Augustine*. Translated by Edward B. Pusey. New York: Macmillan Co., 1961.

Barash, David P. and Lipton, Judith E. *Stop Nuclear War! A Handbook*. New York: Grove Press, 1982.

Barclay, William. *The Revelation of John*. 5 vols. Philadelphia: Westminster Press, 1959.

Brown, Lester R. *Building a Sustainable Society*. New York: W. W. Norton & Co., 1981.

Browne, Corrine, and Munroe, Robert. *Time Bomb: Understanding the Threat of Nuclear Power*. New York: William Morrow & Co., 1981.

Busséll, Harold. *Unholy Devotion: Why Cults Lure Christians*. Grand Rapids, Mich.: Zondervan Publishing House, 1983.

Buttrick, George A., et al., eds. *The Interpreter's Bible*. 12 vols. New York: Abingdon Press, 1957.

De Jonge, Alex. *The Life and Times of Grigorii Rasputin*. New York: Cowan, McCann & Geoghegan, 1982.

Eckholm, Erik P. *The Picture of Health: Environmental Sources of Disease*. New York: W. W. Norton & Co., 1977.

Editors of *The Ecologist*. *Blueprint for Survival*. Boston: Houghton Mifflin Co., 1972.

Falk, Richard A. *This Endangered Planet: Prospects and Proposals for Human Society*. New York: Random House, 1972.

Frank, Anne. *The Diary of Anne Frank*. New York: Modern Library, 1958.

Freeman, Leslie J. *Nuclear Witnesses: Insiders Speak Out*. New York: William Morrow & Co., 1981.

Graham, Billy. *The Holy Spirit*. Waco, Tex.: Word Books, 1978.

Graham, Billy. *Till Armageddon: A Perspective on Suffering*. Waco, Tex.: Word Books, 1981.

Graham, Franklin, and Lockerbie, Jeannette. *Bob Pierce: This One Thing I Do*. Waco, Tex.: Word Books, 1983.

Gribbin, John. *Future Worlds*. New York: Plenum Press, 1981.

Hersey, John. *Hiroshima*. New York: Alfred A. Knopf, 1946.

Ladd, George Eldon. *A Commentary on the Book of Revelation of John*. Grand Rapids, Mich.: William B. Eerdmans Publishing Co., 1971.

Mackarness, Richard. *Living Safely in a Polluted World: How to Protect Yourself and Your Children from Chemicals in Your Food and Environment*. New York: Stein and Day, 1981.

Marine, Gene, and Van Allen, Judith. *Food Pollution*. New York: Holt, Rinehart & Winston, 1972.

Montagu, Ashley. *The Endangered Environment*. New York: Mason/Charter, 1974.

Office of Technology Assessment, Congress of the U.S. *The Effects of Nuclear War*. Totowa, N.J.: Allanheld, Osmun & Co., Pubs., 1979.

Osborn, Frederick. *The Human Condition*. New York: Hugh Lauter Levin Associates, 1973.

Ostmann, Robert, Jr. *Acid Rain: A Plague upon the Waters*. Minneapolis, Minn.: Dillon Press, 1982.

Petersen, William J. *Those Curious New Cults.* New Canaan, Conn.: Keats Publishing, 1973.

Rankin, William W. *The Nuclear Arms Race—Countdown to Disaster: A Study in Christian Ethics.* Cincinnati, Ohio: Forward Movement Publications, 1981.

Renneker, Mark, and Leib, Steven. *Understanding Cancer.* Palo Alto,Calif.: Bull Publishing Co., 1979.

Report of the Study of Critical Environmental Problems. *Man's Impact on the Global Environment.* Cambridge, Mass.: MIT Press, 1970.

Robinson, J. A. T., Bishop of Woolwich. *In the End God.* New York: Harper & Row, Pub., 1968.

Schell, Jonathan. *The Fate of the Earth.* New York: Alfred E. Knopf, 1982.

Science Action Coalition, and Fritsch, Albert S. *Environmental Ethics: Choices for Concerned Citizens.* New York: Anchor Press/Doubleday & Co., 1980.

Sine, Tom. *The Mustard Seed Conspiracy.* Waco, Tex.: Word Books, 1981.

Strong, Maurice, ed. *Who Speaks for Earth?* New York: W. W. Norton, 1973.

Waldbott, George L., ed. *Health Effects of Environmental Pollutants.* St. Louis: C. V. Mosby Co., 1978.

Walvoord, John F. *The Blessed Hope and the Tribulation.* Contemporary Evangelical Perspectives. Grand Rapids, Mich.: Zondervan Publishing House, 1976.

———. *Return of the Lord.* Grand Rapids, Mich.: Zondervan Publishing House.